PRAISE FOR *THE TWENTY*

"In *The Twenty: One Woman's Trek Acr[...]* [...] year-old author shows that—with self-[...] [...] the door on adventure. In this engrossing memoir cum travelogue, Bohr leads the reader on a 13-day trek over Europe's most rugged trails, crossing Corsica's mountains. As she inches along dizzying ledges, navigates slippery scree, and clings to cliff-side chains in hailstorms and blistering sun, your muscles clench until she reaches camp each night. It's a compelling tale of perseverance, of burdens more easily borne when shared, of wisdom gained from loss. As a bonus, Bohr's charming writing introduces the unique island's history and culture. Highly recommended as an inspiring, joyful read for intrepid trekkers and armchair adventurers alike."

—Margaret Rodenberg, author of *Finding Napoleon*

"*The Twenty* is an exhilarating and brave adventure story about Bohr's trek with her husband on the GR20. The characters danced off the page and into my heart and I cheered them as they hiked across Corsica. I'm inspired to take on the 20 after reading this exciting, honest travel memoir."

—Kathy Elkind, author of *To Walk It Is To See It: 1 Couple, 98 Days, 1400 miles on Europe's GR5*

"Bohr's magnetic narrative draws readers in and invites them to live vicariously through her vividly painted word pictures. And though I didn't strip off my socks—pulling white flesh with them—at the end of each day, I journeyed alongside her on treacherous terrain, ascending and descending razor-sharp scree, jagged granite, and sheer, slippery rock slabs. It was as if I, too, felt my cautious way along narrow ledges and lived the leg-trembling reality of the 124-mile trek across Corsica. *The Twenty* is a story of human resilience that swept me away."

—Laurie Buchanan, author of the Sean McPherson novels

"The author takes readers on a physical trek across Corsica and perhaps an even more arduous psychological one that is every bit as challenging as the rugged trail. At 60, she and her husband of 35 years tackle the GR 20, a 124-mile footpath considered Europe's toughest hike. Along the way, Bohr challenges preconceived notions about aging, marriage, and how time can reshape self-image."

—Davida Breier, author of *Sinkhole*

"Like all great travelogues, it will have readers itching to travel somewhere remote and outside their comfort zones."

—*Kirkus Reviews*

"*The Twenty* captures so well the inner trek to life's third chapter. Just as the author finds new strength and courage physically on her Corsican adventure, she simultaneously discovers a deep well of psychological and spiritual strength that promises to keep life vital, growing, and changing. Bohr joins the ranks of aging women who will not go gently into that good night, and instead seizes every day with passion and purpose. An inspiring must-read for those wishing to enter the noble passage of aging with grace and gratitude."

—Stephanie Raffelock, author of *A Delightful Little Book On Aging*,
Creatrix Rising: Unlocking the Power of Midlife Women

"*The Twenty*, Bohr's second travel memoir, is as much a page-turner as her first, *Gap Year Girl*. Her writing is so descriptive that I felt I was hiking the 20 myself (something I would like to attempt even at the age of 66). I shared the author's occasional disappointment and was amazed she didn't give up. A feel-good must-read for all, especially baby boomers who believe that limits exist only in the mind."

—Mary Anne Marciante, International Marathoner and
Hotel Ambassador, The St. Regis Deer Valley, UT

PRAISE FOR *GAP YEAR GIRL*

"[In *Gap Year Girl*,] Bohr steps outside of her comfort zone and explores the world...and she vividly conveys her experiences, such as when she describes the chaotic streets of Morocco and the loneliness of the bucolic French village Saint-Cirq-Lapopie."

—*Publishers Weekly*

"Bohr shines...provid[ing] glimpses of herself as a whole person, not simply a traveler. *Gap Year Girl* is an excellent choice...a travelogue filled with historic places, but its personal stories provide its highlights."

—*Kirkus Reviews*

"You can't read *Gap Year Girl* as a bystander. You're with her every step of the way, for this is travel writing at its very best."

—Kev Reynolds, Author of *The Tour of Mont Blanc*, Cicerone Guides

THE
TWENTY

One Woman's Trek Across Corsica on the GR20

MARIANNE C. BOHR

SHE WRITES PRESS

Published 2023
Printed in the United States of America
Print ISBN: 978-1-64742-432-9
E-ISBN: 978-1-64742-433-6
Library of Congress Control Number: [LOCCN]

For information, address:
She Writes Press
1569 Solano Ave #546
Berkeley, CA 94707

Interior Design by Kiran Spees

She Writes Press is a division of SparkPoint Studio, LLC.

As ever, to Joe, who was on every step of this journey with me and who loves to travel and hike almost as much as I do.

"Five years ago, I took a trip to Corsica . . . Imagine a world still in chaos, a tempest of mountains separating narrow ravines with rushing torrents; no fields, but immense crags of granite and giant undulations of earth covered with scrub or tall forests of chestnut and pine. For a month I wandered around this beautiful island, feeling as if I were at the end of the world."

—Guy de Maupassant, *Le Bonheur*

"The GR20 climbs high into the mountains and stays there for days on end, leading ordinary walkers deep into the sort of terrain usually visited only by mountaineers."

—Paddy Dillon, *The GR20 Corsica: Complete Guide to the High-Level Route*

"The GR20 in Corsica is justifiably one of the most famous treks in Europe. It follows a route along the high mountain spine of this rugged island. It is dramatic and wild, and the local people have their own distinct Corsican culture. The scenery is incredibly varied from rocky mountain ridges, azure lakes, pine forests, and views across to the Mediterranean. [The Twenty] should be on the bucket list for any competent and fit trekker."

—KE Adventure Travel

THE GR20 BY THE NUMBERS

Length of the Trail
124 miles

200 kilometers

Maximum Altitude
7,500 feet

2,300 meters

Gain and Loss in Elevation
62,300 feet

19,000 meters

Number of Hikers who Attempt the G20 Annually
18,000

Percentage of Hikers who Actually Complete the Trek
Less than 50

CONTENTS

Corsica

Isola di Capraia (Italy)

Cap Corse

Rogliano

Punta di Stintinu

Nonza

Bastia

L'Ile-Rousse

Belgadère

Borgo

Punta de la Revellata

Calvi

Calenzana

L'Asco

Golo

Morosaglia

Galeria

Fango

Monte Cinto 2706m ▲

Albertacce

Corte

Cervione

Capo Rosso

Piana

GR20

Vivario

Tavignano

Vico

Cruzzini

Vizzavona

Aléria

Punta di Cagèse

Bocagnano

Ghisonaccia

Capo di Feno

Gravona

Cozzano

Travo

AJACCIO

Santa-Maria-Siché

Crocce

GR20

Solenzara

Tavaro

Capo di Muro

Conca

Iles Sanguinaires

Propriano

Levie

Punta de la Chiappa

Sartène

Porto-Vecchio

Roccapina

Figari

Bonifacio

I.Cavallo

Capo Pertusato

Iles Lavezzi

Isola Santa Maria (Italy)

0   10   20
miles

0   10   20
kilometers

Corsica Map Area

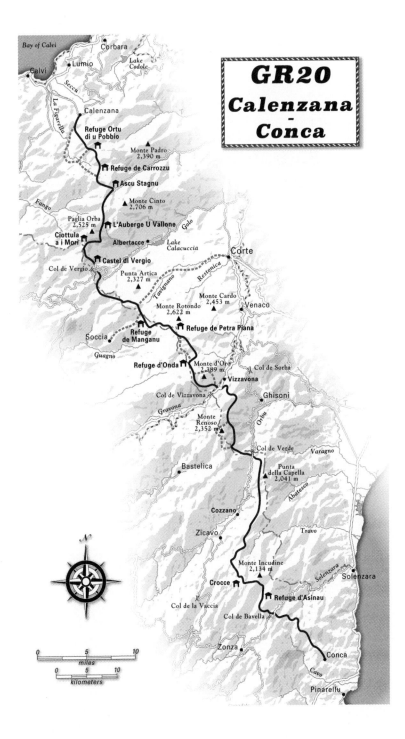

Bay of Calvi

Corbara

Lumio

Calvi

Lake
Codole

Secca

La Figarella

Calenzana

Refuge Ortu
di u Pobbio

Monte Padro
2,390 m

Fango

Refuge de Carrozzu

Ascu Stagnu

Monte Cinto
2,706 m

Paglia Orba
2,525 m

L'Auberge U Vallone

Golo

Ciottula
a i Mori

Albertacce

Lake
Calacuccia

Corte

Castel di Vergio

Col de Vergio

Punta Artica
2,327 m

Restonica

Tavignano

Monte Cardo
2,453 m

Monte Rotondo
2,622 m

Venaco

Refuge
de Manganu

Refuge de Petra Piana

Soccia

Guagno

Refuge d'Onda

Monte d'Oro
2,389 m

Col de Sorba

Vizzavona

Col de Vizzavona

Ghisoni

Gravona

Monte
Renoso
2,352 m

Orba

Col de Verde

Varagno

Bastelica

Punta
della Capella
2,041 m

Abatesco

Cozzano

Zicavo

Travo

Monte Incudine
2,134 m

Solenzara

Solenzara

Crocce

Refuge d'Asinau

Col de la Vaccia

Col de Bavella

Zonza

Conca

Cavo

Pinarellu

GR20
Calenzana
-
Conca

N

0   5   10
miles

0   5   10
kilometers

INTRODUCTION

We were about to turn sixty. And while many celebrate milestone birthdays with a dinner, cruise, or spa weekend, the prospect of leaving our fifties within days of each other made my husband, Joe, and me restless for adventure. It was 2016, and we considered several options. We decided on an extended hike across the French island of Corsica since the backpacking-around-Europe days of our youth, with something new around every corner, remain our standard for travel. We wanted to challenge what it meant to be sixty years old.

We've shared many journeys since we were teens, and they've become enduring bridges between us. Few things have brought us closer than traveling—camaraderie through shared experiences no one can take away. And unless we're with our children, we always go by ourselves. We're our own little world of two surrounded by a sea of others.

But this trip would be different. We'd be part of a group of fellow hikers and looked forward to what we hoped would be a shared adventure.

Mediterranean islands evoke sun-dazzled days and wine-soaked nights, curvy women scantily clad, and bronzed men in linen shirts. While Corsica is not fashionable Capri and definitely not jet-setting Ibiza, it does have its share of white sandy beaches and sapphire-blue coves. However, a very different, untamed Corsica hides behind soaring mountain peaks like broken teeth that most vacationers only glimpse behind sunglasses lounging on the beach. "Wild Corsica" is where rushing streams tumble down cavernous gorges, and silent mountain lakes are bordered by boulders the size of Volkswagens. Dogs sleep in the road, and farm animals range free, making themselves plump for the cheese and charcuterie that are staples of the Corsican diet.

The island's interior is also home to a desolate trek known as the GR20 (*Grande Randonée* number 20)—often referred to as Europe's toughest long-distance footpath. The Twenty's reputation did not dissuade us or dampen our enthusiasm for the journey. I'm a fervent Francophile with a special place in my heart for France ever since I did graduate work in the Loire Valley in the seventies, so the fact that Corsica is one of her eighteen regions added to its appeal. If I can speak French while hiking, all the better.

Trails are blazed with white-over-red stripes and are maintained by the *Fédération Française de la Randonnée* (French Hiking Federation). We'd hiked pieces of other GR trails, including seventy-five miles of the *Tour du Mont Blanc* (TMB) through France, Italy, and Switzerland to circle Europe's highest peak when we were fifty-six. The TMB was a difficult, sometimes grueling hike. But at the end of each day, bruised and battered, we had a hot restaurant meal, soft mattress, and warm duvet waiting. Not so with our Mediterranean adventure. We would rough it for two weeks, for at least eight hours a day on the trail, up and down elevation changes of over sixty-two thousand feet. The numbers were daunting but guaranteed magnificent vistas from sunbaked summits and impressively muscled calves to strut on our return.

Turning sixty is a terrifying anniversary for some. For us, it meant retirement, the end of our helter-skelter, cuticle-chewing workaday lives and the beginning of unhurried adventure curbed only by our wallets and the bounds of our bodies. No longer would travel be rushed as when we had to maximize every minute of our hard-earned vacation days. Retiring also meant celebrating a high school romance that grew into thirty-five years of marriage. We were ready to mark milestones sixty and thirty-five, eager to begin the next phase of our life.

Planning for Corsica began while we backpacked through Europe on an adult gap year in 2012—our "Senior Year Abroad"—which I wrote about in my first book, *Gap Year Girl: A Baby Boomer Adventure Across 21 Countries*. That particular journey was thirty years in the making and required selling the house and our possessions, as well as quitting our jobs. This next step in our adventure progression took fewer leaps of faith since we'd retired days before leaving the US, and no longer had a house to sell. We thought, *We left the country for a full year of adventure; surely, we can do it again for a couple months to train for and then tackle the extreme walking of The Twenty.*

Corsica had been on our travel list for years, and discovering the GR20 in a guidebook quickly bumped it to the top. The derring-do tales of a retired British army general we met on our sabbatical year sealed the deal. He raved about The Twenty and insisted, "You absolutely *must* do it." The general was not a man to be ignored.

Despite our TMB experience, as well as multiday hiking and camping trips in the Grand Canyon, Rockies, and Alps, we knew a two-week trek across Corsica would set a much higher bar testing our mature hiking mettle, not to mention our thighs, and stretching the limits of our "senior" resolve. We were keenly aware that time was of the essence since we couldn't presume our good health would last.

All kinds of debilitations have hit many of our baby boomer contemporaries and led to regret about chances they missed when younger. What used to make them happy is now over: traveling internationally, running, biking with their grandchildren. A skier friend can no longer hit the slopes because of a back injury, and I'm not sure what pains her more: her spinal fracture or having to sit by the fire while the rest of us are on the mountain.

I feel her frustration. I know how angry I would be if I could no longer hike. I've loved it ever since I did my first real trek as a college student—an all-day solo walk from Grindelwald, Switzerland, to the snow line at Kleine Scheidegg at the base of the Jungfrau and Eiger peaks. I was so poorly equipped, but the thrill of the climb—up an Alp no less—hooked me. I liked hiking, and I liked wearing the badge of hiker.

Once I introduced Joe to the sport after college, he bonded with it as I had. There is something so satisfyingly pure about setting off on a trek and finishing it. Add to that the excitement of completing a particularly difficult trail, and it gratifies our shared desire to push ourselves physically and mentally. While there's also a bit of friendly competition between us, we know we have to rein in the "anything you can do" attitude on occasion.

What is the appeal of outdoor challenges? The easy answer is nature's beauty and sublime vistas, but in reality, it's so much more. It's the brisk morning air, the solitude, the restorative effect of the wilderness, the sense of freedom and timelessness; it's how our muscles ache, in a good way, at the end of a long day. Certainly, we hike for the views, but it's also for the chance to be alone with our thoughts, for the opportunity to meet interesting, like-minded people away from their day-to-day lives, for the photos, and yes, for the exhilaration of accomplishing a physical feat and reveling in success.

But the true allure of an extended trek to places inaccessible by vehicles and technology is what it does for our souls. It's a detox, the perfect antidote to the trappings of our modern world—we leave contemporary clutter behind and think clearly about what's important, far from the reach of cellphones and email. With no alarms, no deadlines, no beeps, no bells to interrupt, we put one foot in front of the other while stress and anxiety melt away and we enjoy the wonders of the wild.

Friends and family often asked, "Why Corsica?" And although the French have vacationed there for years, few Americans have discovered this somewhat exotic corner of the Hexagon. The Mediterranean island's two claims to fame are Napoleon and the GR20. The emperor's birthplace has a colorful history influenced by the cultures of France, Italy, and North Africa. Books say it boasts garrulous people, rich, delicious food, delightful harbors, medieval villages, pristine beaches, and several first-rate boutique hotels. But there's only so much a book can capture. We wanted to see it for ourselves.

So off we went in July—two for the road, as usual—in hiking boots, lugging shiny new backpacks, a tent, sleeping bags, and trekking poles, to face a 124-mile trail across a mountainous island in the Mediterranean.

At the time we left home, we thought our preparation was adequate, but as our hike approached, I came to wonder if our bravado might have been misplaced given our age. However, to paraphrase Dylan Thomas, we were determined not to "go gentle into that good night," but to "rage, rage against the dying of the light."

Come along for the journey. Join us for The Twenty.

PROLOGUE

July 30, 2016
Bastia, Corsica

A waterfront café faces a sea of masts and the cerulean sea beyond. The fierce Corsican sun bears down. Heat radiates off the pavement in waves. Joe fans himself with a menu, his blond hair blowing as tears pool in my eyes. *You must not weep*, I tell myself. *You will not.*

The Mediterranean afternoon hubbub is in full swing, yet I barely notice, mired in my misgivings. "You're no athlete," my father once told me, a chubby girl of twelve, when I said I was trying out for the volleyball team. I cried with humiliation, hidden in my room. Even now I feel the sting of his scorn—an indelible adolescent gash. Despite the fact that I *did* make the team and my certainty that he *didn't* mean to be cruel, the hurt remains. How easy it is to become tangled in the fishing net of memory. Is it possible to overestimate its role in shaping one's identity?

My fingertips are white and numb, as usual, and I'm scared. Terrified, actually. I've repressed the doubts about whether I can do this, refusing them air over weeks and months of training. When apprehension did wriggle to the surface, I squelched it, burying it deep, outside of time and space. If I keep my secret to myself, perhaps it will just disappear. Dissipate, if I don't speak its name. Giving voice to my vulnerability and fatigue would make them more real, and I must pretend they aren't. The anxieties are there, the fear of my inadequacy bubbling up as we sit on this island under a heat-magnifying red umbrella, desperate for a breeze. *This is weather that makes people swoon*, I think. *They just slump over when their bodies say, "No more."*

It's taking all I have to sit upright. *You will not cry*, I repeat silently. The thought alone seems to summon my tears.

And we haven't even begun the trek.

Joe analyzes the trail map yet again, as if he'll discover something new. He's so excited, almost giddy, like a child, while I play with a limp wedge of lime with my straw. I sip my Orezza mineral water—gone flat and warm—and stifle a cough stuck in my perennially parched throat.

It all begins in two days, once we meet up with our hiking group. Two weeks of wilderness, two weeks of walking, two weeks of scrambling under the sun over the scree. Six months ago, I thought I could do this. Now I'm not so sure.

I gaze at the hypnotic ebb and flow of the sea, wanting to be anywhere but here. There's a pretty white boat in the harbor, about to set sail. Perhaps it can carry me away. Me and my heated heart. I've been angry about my fatigue, angry about my body letting me down, so angry about it all. But right now, it's fear that overwhelms me. The fear of my physical limitations and of disappointing myself, yes, but most of all, I'm terrified of disappointing Joe. He believes in me, and I can't let him down. But I'm afraid this damned body will, and there won't be anything I can do about it. Still, I've always believed in miracles, I reassure myself, as I unstick my clammy legs from the webbed plastic chair.

We look over the sea, and the sun vanishes. A sudden gust of wind whips the map from Joe's hands and sends my plastic cup flying. And just like that, it starts to rain. A driving summer downpour raises steam from the stones.

Keep close to Nature's heart . . . and break clear away, once in awhile, and climb a mountain or spend a week in the woods. Wash your spirit clean.

—John Muir

PART I: PREPARATION

April 2015: Sixteen Months Out
Bethesda, Maryland

We decide on a frozen winter evening.

Another late night, Joe has walked home from the metro in the dark, after a fourteen-hour day at the DC Navy Yard. His weekend business trip merged into Monday morning work. No time to recover and no time for us. Our marriage has always thrived on making time for each other, but for the past several months, our increasingly crazy work schedules that have us leaving home before dawn have prevented that. His six-foot frame is hunched, shoulders slumped as he stomps slush from his shoes onto the doormat and unwraps his ice-stiffened scarf. Still, he manages a "Hey, Babe." I do adore the sound of his voice.

I've been home for hours grading papers. I love teaching, and I love my middle school French students, but I wish they believed me when I told them I know right away when they use Google Translate. Tonight, I'm frustrated by so many things.

I miss our grown children, their physical absence leaving me in tears this evening. For the third night in a row, I've tried calling our daughter, Caroline, just to tell her I love her. Because of the three-hour time difference between the East Coast and San Francisco, and her twelve-hour shifts as a NICU nurse, we don't connect. When she's available, I'm teaching. When I'm free, she's working. I missed my weekend call with our son, Chris, in Los Angeles because I confused the time of our phone date. Even though they're now adults, I still need to hear their voices often. But distance and schedules demand I wait another five days before we speak.

Joe closes the door, and I blurt as I get up to greet him, "I don't want to do this anymore. I don't want to live so far from the kids. And I hate not having more time to spend with you. We have to make a change."

Joe looks like I slapped him as he drops his briefcase. I pause to blow my nose and wipe my tears. "We've been working for almost forty years, and we need to stop."

"A little dramatic, no?" Joe says, crossing the space between us to take my hand and lead me to the couch. He collapses, overcoat still on. His eyes are closed, head in free fall behind him. "Take a breath, Marianne. Is there a topic sentence?"

He's called me Marianne and not Babe. It's what he says when he knows I'm upset. I know he's exhausted, and I feel guilty for greeting him with my verbal assault.

Little does he know, I spent the weekend while he was away crunching numbers on spreadsheets that map out several financial scenarios for quitting our jobs. Joe, working for the Department of Defense, and I, as a teacher after a long career in publishing, have been savers since we married. Isn't it time to relax and have fun before more years tick by? I have questions about healthcare, pensions, and taxes, but what I constructed with a few educated guesses reveals an appealing escape years earlier than either of us imagined. We'd never talked about retiring early, always assuming we'd work until we were sixty-five.

"The topic sentence is 'Retirement.' I'm really sorry for being so emotional, Joe," I say, knowing few things distress him more than seeing me cry, "but I need to just let it all out. It was a really long day at school, and I couldn't reach Chris and Caroline and you're home so late and I've just really missed you." I lean in next to him and take a deep breath.

"I know. I've missed you too. Just tell me what you want to do." His hand grabs my knee, eyes still closed. As always, he's open to hearing my ideas, even the bold ones.

"Well," I say, hopeful already. "What would you say if I told you we could retire next year and move closer to the kids?"

"I'd say, no way." He slumps down further on the sofa, hands across his chest, fingers interlaced. His inner skeptic is always the first to react. "I haven't looked at the numbers for months, but retiring that soon would be years earlier than we thought, right?" When I don't answer, he opens one eye and sees my stare. "You're serious, aren't you?"

Before I respond, he snaps up his head. "What about our 401Ks? We have to be fifty-nine and a half to get at them with no penalties."

I lean forward, cock my head, and give him a look: *Come on, Joe. Think about it.*

It takes a moment in the fog of fatigue, but the light bulb finally goes on, his soft green eyes widening. "Oh, God," he says, speaking slowly. "We'll be fifty-nine and a half in September. That's only six months away. And I can retire at sixty and get health insurance we can actually afford. Why do I always forget how old we are?"

After a week of weighing pros, cons, and risks, Joe is finally comfortable with my proposal. We review the numbers ("You're sure we can afford this?"), he plays his pessimistic self ("Are we going to feel worthless if we're not working?"), and then we agree on a plan. It's how it's often been in our marriage. I'm the one more at ease with change, the romantic ready to take a chance on big ideas. And his caution and tendency to expect the worst lead us to consider questions that have helped us avoid some missteps.

Done. We're retiring at the end of June 2016. We email Chris and Caroline to give them the news. "Yippee! We're retiring next year and will soon be heading west!"

August 2015: Twelve Months Out

Long ago, I learned that a trip on the horizon makes me happy. If I have no definite travel plans, no dates inked on my calendar, I'm uneasy, untethered to the future. Buying guidebooks, browsing the Internet, planning an itinerary, and mapping out details give me a healthy kind of high. The anticipation of getting away feels like my natural state, and imagining a future trip works its way into my daily psyche. If a difficult conversation or an overloaded schedule leaves me off-balance, I close my eyes and picture taking off in a plane. I'm once again my authentic self, invigorated by the promise of discovery.

"No turning back now," I say to Joe as I walk into the living room late one Saturday afternoon. "We're committed to leaving the rat race and taking off on a trip. I just paid our deposit. Get ready to hike across Corsica for two weeks."

"I am *so* pumped," he says, getting up to hug me. "You know how I love your *big* ideas. Retiring and heading right to Corsica might be the best ones you've ever had."

"And we have a whole year to get ourselves in shape."

"Can't think of a better way to celebrate retirement, turning sixty, and being married to you for thirty-five years."

"Ditto, Joe. Next August can't come fast enough."

"I'll make us a training plan. We've got to be ready for The Twenty." Joe's declaration becomes our rallying cry.

The trail across Corsica deserves enormous respect, and we're taking its reputation seriously. We prefer traveling by ourselves but don't want to be completely vulnerable. We'll go with a small group and a local guide who will make sure we won't get lost.

I pour myself a glass of wine, sit back in my favorite chair, and put my feet up on the ottoman. I close my eyes and think about what we've signed up for.

The GR20—the *Grande Randonnée* (big hike) number twenty, or, in Corsican, *Fra li Monti* (Across the Mountains)—bisects Corsica diagonally and follows its mountain spine from the northwest to the southeast corner. It's one of hundreds of GRs, well-marked trails that crisscross Europe, primarily in France, the Netherlands, and Spain. Although not well known in the US, if you ask a European trekker about challenging trails, The Twenty always comes up. It's a notoriously difficult route and a rite of passage for serious European hikers. Rocky terrain of granite slabs strewn with scree—the small loose stones that cover the slopes—gargantuan boulders, narrow ledges, and steep inclines, some of which require holding onto chains or cables to ascend, have earned the trail its reputation as relentless.

I'm now anchored by a trip on the horizon, at least until the rigors of training begin.

January 2016: Seven Months Out

You really need more exercise, I tell myself in the mirror. I do hot yoga three times a week and lift my share of weights, but I need more cardio. Something to put my lungs through their paces and strengthen my winter-weary legs for the 124-mile trek. I sigh, knowing that since

November, I've barely put a dent in Joe's training plan. He reminds me daily that our hike across Corsica is now just seven months away. And in case it's slipped my mind, he repeats the refrain, which has now become irritating: "Have to be ready for The Twenty."

But it's frozen outside, and I've no will to train. My annoyingly fit husband's done "something athletic every day" for months. But I'm not motivated. This isn't like me. And for the first time I wonder, *Will my age make a difference this time?* I've never hiked for two weeks straight, on such a tough trail, at this age. Will *I* be ready for The Twenty?

My psychological lack of enthusiasm may be due to corporeal reluctance. I've been so achy lately, a sore knee, a tight quad, and now tender wrists and inflamed knuckles. The result of adding push-ups to my workouts? My current physical condition brings the unwelcome thought that, at fifty-nine, I have so many more days behind me than I do ahead. Ugh.

I must have stretched too deeply into my *ustrasana* camel pose last night because my shoulders, down through my upper arms and into my elbows, are killing me. And all this without even stepping into my hiking boots. The state of my body dampens interest in walks in the woods, especially with snow on the ground.

"Is this what you'll be like on Corsica every morning?" Joe teases, still damp from a shower, donning his running shorts.

"Oh, God." He snaps his towel at me.

"If you're like this after sleeping on a mattress under a duvet, how're you going to feel after two weeks in a tent?"

I groan, playing along but choking back frustration. Enough with the push-ups.

February 2016: Six Months Out

The man I've loved for over forty years is thorough when it comes to buying equipment. He researched for months what we'll need for our two-week trek, taking such pleasure in technical details. After all, he's a marine engineer who's built ships all his life. Specs he can do. We start a cyber-Sunday shopping spree, computers open, surrounded by dog-eared catalogs. But before lightening our bank account, we study the kit list one more time.

"Do we really need quick-drying camping towels?" I ask.

"How you think we're going to dry off after washing in the mountains? There won't be any Turkish towels hanging from the trees. And these are super light."

"Just never occurred to me, that's all."

"That's why I'm here. To be the gear guy. And that reminds me, I have my running light but you need a headlamp. What do you want, gray or black?"

We find the lowest prices (light, compressible trekking gear isn't cheap), scrounge for coupons, choose colors, and order our equipment. I look down at my yellow legal pad: Osprey rolling duffels. Forty-eight-liter backpacks. Water bladders with purifiers. Sport bottles with built-in filters. Plastic meal kits. A two-person, ultra-light Marmot tent. Thirty-two-degree Big Agnes sleeping bags. Inflatable travel pillows and pads.

As a final purchase, we add two pairs each of our favorite Darn Tough brand of hiking socks. Brown for Joe, green for me. The first of our gear will arrive tomorrow. I imagine the perfect newness of our purchases, knowing that once we're on the trail, our virgin equipment will be splattered with mud, stained with sweat, bleached by the sun, and frayed at the edges.

But I do realize it will be *my body* doing the hike, not my gear,

no matter how high-tech. Resolve kicks in as I think about how I've
lagged in my training. I can't wait to be on Corsica, to take in its
unique aroma I've always read about—maquis, the hillside scrub,
which earned the island its nickname, the Scented Isle. I *will* be ready,
I promise myself.

I no longer feel my legs, deadened from exertion. And yet, I sense
them trembling. My feet, however, are screaming in pain. Stop! Please.
Not another step on this river of rubble, the sharp fragments tearing
at the rubber of my boots, cutting through to the blistered skin of
my soles, daggers slicing my flesh. The razored scree. The loose stone
that's left after mountains freeze and thaw and freeze again, wearing
down too fast.

From behind a grotesquely gnarled olive tree swarm fat, lumi-
nescent flies. Their buzzing invades me; I can't avoid their staccato
smacks to my face.

Joe and the others are well ahead, over the ridge, and I can no
longer see them. I grip my pounding head and plant my feet for just
a moment, but the stone shards shift, tumbling into the crevasse
opening beneath me. I shift my weight and hold my ground, but then
the scree, like a ruthless undertow, pulls me down, my feet shooting forward. I struggle to catch myself but hold no sway against the
mighty rock current. Frantically, I try to slow down, digging into the
merciless talus, tearing my nails and bloodying my hands. The pull
is irresistible and I succumb to the tumbling flow. I'm falling. Just
falling.

I awaken with a scream in sheet-drenching sweat. Joe gently pulls
me to his side of the bed. "Babe, you're dreaming. Where were you?"

It takes many minutes for the terror to subside, for me to reenter our bedroom. I press my palm to my chest, trying to slow the pounding. I roll over and find that my nagging morning pain is gone. Perhaps my dream shocked it into submission.

Combine yesterday's buying bender with a surge of self-doubt. The result? The scree of my nightmare. What have I gotten myself into? I pull the sheet over my head.

February 20 is our first official day of training together, our first real hike since fall, and we need to soften hiking boots that have stiffened in dark corners of the closet.

Hibernation behind us, we head out to an unseasonably warm weekend. Joe decides after just the first mile that he needs new boots. His current pair is low-slung, and he wants the stability of a higher collar. Mine cover my ankles and provide plenty of support, and even though they're seven years old, the treads remain deep, the seams are intact, and they treat my wide feet well. They'll do just fine getting me across Corsica.

We've left our trekking poles at home since we're doing thirteen easy miles, gentle ups and downs along Rock Creek, from Maryland into Washington, DC. My body is cooperating as a long shower loosened me up. We talk about how different this cool, comfortable jaunt is from what our Mediterranean tramp will be under fierce August sun.

"I don't feel *too* bad about the shape I'm in," I say, cocky as the miles tick by.

"We're both at a good starting point but need to take what we signed up for seriously. This has to be the first of lots and lots of training hikes."

I take several strides in silence, breathing deeply with each footfall. "Did you know the amount of air our lungs hold actually decreases as we age?" Joe half turns to look at me. "Just read that this morning. Something about our diaphragms getting weaker."

"Did they say what *increases* as we get older?"

"Our waistlines?" I pinch my stomach. "Got to get rid of this winter insulation."

"You and I both, because we really need to think hard about how difficult Corsica's going to be," Joe pushes. "I've been reading everything I can get my hands on about the hike, and I think it's going to be even tougher than we thought."

I tell him I've read every single page of the *GR20 Cicerone Guide* we bought last fall. "I picture the hardest part of every hike we've done—the *Tour de Mont Blanc*, the Grand Canyon, El Capitan, Old Man Coniston—all strung together, one after the other."

"Well, we need to keep thinking about what it's going to take."

I stop in my tracks, hands on hips, chin out. "Enough, Mr. Cynic!" I shoot back. "I hear you and I get it. Let's just remember that *I'm* the one that got *you* into hiking, right?"

No reply.

Caroline calls that evening. "How's training going?"

"All good, but your father needs to stop pushing so hard. He's making me crazy."

"He did that with me too, with soccer. Remember? It was annoying, but he was right. You probably know he's right this time too, and that's why it's bugging you, Mom."

She knows us both so well.

The following week with Joe away on a ship, I head out to do ten miles on my own. I take one pole because my knees have been bothering me. Not unexpectedly, they're throbbing six miles out even though I'm on a perfectly flat rail-trail, but I'm surprised when my wrists and hands swell like sausages, especially my right one, the one with the pole.

I cut my walk short as my knees are visibly puffy. It may be time to see the doctor. But we have days of standardized testing at school, and it's not fair to the other teachers to take off. I promise myself that if all this lasts into next month, I'll make an appointment.

March 2016: Five Months Out

The swelling and stiffness are worse, especially in the morning. What is invading my body? I've always been a jump-out-of-bed morning person—it's when I'm most productive—so why is my attacker striking when I'm at my best? I get up earlier than my normal 5:30 to take an extra-long shower to ease the first-light pain. I've begun to dread the wee hours—"my miserable mornings." In the evenings, the inflexibility eases, but oh, the mornings. I swallow a handful of Aleve like it's candy.

I stretch my tender muscles with a tottering amble up and down our apartment building's hallway. I arrive at school early to loosen up further—slowly, painfully making my way around the parking lot, flip-flops slapping at my feet. Despite winter temperatures, I prefer chilly toes to constricted ankles and the agony of a heel. I sling my book-heavy bag over a sore shoulder, relieved to enter the building in darkness. I so love teaching, but pain dampens my enthusiasm for pleasantries with colleagues this morning. By the time class starts hours later, I can move freely with just some minor discomfort.

In the evening, I log a few miles once stiffness has released. But I'm coming down with a cold, the first in over four years. What the hell is wrong with me? Why am I falling apart just as we're retiring?

Hands, shoulders, knees, and wrists, I chant in my own version of the children's jingle. All are on fire. I can't push myself out of bed without wincing.

One Saturday morning, we delay getting out of bed as long as possible to catch up on emails and the news on our phones. It's almost noon when Joe asks, "Do I hear rain?"

Rather than get up to open the blinds, I Google it. "Yup, it's sprinkling."

"Really? Why not say you don't know. I would have gotten up to check."

"I know, but Googling it was easier, and I don't want you watching me get out of bed. I move like an old woman and don't want you seeing me like that."

"Hey, we're in this aging thing together, and you'll never be an old woman to me." Joe leans over with a kiss and then gets up to bring me my mega-dose of Aleve. He sits on the bed and massages my thigh and then my wrists. "Look at me, Marianne." I raise my head. "I know you keep putting it off, but isn't it time to see the doctor?"

"You're probably right. I just think I'm in denial about it all."

"Promise you'll call on Monday?"

I nod and he asks, "Want me to come with you? For moral support?"

"Absolutely not. I'll just get an appointment for after school one day this week."

He holds my face on both sides and plants a kiss on my forehead. I give him a weak smile, troubled by the niggling voice that wonders, *Will I be okay for Corsica?*

I make Joe close his eyes as I force myself out of bed for a shower. The pain in my hands is excruciating as I grab the towel rack for support. I grasp behind my knees, one by one, to lift my legs into the tub. When I return to the bedroom, Joe is there to dry my back and hook my bra. "Would you also zip me up and do my buttons?"

I'm four years old again.

Spring approaches, flowers bud, birds chirp, and I fold in on myself. I stare at my hands, willing away the swelling. They're like sallow medical gloves, blown up and tied with a string. My body refuses my commands: straighten up, walk normally, twist the toothpaste top, uncork the wine. The simple task of turning a knob shoots bolts of pain, like lightning, up my arm. I follow close behind others so they'll open doors for me.

How will I ever grip a trekking pole?

We call Chris to go over the details of his upcoming visit to Maryland, and I tell him about my joints. He's all about health and nutrition, so I know he'll have advice.

"Turmeric is good for inflammation, *Maman*," he says, using his pet name for me.

"Definitely worth a shot." I add it to my grocery list.

My normal approach to aging's indignities—menopause, thinning hair, and a sluggish metabolism—like my approach to most challenges, is to fight them on my own. I've always been uncomfortable asking for help, not liking people to go out of their way for me. My conditioned response when someone offers assistance is, "I'm fine. But thanks." Maybe I just want to appear that I have it all together, and I'm told I'm pretty convincing.

But Joe is right. I must seek a doctor's help when, on Monday morning, my pain spreads to my neck. As real as the intractable ache in my joints is the lump in my throat. It constricts my breathing and has me on the verge of crying all day. Damn this trespasser!

* * *

"Could it be bursitis?" I ask. "It's bothered me before, but never in so many places."

"Sounds situational to me," the doctor says after poking and prodding my sensitive joints. "Try adjusting your sleeping position."

It's not how I sleep, I want to scream, the familiar prick of tears brimming behind my eyes. But then she starts typing and says, "Just to be sure, let's do some blood work."

I exhale audibly. Validation. The tech sticks me to collect eight vials of blood.

"Your inflammation markers are high, so we need more tests," the doctor says.

Vindicated. My "markers" vouch for how I feel. But that thought is instantly replaced with, *Crap—what if something's seriously wrong?* I sit and relinquish more blood, starting to feel like a pincushion. The doctor will call me tomorrow.

I fall asleep in one decade of my life and awaken in the next. I was fifty-nine and overnight, I've turned sixty, determined to do what I've always done. Joe made the transition eleven days ago, which bids me, with throbbing difficulty, to roll over, wrap my arm around him. "So sorry, Joe, but you're no longer married to a younger woman."

"We're not going to let that stop us. Welcome to the sixties, Babe. Our sixties."

"The tests eliminate Lyme disease and lupus, but your inflammation level has elevated further, and your out-of-character cold could mean we're looking at an autoimmune disease. I'm referring you to a rheumatologist with an opening in an hour."

I do research on my phone: Autoimmune. Disease. Can't we go back to the bursitis option? Do I really have a disease? What an ugly word. *An autoimmune disease develops when your immune system decides your healthy cells are foreign and attacks them.* Lovely.

I should take the long view, but my heart jumps right to Corsica. I am so determined to do this thing, but now I'm adding a disease to mountains and hiking. Not a good mix.

I sit on the examining table, bare legs dangling like a child's, vulnerable and shaky, the disposable paper crinkling beneath my bottom. Not how I pictured starting my seventh decade. "When did the pain start? How long does it last? Does it keep you up at night?"

I stand in my hospital gown, the tile cold under my feet. The doctor manipulates my limbs and fingers, pushing and pulling them into awkward positions as he questions me further: "Does this hurt? How about this? Can you lift it higher? Push back. Harder." He sees I'm welling up as he pulls on my shoulders and asks if I'd like some cortisone.

"If it makes me hurt less, then please." The needle bites, once in each shoulder. Relief is immediate, from my neck to my fingertips. Even the tenderness behind my knees eases. I'm the grateful tin man whose joints have been oiled. I do windmills with my arms.

"This will be temporary, but looks like you can go to yoga tonight," he says. I want to kiss him. "But hold on," he adds when I jump off the table. "We're not quite done."

He looks at my chart and gives me the diagnosis.

"You have a chronic disease." He puts his hand on my shoulder as bees thrum in my ears, my head in a vise. But another part of me is smug. I knew it!

"You have rheumatoid arthritis—RA—an autoimmune disorder. It strikes your joints—your hands and wrists in particular."

I finally manage to speak. "But why so sudden?" A lightness slips away, and reality creeps in. I'm sick. Seriously sick. My body has started to fail.

"If you think back, you may recall signs you chalked up to age." Everything these days seems to be about my age. "And then, of late, the disease decided to hit full strength."

Just as I have, he's personified my uninvited guest—giving it a will.

I ask what first pops into my head. "Did I do anything to cause this?" My damned guilt has me, a Catholic manqué, thinking it must be my fault, quietly ashamed.

"Your mother had ulcerative colitis—another autoimmune disorder. They do run in families. If you want to make it someone's fault, blame your mother." He chuckles.

"Great. I'll add it to the list."

On my way home, I stop at a park and limp to a bench to collect my thoughts in the spray of a fountain. Those not walking with confidence catch my eye now that I have my own burden to bear: a young woman with a cane and an elderly couple, arm in arm, cross the lawn. Will that be me from now on? Spending my life sick and in pain? A bitter darkness takes root and tangles inside as I search for an apt metaphor. Am I caged? In prison? The door slammed shut, key turned, dead bolt in place. Or am I just no longer in charge.

A couple young bucks in European suits sit across from me. They eat kale salads, drink smoothies, turn their faces to the March sun. I feel resentment rise. *Can you see that I'm now an outsider? Can you tell I have a disease? But I've taken such good care of myself—a chunky child who forever fought less-than-lanky genes.* Once a young adult, I paid careful attention to what I ate and was obsessively active, trusting I could stay healthy with passion and singleness of purpose. But what a fool to believe I could control it all.

I meet Joe at our local hangout, a dimly lit bar and grill, for a birthday dinner. I wait in the shadows; despite my intention to keep my upper lip stiff, I know my bravery has its limits. I don't want Joe to worry and will try to disguise my own. "Tell me about the doctor's," he says before he's even in the booth. He leans across to kiss me and reaches for my hands. As I fill him in on cortisone, autoimmune diseases, and RA, all seems perfectly normal around us: a familiar happy hour with a favorite waiter, usual drinks and bar fare. *But it's not all normal,* I want to shout as Joe massages my wrists before I lift my cosmo.

"Marianne, we're in this together." Joe's eyes fill as he glides over next to me, draws me close, and his arm circles my shoulder. For the first time in weeks, it doesn't hurt. The tears I've held for hours spill over. "At least we know what we're up against," he says, raising his martini, dirty, with extra olives. "Here's to getting you well, birthday girl."

And I dare propose another. "And here's to doing The Twenty. At sixty!" As our glasses clink, I add, "And I'm afraid RA's along for the ride."

Joe returns my half smile. "Marianne. Maybe we should delay going to Corsica. Postpone the hike until we know you'll be okay. We'll just push it back a year."

"No. No way. We decided, we're doing it, and we're *not* backing out. To hell with RA. But promise me. This is our secret. No telling anyone but the kids about it."

"Got it. It's just between us. Promise. But let's know we can always cancel for this year. Corsica's not going anywhere."

In bed, there's a big sad stone in my center, and I can't stop silent tears. They catch in my hair and then dampen my pillow. The long-term effects of RA should be my biggest concern, but all I feel is vulnerable. And that we won't be able to do the hike together.

Of course, we can always go to Corsica, and I won't let Joe sacrifice the experience. He'll protest, but I'll insist he go on. I'll sit on a beach, do easy walks, meet some locals.

We discuss what we'll do if one of us gets hurt on the trail. "Look at me, Joe," I say in the dark of our bedroom. "If you or I can't hike for any reason other than being really ill or getting *seriously* hurt, the other has to keep going and finish for both of us. Agreed?"

"But, I want to do it together . . . like we do almost everything."

"I do too, Joe, but you have to promise me. Please."

"But—"

"No buts. We're agreeing right now that it's okay if only one of us gets to the end."

I finally feel him nod as he rests his head on my chest. "Agreed."

Drifting to sleep, my thoughts descend to the dark chance I'll get really sick, unable to share the adventures we always have. If that happens, will Joe love me any less?

April 2016: Four Months Out

"Going for a run," Joe calls from the kitchen and then doubles back to the living room to kiss me goodbye. "See you soon."

It shouldn't make me sad, should it? That he's healthy and I'm not? There's a divider between us that never existed before, even if it's one that only I perceive. Suddenly, we're out of sync, and I feel I'm growing old much faster than he is.

* * *

Post-diagnosis despair lingers, but beside it retirement revelry blooms, cortisone pushing pain into remission. I resume resolute training and throw myself into adventures to come.

With retirement three months away, Joe and I give notice at work and start coloring in the details of post-employment life. To be close to the children, our pioneering spirit will take us to California, moving somewhere between them on the Central Coast.

But first, to start our next chapter, we'll leave for France on July 4 to start our training on the Continent. Happy birthday, America. Hello, Corsican adventure.

May 2016: Three Months Out

"Oh, God." Pain shoots up my arm when I push myself out of bed and look down at my hands. The intruder and its mean-spirited spell are back, the cortisone cure having lasted just a few short weeks, tablespoons of turmeric notwithstanding. I hobble to the bathroom, groaning as I grab the dresser to take pressure off my legs. You *are* doing The Twenty, Marianne. Joe will be proud of you, and the kids will too. You'll prove your father wrong.

My doctor puts me on a wonder drug regimen that brings relief in a week. The evil hex has lifted. I feel good except that my shoulders still won't let me hook my bra in the back. I have to swing it to the front. Like when I was eleven. "It's a miracle," I tell Joe, "that so much hurt can melt away with some teeny white dots. Did I tell you they also use these drugs for malaria? At least there's one disease I won't have to worry about."

Joe laughs. "Might be key if we were heading to the tropics and not Corsica."

After another week, the stiffness fully loosens, and I sometimes forget my diagnosis altogether. It's only when I unscrew the top of my coffee mug or accidentally bang my always-tender hands against a student's desk that I remember my intruder.

"You should be fine," my rheumatologist says when I tell him our plans. "As long as you do the training," he adds.

"Have you been speaking to my husband?"

June 2016: Two Months Out

Possessions can own you more than you own them. So, after sixty years of accruing, we're consumed with divesting. We store a few things and sell or donate everything else.

The toughest task is last: sorting the mementos of our children's upbringing. It's difficult to part with cherished keepsakes, those in the seventies Kodak ad: "The times of your life." I sift through the pieces, the years slipping through my fingers: *Letting go of paper traces won't ruin the memories,* I tell myself. *They're there to retrieve when I need them.*

My heart raw after a day of Solomonic decisions, I stage what's coming with us to France in a now empty room, walls echoing as I drop the piles: clothes, hiking gear, and camping equipment. From beneath a heap peeks a picture of school-aged Chris and Caroline, arms around each other, thumbs-up. My good luck charms. I slip the photo in my pack. The final mound is a pile of orange vials—all the miracle medicines without which I'll be an arthritic mess. I'm still amazed at how much better they've made me feel.

I call the kids that night, needing their voices after summoning so many memories.

"Hey, *Maman,*" says Chris. "How you feeling?"

"Not too bad. Compared to March. And yes, I've been taking my turmeric."

Caroline, nurse that she is, asks, "How're the prescriptions working? Loosening you up? Ready for The Twenty?"

"Aren't you Dad's daughter, asking if I'm ready? Meds are good. Helping a lot."

"Great, Mom. I'm so glad and so proud of you both."

But how would Chris and Caroline feel if I couldn't do this hike? Might they no longer see me as a traveler and adventurer, as they do now? And would it launch that inevitable worry children must eventually admit—that their parents are getting old?

"You're a crazy woman," a colleague says on the final day of school when I share our hiking plans. "Sixty-year-olds shouldn't climb mountains. You could get hurt!"

"That's how we know it's an adventure." I smile.

The day ends, but rather than feeling like something momentous, I tell myself that retiring is just another gentle transition. I miss my students after every year—those who move on to high school—and I'm accustomed to academic years sliding into summer breaks.

But as I sit in my car in the parking lot, gripping the steering wheel, it hits me: I won't be back in the fall. I'll have moved far away, likely to never see most of my students again. I resolve to continue teaching in some form because I need student energy in my life. I see a group of students in the rearview mirror and wave, my eyes welling. Ethan and Hanna, Gaby and Laura, Meghan and Jack. *Au revoir, mes étudiants.* Until I see you again.

While I take care of vacating our apartment, Joe goes to the office for the final day of a thirty-eight-year career. We enjoy one last local happy hour. "So?" I ask, after toasting to retirement. "How does it feel to have office life behind you?"

"Well, I'm definitely happy to no longer be the guy who turns the lights on in the morning and off in the evening as well."

"Not going to miss those fourteen-hour days, huh?"

"Fourteen-hour days I don't mind, as long as they're not behind a desk."

"Are you worried at all? About anything?"

"Actually, I was thinking on the metro today that it's going to be hard to switch from so many years of saving *for* retirement to spending what we've saved *on* retirement. Withdrawing rather than depositing. And I worry about whether we've done all our calculations correctly. I know you're an Excel whiz, but still . . . is this going to work out?"

"We've checked the figures so many times, so we just have to say, 'We're doing this.'" I raise my cosmo and clink his martini. He gives me a big smile and nods.

In the final days before departure, I feel rootless, tied by a tentative thread to this neighborhood that's been our home for four years. In the hot, humid evenings, I roam the streets, savoring every step because we won't be back. After our trip, we'll be headed for California. I stop in a park to crush lavender blossoms between my fingers and brush them beneath my nose. The scent transports me to southern France and aromatic Corsica.

July 2016: One Month Out

I'm a sixty-year-old retiree riding into the proverbial sunset with her high school sweetheart. We, our gear, and my bag of prescriptions are on our way to France.

As we board the plane, all ties to preretirement life relax and then dissolve as Washington, DC reduces to miniature out our window. "Finally on our way." I sigh as Joe leans close. "I am so, so excited for our trip and cannot wait to see beautiful Corsica."

But lest I get too starry-eyed with sun-drenched imaginings, I remember Joe rousing reality. "It's going to be a long, hard hike." *Especially in my condition*, I think. But all that be damned. I'm doing it.

I open my guidebook and for the first time read the history of the trail. Frenchman Michael Fabrikant, Alpine mountaineer and Corsica aficionado, marked the route in 1970, much of it cobbled together from age-old trails cut by shepherds. Two years later, he received economic support when the *Parc Naturel Régional de Corse*, which covers nearly 40 percent of the island, was created to preserve the environment and exploit its beauty. By luring hikers (and their cash) to the island's interior, the mountain economy would be supported, and dying mountain villages and their traditions might be saved. The park authority rebuilt *bergeries* (shepherd's shelters), restored remote chapels, engineered and blazed the trail, renovated old mountain huts, and built new ones. Sixteen publicly run and a handful of private refuges now dot the island's scoliotic mountain backbone. They are staffed and have water, toilets, showers, food, self-catering facilities, and camping areas.

"How long you think The Twenty's been around?" I ask Joe.

"I don't know—a hundred years?"

"Only since 1970. Not so old after all. Younger than us." That age thing again.

Perhaps it's the hours in a plane that have my RA flaring. I quickly learn that my meds are not miracle workers and that there will be good days and bad. Arrival in Paris is tough.

"Exercise is good," my doctor said, "to keep your disease from acting up." So I look forward to meandering the streets of the City of Light to ease my aching joints as we slip into town on the train. We've visited Paris for almost forty years—first as college backpackers. While it can be hard to go back, revisit old haunts, and accept the passage of so many years, we focus on painting fresh tableaux with brand new memories.

I reflect on the places we've stayed in this city and recall our very first hotel. Perfectly situated on the Seine, it was a shabby little no-star walk-up. Breakfast was included in the pittance we paid. On our first morning, the chambermaid entered with no warning to deliver croissants and cafés au lait. Joe was soaping up in the curtainless shower in the corner of our room itself. "Bonjour!" she warbled with no embarrassment. Joe's face was the color of the strawberry confiture. I couldn't stop giggling all day.

We arrive in Provence, the dry, hardscrabble terrain similar to what we'll find on Corsica. The warmth of the Luberon Valley embraces us as we resume our training in the rocky hills immortalized by the Impressionists: Cézanne, Renoir, and Van Gogh. They're nestled in a quiet corner of countryside where breezes rustle squat olive trees with shimmering leaves, green on one side, silver on the other. Hilltop villages and thick-walled *mas* (southern French farmhouses) lost in time rise from fragrant, geometric lavender and sunflower farms, and vineyards form mosaics of purples, yellows, and greens. During yoga *savasana*, whenever my teacher said, "Go to your peaceful place," I always drifted here, where I sense I belong.

But what is usually my sanctuary of choice becomes the ruthless training ground for two determined hikers. We do an all-day, fourteen-mile hike up the practically perpendicular mountain massif that rises four thousand feet above the valley. We climb briskly at first, conditioning enthusiasm nipping at our heels. But then the gravelly trail heads straight up through thick scrub with no switchbacks to alleviate the rise. I put my heels down first, my feet at thirty-degree angles to my shins, my calf muscles stretching and then tensing just short of a cramp. But I decide this won't work. I ascend on tippy toes.

I say to Joe while I'm still close behind, "I thought retirement was about taking it easy." After just ten minutes, he's well ahead of me and after fifteen is no longer in sight.

Tough ascents are my hiking Achilles' heel. Joe finds the descents that pummel his knees more difficult, so I usually blaze the way down. But for now, I'm the caboose.

On climbs like this, Joe stops every fifteen minutes so I can catch up, and I'm sure I'll see him soon. But after half an hour, my face red beyond the effects of Provençal heat, for the first time ever, I'm upset and then angry about hiking solo. My RA assailant has me particularly tired and stiff today, slowing my already poky pace and leaving me farther behind than usual. Joe must be taking two steps for every one of mine.

"*Il est parti, le monsieur?*" asks a trail runner, passing me on his way down. He left, your guy? I guess he saw Joe up ahead.

"*Ouais, il est parti,*" I say with a shrug. Yeah, he's gone.

"*Tant pis,*" he says—too bad—and quickly disappears.

Butterflies entertain me, suddenly flittering everywhere. A delicate peach one with a black spot on its wings keeps me company. It dances its way up the trail and distracts me from my burning lungs. I whisper butterfly in several languages, all of them some of my favorite words. They roll softly around my mouth: butterfly, *farfalla, mariposa, papillon.*

My winged companion stays close until I reach a clearing with a view back over the valley. I spot our inn and its orange tile roof in Ménerbes, now a speck among miniature farm buildings, and just like that, any irritation I feel toward Joe evaporates. How often have I told him not to coddle me?

I turn to continue and see him sitting just ahead on a curry-colored rock.

"Where are our crampons?" I call, happy to see him although annoyance needles.

"Sorry I didn't wait for you. I knew if I stopped, I'd never get going again. Really. I can't believe how steep this thing is—the angle is absurd. Forgive me?"

I step toward him and smile. "Just hope there's a soft place to sit at the top."

"Actually, I hope there *is* a top." His optimism astounds me.

After another hour of vertical agony, we arrive above the tree line at the crest, I just after Joe. We look north, all the way to the bleached bald pate of *Mont Ventoux*, our next major climb, and then to the snow-capped Alps towering in the northeast. We munch on protein bars and then take a roundabout, zigzag route down. Finally, I'm in the lead.

In the Luberon, rosé wines flourish, ripe, oil-soaked olives and crusty bread precede every meal, roasted vegetables crown seafood platters. My taste buds tingle, anticipating every dish. On a really good day with my head high and my spine straight, I'm all of five foot three. I've forever wished I were taller so I could eat more, especially when I'm in this part of the world. With five more inches, I could actually have dessert without worrying about my thighs. But with the GR20 looming, I have to take extra care to keep the pounds away. I'll have to carry any ounce I gain up Corsica's unforgiving slopes.

When I was growing up, three activities consumed our household: making a meal, eating a meal, and cleaning up after a meal. That's it. And no one left the table until all plates were clean. My parents insisted that their eleven children eat three meals a day, with plates full of carbohydrates to fill empty bellies: meat, potatoes, gravy, white bread with margarine, and dessert. Always dessert. The speediest among us vied for seconds—if you finished first, you held your plate like Oliver Twist. "More, please."

Once, one of my little brothers, inconsolable when told he had to finish his dinner, dried tears running down his cheeks with a piece of bread. *Think of the children in Africa!* I cared about children without enough to eat and would gladly have given them my food. Three squares on my small frame were never a good idea. Add to that my father's Mexican Indian heritage and the squat body type that dominates family photos when he was a boy, and my chances for being thin were doomed. I've struggled with it all my life.

We move on to Roussillon, an ocher hilltop hamlet, on Bastille Day (July 14), the celebration of France's independence from the king. I lean over the windowsill toward a young *maman* and her two sons, one with a baguette under his arm, the other munching a croissant. They clench tiny French flags and sing "La Marseillaise." "*Le jour de gloire est arrivé!*"

We celebrate the holiday with a hike through Roussillon's hills and catch up with the twelfth stage of the Tour de France. We join the crowd on a grassy rise overlooking the route. We first hear their hum and then see them hover over outlying vineyards, craning our necks to see the thumping whirlybirds following the riders. Cowbells clatter. Crowd noise swells, and then finally, the sleek peloton approaches behind a rolling wall of security. The spectators go wild, the athletes fly by in a blaze of color, and in a flash, we're left in their wake. The crowd quiets, families disperse, and the race moves on.

Sun-soaked after an ebullient day celebrating Bastille Day, we relax over dinner with a bottle of rosé and collapse into bed. At one in the morning, we're awakened by a call from Caroline. "I just want to be sure you're both safe."

Why wouldn't we be? I think in the fog of a dream. "We're fine, sweetheart. Everything all right?"

The day's frivolity is shattered. The tragedy in Nice sinks in slowly, the realization of what's happened on the Promenade des Anglais. We assure Caroline that we're hours north of the Côte d'Azur and ask her to call Chris. *Liberté, égalité, fraternité. Je suis Nice.*

The Provençal sun is fierce. Despite slathering sunblock, our skin darkens as we spend hours climbing. "Except for my blond hair, there's no doubt about my ancestry," I say, stretching my red-brown arms in front of Joe. "And even your Irish skin is tan."

He's studying the spreadsheet he built for Corsica. It lists the daily terrain, where we'll sleep [in tents, *gîtes d'étape* (private hostels), and former ski lodges on two luxurious nights], and whether we'll have our duffels. If where we stop for the night is accessible by road, our guide will have them transferred and waiting. If not, we'll do without.

"Nervous about anything?" I ask, looking over Joe's shoulder at the spreadsheet.

He stands to hug me. "Maybe that I'm not the athlete I used to be?" He laughs. "Actually, I'm mostly worried about your health holding up and if we can do this whole thing. The most we've done is seven days in a row. Like the TMB. Can we do thirteen?"

"I'm nervous about that too. We'll be totally beat every night and will have to get up and do it all again the next day. But since Paris, my RA's been behaving, so. . . ."

"We'll just have to pace ourselves and hope your joints keep cooperating, right?"

I nod. "And how about your vertigo? Any nightmares about narrow ledges?"

"Thank God, no. But I have been thinking about electrical storms. Just read a blog post about a couple caught in one on The Twenty. It ended well, but it did put me on edge. You know how I am about lightning. Did you know it's called astraphobia?"

"Had no idea. But what if we just keep everything we're worried about between us and not talk about it? You know, our age, my RA, your vertigo, and astraphobia. They'll be our secrets, and maybe they'll all just go away."

"Agreed. That would be good. But, let's sort out our stuff just one more time. To make sure we've got everything we need and nothing we don't. Can never be too sure."

We spread our gear across the bed. The tent is in the middle, Joe's pile on one side, mine on the other: sleeping bags, pillows, towels, sporks, lamps, poles, clothes. We study it all, debate the merits of each item and think in terms of grams. Every one we carry will make each step harder. We tear off tags; we'll share a knife, so we put one aside; I take the carabiner from my water bottle; I rip out half my journal's pages; we put moleskin and wet wipes in baggies; we stuff our sleeping bags in our packs and Joe attaches the tent to the outside of his with bungee cords. Tomorrow: up Mont Ventoux, fully loaded.

We arrive in Bedoin, cycling mecca extraordinaire. The village is overrun with MAMILs (middle-aged men in Lycra) on expensive bikes in flashy, tight, never-attractive jerseys and shorts. We're the only walkers—this is Tour de France territory, after all—and take to the trail, leaving the road to the cyclists. This is the toughest hike yet.

Except for an aromatic stretch on pine needles, we're on steep, stony slopes up Mont Ventoux.

On our way back down to the village, we tackle a sharp decline. The scree is slippery, and even with help of our poles, Joe and I slide in tandem, falling on our rumps, cushioned by our packs. We're two turtles on our backs, unable to get right-side up. We roll to our sides, laughing. "Sometimes I think the prep alone will kill us," Joe says.

"Exactly. I just want the real thing to start because I'm so over training."

"You know, we have yet to run into any Americans on our hikes."

"Most Americans in Provence come to relax. Smart Americans, that is."

We make it to Nice, her sadness palpable. Along the sea, we walk down the broad Promenade des Anglais, site of the July 14 massacre, where a cargo truck was deliberately driven into a Bastille Day crowd not two weeks earlier. Eighty-six died, and over four hundred were injured. The makeshift memorial of flowers, pictures, and teddy bears lines the boulevard as we linger and then make our way around the headland to the old port.

Hôtel Le Saint Paul, her pink facade facing the Mediterranean, is a faded lady past her prime. Look closely and you'll see her beds are made with limp linens, balusters are missing chunks of plaster, and potted plants drop dry leaves onto cracked tiles. Guests come for her views, but we like her budget prices and proximity to the ferry to Corsica.

Joe goes for a final run around the port, and I realize that when I next don my trekking clothes, it will be to start the hike. I consider my body in the full-length mirror before a shower. Summer's sun has bleached my hair lighter, and I'm as lean and brown as I've ever been. And yet, the firm lines of youth have softened. My thighs still threaten to fall over my knees, and I know that no amount of exercise will ever totally tighten my tummy. I make muscles with my arms, raising gentle brown mounds, but the flesh underneath is jiggly and pale, like laundry on a line. Still, I've never trained harder for anything, and I have to believe my body will come through. I'm ready for The Twenty.

It's departure day, and my wrists ache in the sharp sea air. I have a hard time with my pack, so Joe hoists it, and I slip it on. We drag our duffels to the dock, and I alternate hands every few yards to share the strain. My invader is coming with us. Damn you! The smell of tar, the briny taste of the breeze, the screech of gulls, and the oil-sheened water assault my senses. Joe snaps pictures of ships as they come and go, sounding their horns in passing.

At last, our ride approaches: the Corsica Ferries Mega Express Two, smoke rising from her stack. Anxious chills tickle my spine as our mobile bridge to Corsica looms—a heavy machine silently, gracefully gliding. She towers above the breakwater and then cuts an arc into port. Her propellers reverse, her bow thrusters kick in, churning up a wake. The diesels throb, pushing her bulk gently to the dock. Steel plates grate, and from the ferry's gaping maw, a parade of cars, campers, motorbikes, trucks piled with produce, and a throng of pedestrians disgorge. The gangway becomes a hurly-burly traffic jam.

"Is there anything as exciting as traveling by ship?" I ask Joe. He smiles, thinking I've said it just to please his inner mariner, but I do anticipate the journey. Watching ships set sail always fills me with longing for new destinations, and this time, we'll be aboard.

The broad yellow stripe on the ship's blue stack surprises me. It features the profile of an African Muslim—*la tête de maure,* a Moor's head—with a white bandanna across his forehead. Joe tells me the likeness is also on the white Corsican flag. The island known to the French as *La Corse, l'Île de Béauté*—is represented as a Moor. It gnaws at my sensitivity about race and ethnicity. I research its origins on my phone.

I learn that the island's standard has a checkered history. The *Testa di Moru*, the Moor's head in Corsican, first graced the flag of its Italian island neighbor, Sardinia, in the Middle Ages. It seems a curious choice, but it connoted a strong, independent people. When the King of Aragon defeated Muslim armies, he added their coat of arms to his own. A blindfolded version was adopted when he conquered Sardinia, and the design jumped north to Corsica. Eventually, defiant separatists embraced the bandeau-across-the-brow to symbolize independence when the island became part of France in the 1700s.

I've always bonded deeply with France, even suspecting I was a French peasant in a former life. It's now time for my pilgrim's heart to make room for a new piece of her, stretching my connection to its island to the south, between the Ligurian and Tyrrhenian seas: a little bit French, a little bit Italian, and distinctly Corsican. Its 3,400 square miles of craggy terrain with 620 miles of coastline would easily fit inside Connecticut. Its outline is a clenched fist, with the twenty-five-mile-long Cap Corse peninsula a knuckled index finger pointing north as if to warn outsiders, "Beware!" Including its cautionary digit, the island measures 114 miles north–south by 52 miles east–west, the fourth largest and most mountainous island in the Mediterranean. Although warmer than mainland France, it receives much more rainfall, and its mountains are streaked with snow year-round.

I massage my wrists as we queue up to board on the busy quay, Joe's arm around me. I feel apart from the easygoing holiday hordes of designer sunglass-sporting vacationers streaming off the ferry smelling of sunscreen. I imagine the visits of those rolling down the ramp. How many were on the island to explore its interior? Did any do the GR20? Did they start *and* reach the end? What are their stories? What will be ours?

We're on adventure's gangplank, about to jump off, with only limited notions of what lies ahead, 150 miles across the sea. We're blank pages upon which Corsica will write her complicated story. The Greeks called the island *Kallisté*, the most beautiful; Balzac described it as "a French island basking in the Italian sun"; Matisse said the island is where, "all is color, all is light." Soon we'll see for ourselves.

After four hours at sea, land appears on the hazy horizon, a phantom island rising from the depths. Indistinct gray shapes jutting out of the Mediterranean soon become mountain silhouettes—one after the other, surging between sea and sky.

We head outside to get a better look. Joe says, "Those are some serious rises. Wow. I read that Corsica is basically a mountain in the Med that plunges into the sea, and now I get it. Something like two-thirds is covered by peaks, and some of those suckers are nine thousand feet. My legs are cramping already, and those pinnacles are doing a job on my vertigo."

As the barren, jagged heights come into focus, I'm weak at the prospect of crossing them. "Until we started thinking about doing this, I never knew Corsica had mountains at all. . . ." We trace the island's coast of ragged reefs on the way to the northeastern port city of Bastia. Huddles of houses and stone churches cling precariously to ridges that dive straight to the sea. I drift off thinking about my love for France and how comfortable I am when I'm here. But suddenly, Corsica feels strangely foreign. I shiver and my eyes close.

"I'm going inside to check the map I saw on the bulkhead," says Joe.

A woman takes his place at the rail and asks in French if we'll be visiting family.

"No," I say. "We're hikers headed to the GR20."

"*Ooh là là*," she says, cocking her head. She pumps her fist in a tight perpendicular line toward her body, the French gesture for difficult. "*C'est dur, ça.*" That's hard. She tells me she enjoys hiking too, but never does anything difficult. She warns that it gets cold in the mountains, even in midsummer. "And very windy," she adds. "*Bonne chance!*"

As I watch her disappear through the lounge door, without warning, suffocating panic rises. I'm suddenly light-headed, struggling to breathe, my RA invader attacking.

Stop this ship; I want to get off. I can't do this. I'm not well enough. I'm too old. I clench the rail. No escape.

I join Joe inside for a steaming cup of tea. I wrap my hands around it, struggle not to shake in the air-conditioning, force myself to inhale, exhale, be calm. I keep my anxiety to myself, reluctant to dampen Joe's boyish enthusiasm as he goes out to watch our arrival.

What would I say to my children if they felt as I do? Perhaps a version of what I told them growing up: If you always avoid feeling scared, you'll never try anything new.

Inhale, exhale, be calm. My breathing slows as I continue my self-talk. You're starting a tough physical challenge, but you can handle it. You can. Breathe in, breathe out, be calm. You'll be tired, but you'll pull through. You'll grow new muscles and find new strength. You'll do your best on every one of the thirteen days. Every. Single. One.

I take an extra-deep breath, drain my tea, brace myself against the wind, and join Joe on deck.

Because in the end, you won't remember the time you spent working in the office or mowing your lawn. Climb that goddamn mountain.

—Jack Kerouac

PART II: CORSICA
ARRIVAL THROUGH DAY FIVE

July 30–31
Bastia, Corsica

The familiar glee of arriving in a place where not a soul knows us surges. After a year of anticipation and months of training, we've made it to Corsica, whispers from the continent behind us. The marine layer has burned off, and a clear blue afternoon welcomes us, the sun's hot white light blinding the walk to our port hotel. Wherever we see a French *tricolore* flying, there beside it is the quirky Corsican flag.

"Did you know Corsica was the first part of France liberated from the Nazis?" Joe asks. "The Germans first left Ajaccio and then headed north. And Bastia was where they left for good."

"Didn't know that. But I do know I can always count on you for colorful historical commentary."

We pass a monumental marble statue of the island's most famous son—Napoleon Bonaparte, looking out to sea in a Roman toga—holding court over the town's central Place Saint-Nicolas. It's my turn to add some background knowledge. I tell Joe that the future emperor's father, Charles-Marie Bonaparte, was deputy to revolutionary leader Pascal Paoli and thus, Napoleon began his life as a patriotic islander (although he would become fiercely anti-Corsican as the leader of France). And that, while born and raised in the capital city of Ajaccio, it was from Bastia's town's harbor that young Napoleon set sail for his formal education at a military academy in France.

"Never knew you were a Napoleonic scholar," says Joe.

"Neither did I. Just became one on the ferry over."

We have the rest of the day to explore, adjust to being on the island, and relax before meeting our group tomorrow. The town's labyrinthine Vieux Port, overlooked by colorful houses and the ramparts of a citadel built in the 1500s by the city's founders from Genoa, teems with quayside terraces under awnings, all of them overflowing with patrons chatting, laughing, and enjoying seafood and drinks. Despite the fact that the pastel buildings are not as post-card perfect as when seen from a ship—in fact, many are close to crumbling, and laundry lines hang from pipes and window grills—we warm immediately to this lively Gallic-Italian city. Wandering vibrant Bastia is a delight.

My anxiety calms, but the shaky feeling lingers, my stomach fluttering randomly. We sit scorching in the late afternoon at a waterfront café, part of the afternoon hubbub, watching ferries come and go—in from Genoa, Marseille, and Nice and then back out again. Joe studies the trail map, his brows drawn together in concern. A pretty white sailboat catches my eye. My father's dismissive assertion—*You're no athlete*—rings in my ears until a sudden summer downpour sends us scurrying.

We get into bed that night, and I finally share my anxiety with Joe, pouring it out until I'm empty. And as he always does, he calms me with gentle reassurance, putting his usual pessimism aside. He reminds me how hard we've worked and that we're doing this together. "We're just both going to give it our best. What more can we do?" He rubs my back as we drift off to sleep, belief in my ability gently making its return.

"No way you can run two miles without stopping—that's eight times around the track," dared a high school friend on the track team, shaking her head as she folded her arms across her chest. "Five dollars says you can't." It was 1971, I was fifteen, and five dollars was the equivalent of babysitting for six hours. My frame was hardly athletic, but I would show her. And my father too. I'd show anyone with a challenge that inside that soft, pudgy exterior was a young woman determined to prove she was an athlete. And I did.

"Still have butterflies?" Joe asks the following morning over cafés au lait and croissants on a café terrace near our hotel.

"A couple more than a few. A flight, a flock, a gaggle, or whatever you call a lot of them." I laugh. "But I'm telling myself it's excitement and not fear. Seems to be working."

We'll soon rendezvous with our GR20 guide and five other hikers at the airport, keenly aware that how the next two weeks play out will have much to do with our companions. I think about meeting them with equal parts anticipation ("Do you think there'll be other women?") and trepidation ("Will they be friendly?"), interrupted by occasional jolts of terror when Joe says, "What if they're all twenty-year-old hard bodies and they leave us in the dust?"

"What happened to my cheerleader from last night? We'll just show them what sixty-year-olds can do."

I'm distracted by the conversation of men at a nearby table. My back to them, I hear their tone and picture tough, swarthy dudes with five o'clock shadows at eight in the morning. I'm sure they're smoking unfiltered cigarettes in their wife beaters, plotting something nefarious. I shift my chair to take in the scene. They are indeed smoking as they sip espressos, but they wear faded pastel polos, baggy shorts, and leather sandals with dark socks. They're the Golden Boys of Bastia, likely grandfathers all. Clearly, they're good friends, now greeting a new arrival with backslaps and exaggerated welcomes. They read their papers and discuss the news with gusto and a distinctly Corsican rhythm, but I'm not privy to a word they say. Corsica is twice as far from France's Provençal shore as it is from Italy's Tuscan coast, and thus it makes sense that while Italians follow the language with some difficulty, the French (and I) understand it not at all.

I open my *Cicerone Guide* and reread that although the island's lingua franca is French, most residents speak Corsican (officially lingua corsa) at home, and schools are generally bilingual. Often mistaken for a French dialect, Corsican is a Romance language but was not written until the late 1800s. Only half the island's population of 330,000 (which almost triples in the summer) was actually born here, many with French first names and Italian surnames. Most identify themselves as Corsican and only if pushed do they admit to also being French.

"Enough of reading about this place," I say to Joe, closing my book. We take final sips of coffee and brush croissant flakes from our laps. "Time to meet our fellow climbers."

"Hello," says a mid-thirties man with a broad, contagious smile and very white teeth—a French surfer dude with youthful, good looks and unruly, sun-streaked locks. He speaks English carefully with a lovely French accent and offers strong handshakes. "I am Julien, your GR20 guide." He pronounces it the French way, *jay-er van.* "You are *definitivement* the first to arrive at the meeting point." We introduce ourselves, and he checks off our names on his clipboard. "Marianne and Joseph, *enchanté*, nice to meet you. Marianne is a good French name, *non*?"

"*Mais oui*," I say, referring to an enduring French symbol, the female embodiment of the Republic. "*L'esprit de la France*." The spirit of France. I return his smile.

"*Ah, bon!*" he says, genuinely pleased, his manner easy and warm. He insists I address him with the informal *tu* and not the formal *vous*. "I love it when someone in my group speaks French. It makes it very much less *stressant* for me," he says in English for Joe's benefit. "So, let me ask you. Is there anything I need to know about you before the hike? *Les allergies*? Some medical issues?"

Joe and I shoot each other a look. Not a word! Nothing about RA. Nothing about vertigo, keeping each other's confidences.

"*D'accord*. Okay good, so I will return soon. I will go to look for the others."

I watch Julien walk away, his lean frame in turquoise hiker shorts, orange tee, and black flip-flops, a canvas messenger bag slung across his torso. Whorls of blond hair cover his toned calves, and his bronzed skin signals the hours he spends outdoors. For just a moment, I think about the twenty-five years that separate us and momentarily lower my eyes, sighing.

I once again bury my nose in my guidebook to reread for the umpteenth time the section on the hike's start until Julien returns, sandals slapping, with three others in tow: two men and a woman. A woman!

We're guarded as we exchange names, size each other up, and assess relative ages, hiking abilities, fitness, and experience. Where do we fall on each continuum? There are *definitivement* no twenty-year-olds! Those youngsters go without guides. I squelch any fears I'll be less capable than the others, allowing my reserve of confidence to hang tight. Bravado and drugs will get me through this, if I let them. I'll prove my father wrong, imagine I don't have RA, and drive myself hard. I *can* do this and I *will*.

Joe pulls me aside. "Bet you're happy you're not the only woman."

"You're so right about that! Some girl talk will do me good."

"Ha. Someone to talk to besides me."

"You know I'll never get tired of talking to you." I put my hand on his shoulder. "But having a buddy will definitely be good."

Julien tells us that two of our group haven't yet arrived. "You will meet one person at dinner tonight and the other one at breakfast tomorrow."

In the meantime, we've met Phil, a fortysomething self-employed accountant from England's Midlands with a sometimes-impenetrable accent; Jim, a thirty-nine-year-old American living in Dublin who works for a tech company; and Sarah, a retired Oxford physician about my age (and height) with a grip like a vise. I pride myself on a strong handshake, but my knuckles are tender, and I almost cry out in pain meeting Sarah. We all have considerable experience on the trail, but our compatriots' trekking résumés include exotic exploits like Nepal's Annapurna Circuit, the Rila Mountains of Bulgaria, and Patagonia's Tierra del Fuego. We throw our week hiking around Mont Blanc on the TMB in the mix to establish our own international hiking bona fides. I look over at Joe, and he looks skeptical. I wink to say, *We'll be fine.*

Calvi, Corsica

A minivan takes us across wild terrain until we reach "the garden of Corsica," the sunny, honey-hued region of pastel villages—la Balagne, in the island's northwest corner. The sporadic conversation for the hour-and-a-half transfer on twisty roads through citrus orchards and olive groves centers on how and when each of us arrived on the island and our backgrounds, trekking and otherwise. Joe and I say, "We're retired" but have a hard time with verb tenses when we talk about jobs. There's that fine line between who we are and what we do. Does he say "I am" or "I was" an engineer? Do I say "I am" or "I was" a teacher? We opt for the present tense, deciding that just because we're not working doesn't mean we've relinquished our professions.

Our driver drops us at a nondescript budget hotel in Calvi, the capital of Balagne, founded by the Romans in the first century. The sophisticated seaside resort town, dominated by an imposing fifteenth-century Genoese fortress protected by massive bastions, has sweeping views of both the sea and the mountains, is home to the French Foreign Legion and a quick drive from the trailhead in Calenzana.

The sixth hiker, Chris from North East England, joins us for an early evening walk. At thirty-five, he's the youngest of our group, a tall, sandy-haired man on hiatus from his globe-trotting job testing oil rigs. We follow the edge of a pine grove until we reach the arc of the broad beach, its pearly-white sand fine and shallow water crystal clear. Tourists crowd the port esplanade, many of them off yachts anchored in the harbor. Joe sticks with Julien, and I hang back to chat with the others. Sarah comments that she's never seen so many deeply tanned, leathery men and women in her life, most of them older than we are. "Looks like Corsica's a sunbather's paradise," she says. "They must live on the beach from May through October to get so brown."

"Better not criticize. We may look like them after just two weeks in the sun," I say.

Julien leads us through tight cobblestoned streets and then down an alley to where we'll have dinner. Just before arriving at the restaurant, Joe doubles back and pulls me aside, grinning ear to ear. "What's up?" I ask. "You look like you just won the lottery!"

"I feel like I did! Julien says we don't need our tent and sleeping pads."

"What? Why not? We've lugged that stuff around for a month."

It's a rare occurrence, but my glass is half empty and Joe's is spilling over.

"All the refuges have tents with mats already set up, and Julien will assign us one when we get there. That saves us nine pounds of weight—five for the tent and two for each pad. Do you know how much lighter our packs will be? Especially mine without the tent."

"That's great, Joe, it really is—I just can't believe how much money and care we put into buying things we won't use."

"Hey, we'll just have to get more serious about camping when we get home."

"I know we haven't even started, but am I crazy to already be looking forward to celebrating when it's over? I just have to be able to picture a gourmet feast and a long, hot bubble bath to soothe blisters I can only imagine right now."

"Nope, not crazy. Whatever it takes to get us to the end."

Over an abundant meal of Corsican specialties—grilled fish, sausage, and potatoes—on a vine-draped terrace, we banter about food and drink in the manner of adults who have just met. About how sophisticated French cuisine relies on rich sauces and complicated preparation, while the island's specialties feature simple herbaceous flavors. But as wine and beer flow, tongues loosen, personalities emerge, and awkwardness melts away. Chris says little but it's clear he likes his beer. He downs multiple Pietras, Corsica's signature brew, while the rest of us, save Phil, whose drink of choice is Coke, sip wine.

Phil, it turns out, is the most extreme mountaineer among us. He's climbed all over the world and has significant technical experience, including overnights on glaciers and hanging off rock faces. He's always been single, and I wonder if it's because he's forever running off to scale a mountain. His salt-and-pepper hair is tightly cut, and he has an infectious laugh and quirky wit. From the moment they meet, Joe views Phil with a mixture of fascination for his hiking cred and delight for his willingness to be teased. Joe always needs a partner in humor, and he's found one for this trip.

"How do you expect to keep a girlfriend when you're always away?" Joe asks.

"Oh, I take them climbing sometimes, but they always end up crying," says Phil, his upper lip curling in a grin.

"Well, I'd be crying too if you were my date."

Jim, also single, has a shaved head and big blue eyes, is a bit soft around the middle, and seems to take our undertaking less seriously than the rest of us. He's hiked quite a bit and appears unconcerned about the days ahead. "Nah," he says when I ask if he's worried about the next two weeks. "Can't be any harder than what I've hiked already."

Sarah, petite with a strawberry blond pixie cut, pale skin, and admirably muscled calves, has a way of cocking her head and closing her eyes, elfin-like, when asking questions. She has me chuckling right away as we bond over discussing our love for our grown children.

"Hard to believe now, but when I was a teen I told myself I never wanted children," I admit. "But that's a story for another day."

"Well, clearly you were sensible," she says, "stopping at two." I can't help loving her posh Oxford accent and expressions as she continues, "Don't know what possessed me in my salad days, but I had four, including a set of twins." We chat about the challenges of raising children while working full-time, she at all hours as a physician and I in the frenetic worlds of publishing and then teaching, and discover a shared weakness for wine. We clink our glasses when Julien assures us we can look forward to copious carafes at the end of each day on the trail. "The *réfuges* sell beer, soda, snacks, and of course, wine."

With that, I pour the others and myself a second glass, thinking that maybe with my new friend Sarah and my drink of choice, this hike won't be so tough after all.

I always had difficulty in school. Not with classwork—that came easy. Rather, my painful shyness hindered making friends, signaling others to stay away. You would think that growing up the eldest in a house filled with children forever multiplying would have kept me plenty companied, but I longed for regular friends. "You have so many siblings," my mother always said. Couldn't she see it wasn't the same?

I'd had six childhood homes across five states by the time I was twelve. Six homes and six schools. Frequent moves required by my father's job with General Electric might have made me good at meeting people, but they did just the opposite. I was in sixth grade, walking, yet again, into an unfamiliar school, this one in Smithtown, on New York's Long Island. There were no nuns in the hallways, no crucifixes over the blackboard, no icons of saints, no crowns of thorns, no posters with hands bound by a rosary. I was plump with a bad perm, in my new outfit from JCPenney—a gold plaid jumper over a white Peter Pan blouse. Sears and Penney's were the only shopping options since they had "chubby girl" sections. I wanted to hide in the dressing room whenever we shopped for clothes, mortified when my mother asked a clerk, "Would you point us to the chubby sizes?"

I was the only one in class in a dress and knee socks. Everyone else wore pants. The class stared, as they always did, at the awkward new girl—a Catholic school kid in an alien land—a public school virgin. My mother told people, "Marianne's in," voice lowered, head leaning forward, "public school." Yet again, I wanted to hide. "There's no room in Saint Patrick's." Was I damaged goods because I went to "public school?" Always in quotes, like a foreign language.

It wasn't until halfway through sixth grade that I learned the world wasn't divided in two: Catholics and Publics. How was I to know Public wasn't a religion?

"Thank God there are two of us in this group," Sarah says, interrupting my thoughts. "Two middle-aged women on an adventure."

"I know, right? I'm so grateful to have you along."

"Way too much testosterone with just guys. But let me ask you: How much longer you think we'll be able to get away with calling ourselves middle-aged? At what point do we cross over to elderly?"

"I figure the elderly label is always out there about ten years older than where we are at any given moment. It'll always be just over the horizon somewhere."

"Amen. Let's just keep it at bay."

I sit back in my chair, relaxing my shoulders. Knowing I'll be on the trail with Sarah calms me. I'm reassured about tomorrow morning's start.

Monday, August 1
The Hike–Day One: Calenzana to Réfuge Ortu di u Pobbio

↗ **Ascent:** 5,249 feet

↘ **Descent:** 1,119 feet

→ **Distance:** 9 miles

Guidebook Description: This day is a fine introduction to the rigors and delights of the GR20—it's your baptism of fire.

I awaken an hour before the alarm is set to sound at 4:30, my mind reeling about the day ahead. I can't get back to sleep. Am I excited or just terrified? Nerves. Damned nerves. I roll the stats over and over in my head: thirteen days, eight hours a day, 62,300 feet of ups and downs, 124 miles. I'm an optimist, but right now I'm a worrier—about pack weight, about my joints holding up, and overall about "the toughest hike in Europe." I think back to what Julien told us at dinner. Our three most important necessities are boots that fit, staying motivated, and a positive attitude. "You must be prepared to work hard, but your motor will be more in your head than in your legs."

While I toss and turn, I hear the ding of a text from a friend back home. "You go girl. You got this, Mar!" it says with two smiley faces. Her message delivers a kick of needed adrenaline. Perfect timing. The alarm finally rings, startling me even though I expect it. Time to trade what we've visualized for so long for the reality of the trail. I send a quick text to Chris and Caroline to say we're heading off soon and that we can't wait to tell them all about it. I practically leap from bed into the shower, so ready am I to start the day.

I luxuriate in the hot water, forehead pressed on my palms against the tile, my back in the scalding stream. I take in the heat, acknowledging that even tepid showers will be rare on the trail. I feel as if I'm starting school, and, as on every single first day of grammar school, tears run down my checks.

I hug the edge of a lunch table, my outsider status apparent. Busy sixth-grade conversations hum around me, but I'm invisible, apart from the breeziness of others: effortlessly cool girls with high ponytails and cocky, white-toothed boys for whom friendship and popularity are givens. I just want to fit in, but they ignore me. The new girl. I have a hard time breathing, feeling out of control. What's going on? Am I dying or worse, about to go crazy? I can't tell my mother. Don't want to upset her. She has too many worries already. I spend recess at the edge of the woods on the far side of the playground. I jab at dry leaves with my toe, fighting nausea as hot tears flow. My head hurts and my heart races as if to escape my chest. I've read about fight-or-flight in *Seventeen* magazine. Is that what this is? But there's nothing to fight and I've nowhere to run.

I leave the shower running so Joe can hop right in. I use two towels to dry, one for my hair and one for my body, knowing that the next time I wash, I'll have just one compact, quick-drying camping cloth.

What will go in our backpacks is carefully laid out on the linoleum floor. I jam my Big Agnes sleeping bag in the lower compartment—she just barely fits—and manage to zip it closed. I fill my two-liter reservoir and one-liter plastic bottle with store-bought water to start. Today's going to be long and hot, and we'll pass only one spring early on, so Julien recommended we carry at least two liters. On subsequent days, there will be well-timed springs for refills, but on day one, I don't want to skimp. So despite the added weight, I'll carry three.

Joe and I exchange no words as we review our checklist yet again and continue to pack, layering what we'll need for the next three days. Our lodge on night three is reachable by car, so our duffels will be waiting. But until then, we'll carry what we need.

My forty-five-liter burgundy pack filled, I slip my thumbs-up picture of Chris and Caroline into a Ziplock bag—my wallet for the trail. I braid my hair using my favorite wood-handled brush—the one personal luxury item I've allowed myself—into two neat plaits and tie a bandanna round my neck. I look over at Joe lacing his boots. He crosses the room for an extended hug. I don't want to let go.

My face flushes and hands tremble with anticipation as we head down to breakfast, my shiny first-day-of-school Mary Janes replaced by well-worn hiking boots. I do my best to hold my head high, heeding a former colleague's counsel: Always walk in like you belong. Coffee, croissants, a crusty baguette, ham, yogurt, and wedges of Corsican *tomme de brébis* (powerful, nutty sheep cheese) are on the tableclothed serving table, left by the hotel for zero dark thirty hikers like us. The hushed, predawn dining room is dimly lit and filled with square wooden tables. The chilly temperature exacerbates my trembling, and I can't wait to get my hands around a cup of hot tea.

What becomes a two-week sequence of who arrives when for our morning meal is quickly established. Julien, blond hair wild in sleep-induced tufts, fixes his coffee and chunks our bread. Phil is at the ready, seated, calm, smiling, sipping his tea as Joe and I join him.

"Hungry?" Joe asks Phil, eyeing his abundant plate.

"Need to keep up my energy," he says with a laugh, "and you should too." It's the first piece of advice our Midlands friend gives us, and I'm sure it won't be the last.

Joe pours himself a mug of coffee and a cup of tea for me. My hand shakes as I bring the tea to my mouth, drops of hot milky brew falling to my lap. I force myself to eat something though my stomach rebels.

"*Les toilettes?*" I ask Julien. Not a good way to start the morning.

Next to arrive is the eighth and senior member of our merry band, sixty-three-year-old attorney Kees from the Netherlands, who got in well after midnight. He's a very tall, slim man who towers above Joe's six feet and for whom the word "taciturn" is apt. He has the sad face of a bloodhound, with large droopy eyes behind funky black glasses, and unnerving gravity. What might he look like if he managed a smile?

Jim joins us shortly thereafter, desperate for coffee, and then Sarah totters in, her eyes small, still fuzzy with sleep. "I do *not* function until I have my morning tea," she says as she wraps both hands lovingly around her cuppa. "But I actually do best with three," she adds, holding up her middle fingers to emphasize the number. And so we've been duly warned that hiking cannot begin until Sarah has her caffeine fix. She chatters on about the tasty cheese ("absolutely scrummy"), buttery pastries ("even scrummier"), and how she slept like a rock. Jitters about the day ahead have my tongue.

Joe sees Kees pull a GR20 guidebook from his pack and asks, "So, Kees, have you read it?" Our Dutch teammate is clearly exhausted as he takes off his glasses, eyes unfocused. "No. I have not. I bought it but never opened it. It's a pity," he says, too tired to speak further. My eyes meet Joe's and I know what he's thinking. I've read that book so many times, I can practically recite it by heart. Does Kees understand what he's in for?

As Julien gets up to check on Chris, the only one still missing, we hear, "Cheers," as the leggy Brit saunters in, pours his coffee, and sits at the head of the table. No buffet for him. He's brought his own energy bar.

"Did a little partying last night, did you?" asks his assigned roommate, Jim, in a feigned Irish brogue.

"Actually," says Chris, all eyes on him, "I did." He gives a little smile and takes a bite of his bar. It's all we'll get.

Julien picks up his pack, signaling time to go. "Guys, lunch is next to the buffet," he says. "Take a box of salad, some fruit, and a bag of cookies. I'll take everything else." My stomach is in knots and I can't even think about our next meal. So much for last night's chat with Sarah calming me down.

Our van's headlights cut through early morning mist on the ride from Calvi to the Calenzana trailhead. It's where we'll start climbing the mountain chain that bisects the island from the northwest in Calvi to the summit of Monte Cinto at nine thousand feet, and then heads southeast toward Porto-Vecchio. The Twenty's 124 miles are broken into sixteen stages, or étapes—the ground we'll cross on any given day—nine in the north half and seven in the south. Joe and I debated whether to go with a guide that started in the north and went south versus going with one that went from the south to the north, weighing the pros and cons of each. The northern half is alpine, rocky, and rugged with punishing ascents and descents across tricky, tormented terrain, while the southern section includes longer stretches but with more moderate, verdant miles and fewer grueling angles. Some believe it best to face the difficult northern section first with a fresh body full of energy. Others insist that a gentler southern start gives hikers time to build muscle and adjust to the complexities of the trail.

We chose the traditional route, as do most hikers, starting in the north. Étapes one through six are reputedly the toughest, but also the most beautiful and dramatic. They are rocky and steep with more elevation change over fewer miles. Numbers seven through sixteen continue southeast to the village of Conca, where the trail ends. In general, the ups and downs of the southern portion are less vertical and the path is more defined with fewer down on all fours, hand-over-hand scrambles.

If you do one étape a day, the hike takes just over two weeks, but our itinerary includes three double stages, so we'll be on the trail for thirteen days. Many hikers we'll meet will be day-trekkers doing just a couple legs, preferring to achieve the full distance by tackling a few étapes each summer. Only a small percentage will be thru-hikers like us, determined to do The Twenty in one go. In fact, the dropout rate is substantial—less than 50 percent of the eighteen thousand hikers a year who attempt the trek in one stretch succeed, and most of them cut the endeavor short because of foot problems. *Hmm*, I think. *One out of two. Does that mean several of us won't complete this thing?*

On the drive through olive groves and vineyards, both heavy with fruit, Julien tells us it's rumored that gangsters from Marseille, members of the notorious organized crime group Le Milieu, have homes in Calenzana. "Very beautiful homes with very fancy cars," he adds. I recall a colleague who said, "I hear you're going to Corsica— don't forget your bulletproof vest." And although the island has a reputation for violence, especially citizens who want separation from France and clans that kill for family honor, surely his comment is a caricature.

"There are many guns on Corsica," Julien says. "You see the marks on the stop sign? There," he points. "They are from bullets. Almost every sign is hit. Corsican people love to shoot, they love fireworks, and *en fait*, they love everything that goes *boom*! Especially the FLNC—le Front de Libération Nationale Corse. They are the people who want La Corse to be independent."

Chris says, chuckling, "So maybe Corsica should be called the Island of Bandits and not the Island of Beauty."

Admittedly, there is tension among Corsicans over being a protectorate of France, but is violence actually rooted in the fiery Corsican soul, or is this just a stereotype? I think about the island's difficult history and the conquerors who plundered its indigenous people and their possessions. Despite limited natural resources, its harbor-rich coast and proximate sea-lanes have strategically valuable positions at the crossroads of Mediterranean trade routes. Corsica suffered serial invasions, century after century, by more technologically advanced aggressors: Greeks, Carthaginians, Romans, Goths, Vandals, Arabs, Byzantines, Aragonese, Moors, and finally the Genoese who ruled the island for five centuries until the early 1700s. But, as in America, the imposition of new and unpopular taxes led to fierce protest and eventually revolution.

A constitution for an independent state was drafted in 1735, followed by years of insurrection. Finally, for fourteen glorious years, from 1755 to 1769 under Pascal Paoli, leader of the fight for independence, founder of the University of Corte, and akin to the island's patron saint (Corsicans call him *Babbu di a Patria*—Father of the Nation), Corsica was free and enjoyed the sweet taste of self-determination. It's no wonder that nationalist fervor and a bold, rebellious spirit with quick-tempered contempt for outsiders are at the heart of the Corsican character.

How much of the island's past has contributed to its people's personality, and how deeply does collective memory affect one's sense of identity? Corsicans are distrustful because years of submission produced a yearning for independence, now a shared value. Certainly Americans' romantic belief in the frontier myth and our respect for individual freedoms both have roots in our country's beginnings.

As we approach Calenzana at an altitude of 920 feet, Julien reviews our day. "It will take us about nine hours to go up fifty-three hundred feet and then down eleven hundred feet to reach the Ortu di u Piobbio Réfuge."

"How many miles is that, Julien?" asks Jim.

"It will be nine miles. With our early start, a lunch stop, and some breaks for snacks, we will arrive by the middle of the afternoon."

I note that Julien never uses English contractions.

Joe shakes his head and says to the group, "Even our most challenging training hike wasn't half as tough as today will be."

Sarah asks from the back seat, "You trained for this?" I bite back a grin, having to assume she's joking.

Joe turns to me with an arched eyebrow, and I can tell that number one, he's taking her comment at face value, and number two, he thinks she's mad. If he's told me once, he's told me a thousand times, "We need to give this hike the respect it deserves or it'll crush us. Forewarned is forearmed." Sarah, apparently, isn't lucky enough to have trained under Joe.

"We've been hiking pretty hard, especially the last month. You really haven't trained, Sarah?"

"Afraid not," she says, laughing. "How tough can it be? Fortune favors the bold, I always say."

No one else comments, and I wonder if we're the only ones taking this so seriously.

Perhaps they all have just the right combination of ignorance and audacity that allows them to shrug it off. Joe and I are competitive spirits with fears of failure that bubble up from deep within our personalities, perhaps because we're both eldest children. And while we contend with each other now and then, we're usually competing with ourselves. We couldn't imagine walking across Corsica without adequate prep.

We step down into Calenzana's sleepy village square. The first thing I notice when we retrieve our gear from the back of the van is that Jim, in a wide-brimmed hiking hat to protect his bald head, has only one hiking pole. Phil has none.

"Are you going with just one stick, Jim?" I ask.

"Oh sure. Always use just one."

"And you, Phil? No poles at all?"

"Nah, never use them. Never have. No need."

And I have no words. There's no way I could do this without the support of both my poles.

"So, how'd you become such an intrepid explorer?" Joe asks Phil.

"My dad took me and my brother up mountains from the time we could walk. Every weekend and in the summer after work, the three of us went climbing. Now it's all I want to do with my time off. It's why I'm a freelance accountant—I set my schedule so I can have plenty of time to hike."

What we enjoy as children wields an indelible hold, but perhaps what we missed has an equally determined grip. I suppress a sigh, wishing I'd had such adventures with my father.

"Phil, why do you think you still like mountains so much?" I'm always intrigued by why certain passions interest some and not others.

"Besides the fact that I grew up with them and that they bring back good memories, the mountains help keep things in perspective. And they aren't picky about who they favor. They humble everyone. They're big, beautiful, and dangerous, and you're just a small passing climber. Always good to be reminded of just how insignificant we are."

The more I get to know Phil, the more I like him.

"How great is it that we're next to a church for a parting prayer," I say to Chris as we approach the local chapel, the Oratoire Saint-Antoine. "I'm going to need all the help I can get." He smiles politely with no response and then steps aside to execute a series of martial arts side kicks, arms crossed at his waist. Joe asks us to line up along the church's stone wall for a predeparture picture. St. Anthony is the patron saint of all things lost, I recall from my years as a Catholic schoolgirl. *Perfect*, I think as my legs tremble. *We're not lost yet, but, St. Anthony, we'll need you to watch over us so we won't be.*

I walked up the left side of the center aisle of Saint Clare's church to receive communion, my fingers pointed to heaven, palms pressed in prayer at my waist. The usher waved me over to the right side where the line was moving quickly. I trembled, broke out in a cold sweat. I'd never find my way back to our pew in that huge new church from way over there, but I shifted right, good at doing what I was told. I took the host on my tongue, turned, and followed the line toward the back. The congregation was a sea of unfamiliar faces, all of them, I was sure, looking at me, a silly little girl who couldn't find her way.

I searched for my mother's white mantilla, my father's black hair on the far side of the nave. My eyes glazed over. Where were they? I kept walking, looking, searching, terrified until I walked out the door to the vestibule. I crumbled in a corner, crying.

"Ready to go—*on y va*," Julien says. A statement, not a question.

"Shoulder to the wheel time," says Sarah. "*On y va*. Let's go."

And so, like all those determined souls before us, we're about to walk across this island. My anxiety mounts, and my belly pushes toward my throat as I slip my arms through my pack's straps. I've declined Joe's offer of help because my arthritic shoulders are only mildly sore, and I want to do this by myself. The double dose of drugs I took this morning are definitely doing their job. I flex my fingers, circle my wrists, and whisper thanks to my marvelous meds. *My load isn't too bad at twenty-eight pounds, including three liters of water*, I think, fastening my hip belt tight. About a quarter of my body weight. No sleeping pad and all that paring down made a big difference.

Joe leans in close to say, "So we're actually doing this, aren't we? Ready for The Twenty?" He flashes a wide grin, holds up his palm, his trekking pole dangling from his wrist, inviting a high five.

"Of Course-ica!" I slap his hand, giggling at my corny joke. "I knew I'd have to say it at least once on this trip." Joe rolls his eyes and pulls me in for a departure kiss.

"*Allez-y*," I say, and Joe echoes, "Let's go."

We pass the shuttered café on the Place de l'Église in the pre-dawn light, our departure too early to overlap with even the village's most dedicated coffee clientele. I catch my reflection in a storefront window above a display of honey and olive oil and see a woman with braids and muscled but decidedly short legs. She's Heidi, about to join her grandfather and her goats. But despite her gear, does she actually look like a hiker? Or is she—am I—just playing a part? How simple to create an illusion, how difficult to maintain. But I shake the thought, tighten the grip on my poles, and move ahead.

We continue across the square, turn left on a narrow side street, round a corner, slip down some stairs, and there it is: the trail's first blaze. A double stripe of a thick white band painted over an equally thick red one, a white arrow pointing forward and *Fra li monte* (across the mountains in Corsican) painted on a wooden plank hanging on the cement wall.

"This is it, Babe," Joe says. "We're off!"

I shiver with excitement and sense that something monumental is about to start. We transition from Calenzana's cobblestones to a narrow sandy trail and start climbing right away. There's no gentle introduction when you enter from the north. I think about the variety of terrain we'll tackle on the miles ahead: loose scree, sharp granite, steep, slippery rock slabs, and névés. I follow the others and throw myself into the climb, but our energetic start suddenly stops. Just in front of me, Sarah stumbles, keels over, and I practically fall on top of her.

"Bollocks! One of my sodding poles collapsed." I help her tighten the locking mechanism, but it won't hold no matter what we do. Every time she puts weight on it, it gives way.

By now, our single-file string of eight has stopped, strewn up the trail in a grove of leafy chestnuts. Julien retreats to Sarah's rescue. He twists and turns her stick, pushes and pulls, and finally gives his verdict. "It is finished. You will use one of mine."

"Well," Sarah says, "I suppose I win the award for 'fastest equipment demise.' We haven't even gone a hundred yards. Should have checked them before we started."

I look ahead and see Joe and Chris shaking their heads about voluble Sarah. As for me, I love her candid chatter.

Off we go again. *"C'est parti."* Single-poled Julien is back in the lead; Phil, Joe, and Kees are close at his heels; Chris is some yards behind; Jim lags after him; and Sarah and I trail them all through tall, slim laricio pines. I soon manage to trip over a root in the seconds it takes to lift my eyes from the path to the jagged peaks ahead, still dark in morning shadow. *Damn*, I think. *Be careful. You can't have two of your strengths—surefootedness and balance—fail you from the start.*

"You all right?" asks Sarah, turning around after hearing me stumble.

"I am, but aren't we just the perfect pair of hiking champions? You bust a pole and I almost fall on my face in the first fifteen minutes. Shall we just give up now?"

Sarah laughs. "Rubbish. I actually do things now I would never have dared when I was younger for fear of being crap at them."

I nod. "I hear you. But there are definitely things I still avoid for that very reason."

"Took me awhile, believe me. Had to work at it. Now I just try what I fancy and if I'm not as good as everyone else, I don't much care. Just like I no longer care about the size of my bum."

I giggle but think about how I refused to let Joe take a picture of me from behind at the hotel this morning. No pictures of my butt! Apparently, I'm not yet as evolved as Sarah.

The sun is now up, filtered by scattered trees casting long shadows. "We'll show the guys what we're made of once we really get going," Sarah says.

"Maybe we're just late bloomers, you and I."

Sarah agrees and points ahead, "There's one of our objectives for today—climbing up and through that col."

"We're supposed to be hiking at an average altitude of between thirty-five hundred and seven thousand feet. Doesn't seem bad as an average, but it doesn't really paint an accurate picture of all the ups and downs. Like getting up to that pass."

The trail remains tight and has become rocky, so I keep my head down, fearing that if I look up to our first waypoint, I'll trip again, falling hard this time. I need at least another hour to really get my hiking legs under me.

Conversation with Sarah is easy. She speaks with no trouble as we climb, while frequent deep breaths punctuate my exchanges. I learn that while she may not have trained for The Twenty, she's a strong athlete—an avid biker who just days before finished a weeklong trip across Normandy.

"I go on lots of biking treks, mostly in France, with mates who invite me as their medic—all expenses paid. It's a nice gig. I was an au pair for a few summers in Paris, so they also like having me along for my passable French."

"I knew we'd have lots in common, Sarah." I gasp. "I speak French too." Gasp. *"Nous sommes de vraies copines."* We're true buddies. Gasp.

"Fabuleux!" she says. *"C'est magnifique."*

"So. It sounds," gasp, "like when you said," gasp, "you didn't train for this," gasp, "you forgot to mention," gasp, "your miles on a bike."

"I am pretty active, but I knew this trek was going to be difficult."

The tinder-dry path has turned into a jumble of rocks underfoot with no trees for cover. Our dialog dwindles, and even Sarah's breezy chatter quiets. All I hear is my own labored breathing and the rhythmic patter of my poles: *tick-tick-tick, tick-tick-tick.* With each touch of the steel tips, my inner discourse vacillates between, *We're finally on The Twenty* and, *No way I can do this for thirteen days straight.*

I've been counting the red-and-white trail blazes as we pass them, one every forty yards or so. *Fifty-seven . . . fifty-eight . . . fifty-nine . . .* how many might we see by day's end?

Julien, Joe, and the others at the front of our uphill parade ascend with measured, deliberate strides I can't mimic. The incline has become sharper, taxing the flexibility of my calves and the capacity of my lungs. I slow to a crawl as Sarah maintains her pace, leaving Jim and me well behind. Her athletic prowess is impressive, and I try to lengthen my stride in response.

I look ahead and see that Phil is now in front of Julien, leading the way as he practically dances up the stony incline. Climbing a mountain is exacting work, but he gives the appearance of effortlessness as he hops from one rock to the next.

"What is he, part mountain goat?" I ask Jim as we watch Phil. "Look at him go up—and with no poles!" He has both hands in his pockets, whistling as he hopscotches along.

"He's definitely the most experienced of our group," Jim says. "He told me about the technical trips he's done with crampons and axes."

"I figured as much once I heard him say he'd slept on a glacier." I pause. "Thanks for hanging back with me, Jim. Appreciate it."

"Hey, I'm not hanging back. This is my pace and I'm sticking to it. Whenever I hike with a group, I'm always in the rear. Bothered me at first, but I'm used to it now, and there's always someone else back here with me."

"Well then, it looks like you and I will be spending plenty of time together."

Jim laughs, and Joe turns to wave as he has every fifteen minutes or so since we started. I think about the hiking habit Joe and I have developed over the years. He knows I don't want to be handled delicately, don't want him thinking I can't hike what he can, and certainly don't want him waiting for me at every turn. Just as people hovering as I work has always driven me mad, so it is on the trail. Joe's done what he should, knowing I never want to be babied, leaving me to tackle this tough rise on my own.

We self-proclaimed slowpokes stop every ten minutes or so to turn and take in the view. And, of course, catch our breath. We look over the valley behind us, all the way back to Calvi and its half-moon bay ringed by a white sand corona. Surveying how high we've come helps validate our heaving chests.

The sun finally climbs its ladder in the sky, rising triumphantly over the trees, bathing all in a warm golden haze. The day's start was cool, but the brutal Corsican sun has steadily boosted temperatures into the eighties. Under burning rays on a trail with no shade, I'm sweating like a farm animal, sucking down water like a sprinter.

The signature whir of the Mediterranean—the mating call of male cicadas—accompanies our climb. The membranes of their bellies need eighty-degree heat to perform their song, so they only croon during the day. The electric thrum of *cigales messieurs* serenading *cigales mesdemoiselles* keeps me company, and I concoct cicada love stories to entertain myself.

Jim and I continue winding up switchback after switchback together, around rock slabs tinged pink with lichen. The exertion leaves me bathed in sweat. The turquoise cotton bandanna around my neck is soaked, my braids leaky faucets dripping perspiration from their ends. But I'm feeling good, keeping fatigue at bay.

We catch sight of the group ahead. They've stopped at today's sole spring, the Funtana di Ortivinti, just an hour into the hike. An icy flow spills from a rubber hose sticking from a fern-laden verge, creating a muddy pool on the trail. I release my Osprey and drop it like a stone to the ground. The back of my tee is drenched, and the air provides cooling relief, but I can't wait to douse my head. I splash my reddened face and arms in the freezing fount and then soak and wring out my bandanna. I wipe my face, drape the cloth over my head, and enjoy the refreshing chill. I fill my bottle, icy water splashing over my hands, leaving wet streaks on my dusty legs.

Joe waits for me to cool down and then checks in. "So far so good?" he asks with a big smile. I can tell he's enjoying himself. "You and Sarah seem to be fast friends."

I laugh and manage a smile. "I think so far *so slow* is a better description. And yes, Sarah's great. So is Jim."

"Well, you're not alone, and that's good. I would have stayed back if you were by yourself. You didn't mind, did you?" he asks, sounding guilty.

"Absolutely not." I shake my head and mean it. "You know I want you to go at your own pace so I don't feel like I'm holding you back. And don't get me wrong. I'm really grateful to be with those two, but I'm just afraid I'll always be one of the weak links."

"You are *not* a weak link. You're right there with two others. This is unbelievably hard."

"Stop," I say, my voice rising. "Really. I'm fine. No excuses. We knew this was going to be tough, and we each have to deal with it in whatever way works best."

"Exactly. You know how I have to keep moving on climbs like these. If I stop, I might not get my legs moving again. It's part of why I like being up there with Phil and Julien. They motivate me to keep going and keep up."

I really do understand, and I do like the chatter with Sarah, but there's a selfish little part of me that wishes he'd decide to hang back. . . .

He touches his palm to my cheek. "You're doing great. We both are."

"Snacks!" Julien says, interrupting our exchange as he opens his pack. He breaks out sticky dates, dried figs, salted nuts, butter cookies, and apples.

"Make sure you eat something for your energy," he says. "We have much more climbing before lunch and the *piste* [trail] will get even harder."

Harder? I think. The ascent to this point was ruthless. How much harder can it get?

My jittery morning stomach has calmed and is now growling audibly. I bite into a fig, the grainy essence of a favorite cookie filling my mouth, but it's way too sweet. Even without today's physical demands, I always prefer a salty snack to a sweet one. I've lost so much water, and salt is what I crave. I take a fistful of nuts from the plastic bag Julien offers as he starts answering questions about his background.

"I grew up in the South of France," he says, "My town is Manosque, in the Luberon."

"We were just in the Luberon," says Joe, explaining when asked that we retired at the end of June and have been traveling since July Fourth.

We enjoy a few minutes of quiet while we concentrate on nourishing our tired bodies and then get to know Julien better.

"In winter, I teach skiing and am a mountain guide," he says. "Manosque is close to the Alps, so I learned to ski when I was a boy. There is almost no skiing on Corsica now, so I must go back to the mainland in December."

"How about your holidays?" asks Phil. "More hiking and skiing?"

"Actually, now I do, how do you call it in English? I do *keet*."

"What in the world is *keet*?" asks Jim.

"You mean kitesurfing, Julien?" I ask, translating his French pronunciation of kite.

"*Exactement!*" Julien beams like a boy. "*Je fais du* kitesurf." It's
clear we've hit on a cherished subject. He goes on to explain that
kitesurfing is his new passion and that he'll be certified to teach it
soon.

Not only does Julien look the part, he actually is a surfer dude.

"That sounds brilliant! Sign me up," says Sarah. "Always ready
for a new adventure. I keep trying to fit them all in before my body
says no." And to no one in particular, she asks, "Why does time pass
so slowly when we're young and then fly by when we're old? It's like
the minute I said I was fifty, I was suddenly fifty-five. And then two
seconds later, I turned sixty."

I join Sarah, perched on a rock, and offer nuts, saying, "It's upsetting sometimes, isn't it? As if life is speeding up, like a car with its
accelerator stuck and there's nothing we can do to unjam it."

"Exactly," Sarah says as she nods, popping a handful of nuts in her
mouth. We sit quietly for a moment.

"Clearly, this isn't the first time you've tackled a mountain," I
finally say. "You're a beast on this climb!"

"Ha!" she says, head tilted back. "Perhaps on the ascents, but
wait'll you see me and my wobbly knees on the way down. Especially
when balance is involved. You'll all be way ahead of me, and we'll see
what you say then."

"We all have our strengths, don't we?"

"So do you prefer Corsica or France?" I ask Julien after he tells
us he's lived for seven years in Ajaccio, the island's capital and
Napoleon's hometown.

"But we *are* in France, Marianne, do not forget. Corsica *is* France."

"Oh, geez," I say, blushing despite my tan. "Of course we're in France!"

"Please do not worry," he says as he stores the snacks, our signal to grab our packs and get going. "I also forget and say the same thing sometimes. And so do many Corsicans who like to think they are a different country."

"But is it really more about their culture than their politics?" Joe asks. "Hasn't the government invested a lot in the Corsican economy over the past fifteen years or so?"

"Yes, you are right. They have. And yes, it is mostly about the Corsican identity. They want to be seen as very much separate from the rest of the country. And I think most of the *séparatistes* know it would be difficult for Corsica to have its own economy."

"So it's an emotional issue," I say.

"Yes, I would say so. But I will tell you that I do like Corsica better than the continent. Do you know the French writer, Antoine de Saint-Exupéry?"

"*Mais oui*," Sarah and I say in unison.

"Well, he wrote, 'The sun made love to the sea so often that it finally gave birth to Corsica.'"

"Wow. That's beautiful," I say, the image indelibly etched.

We head up a sharp switchback, deep into the spiny maquis (*macchia* in Corsican), meaning thicket, for which Corsica is famous. It's the island's aromatic answer to the chaparral of the American West and whose name the French Resistance in WWII adopted—the Maquis—as they fled and hid in impenetrable hillside brush. Great carpets of the briary scrub cover 20 percent of the island with juniper and myrtle shrubs along with a potpourri of compact flowers and wild herbs in muted shades of green, yellow, pink, and thorny flares of purple: buttercups, mint, rockroses, lavender, rosemary, basil, and sage. The broiling late morning sun stimulates shimmering waves of fragrance from the prickly plants underfoot.

Julien stops our procession so all can catch up. He tells us that the maquis is deeply ingrained in Corsican folklore and cultural identity. The sweet-smelling vegetation, used to season stews and cakes, manages to grow and thrive below 3,300 feet of altitude in even the slimmest wrinkle of rock, impervious to drought and constant sun. Their roots dig deep into the terrain, forcing their way through the stones, as tenacious as the island's inhabitants themselves.

I so want to meet some of these resolute people, but will our paths cross on this journey? We have yet to have a real conversation with a Corsican.

"Pigs eat these plants, and they give the local sausage a unique flavor. The only other things the pigs eat are chestnuts and acorns, and maybe some wild fruits. We will have some *prisutta* and *salsiccia* sausage for lunch. You will love it. You will see."

"Wild pigs or farm pigs?" asks Jim.

"Both," says Julien. "*Les sangliers*—the wild boars—and the pigs of the farmers all walk around free on the island and get fat from all the nuts on the ground. I am sure we will see a lot of *châtaigniers*—chestnut trees—in the next days. The Corsican people love this tree, even though it was the invaders from Genoa that brought it here. When there was nothing to eat, chestnuts and the flour they made from them helped people not starve many times in history. There is a *proverbe* that says these trees touch a Corsican's life every single day from the time they are born."

"What do they make with the flour?" asks Chris.

"You should know, Christopher. Your favorite—Pietra! They

make beer and also beignets, breads, cakes, and other desserts, like puddings."

Do we have something like chestnuts in the States? I wonder. *Something we identify with and that touches us every day? Corn? Wheat? Amber waves of grain?*

"Since we're talking about animals, would you tell us about *transhumance* on Corsica?" Sarah asks.

Transhumance. I've never, ever heard the word in all my years studying French.

"*Certainement,*" says Julien. "*Transhumance* is very important for the life of Corsica because the island still has lots of shepherds and farmers. Many *transhumance* trails cross the GR20."

"What exactly is *transhumance?*" I ask. Joe, Jim, and Chris all look puzzled because clearly it's new to them as well.

"I think transmigration is the word in English," says Sarah. "It's the seasonal movement of livestock between the mountains and the sea."

"Sarah is right," Julien says. "We will see a lot of farm animals on the trails because they walk up into the mountains in summer when there is no rain and it is too hot near the coasts. Many parts of the GR20 are on *transhumance* trails. In winter, shepherds move them down the trails to their pastures near the sea. The government gives farmers money to help pay for this to keep the tradition. Corsicans love the *transhumance* because it reminds them of their ancestors. It is an emotional word and custom for them. Many years ago, Corsican men went high in the mountains in the summers or down near the beaches with their animals in the winters. They stayed with them for many months. The very long separation from their families was difficult."

"How long does it take to get the animals up and down?" asks Phil.

"Sometimes weeks. And I will tell you, it is very interesting to see it in the spring and in the fall. All these animals moving up and down the mountains."

Spending tax money to preserve tradition? Unless there's a clear economic benefit, the chances for such subsidies in the US are slim. Patrimony might be important to Americans—but most don't want to pay to preserve it.

As we continue through the scrub, Julien points to the confetti-like profusion of mustard-colored plants dotting the sun-drenched trail. "Crush the dried flowers between your fingers." I bring the resulting powder to my nose and am instantly taken with the curry-like aroma.

"I must also tell you about Corsica's very rare essential oil that comes from these helichrysum flowers. It is called *immortelle*. Do you know this? They sell it all over the world."

The men don't respond, and I shake my head.

"Definitely heard of it," says Sarah. "Some of my patients swear by it for soothing inflammation." Maybe I should get some for my joints. "I've also heard it can help post-surgery wounds. Someone called it 'the golden flower of healing,' but I never knew it was from Corsica."

"*Exactement*," says Julien. "It is very powerful and it is very *cher*."

"Why expensive?" asks Chris.

"Because they have to boil many, many plants to make just one ounce. They also use the flowers for *les remèdes à base de plantes*. Marianne?"

"Herbal remedies."

We continue on, and I can't help reaching down to touch the compact flowers again and again to release their spicy scent. My botanical dawdling—stopping to smell the curry—solidifies my status as group laggard, but I'm determined to taste and smell everything I can.

It's taken almost all morning, but we finally pass through the col—the green saddle pass at Bocca a u Saltu at 4,100 feet. One significant hurdle behind us. After a brief descent through a pine forest, we face our next challenge: a messy, relentless rocky rise with no discernible trail—a slope of choppy, exposed granite with nothing resembling a pathway. All we see are the distinctive candy cane blazes dabbed on a few rocks, and so we spread out across the slope. I recall our guidebook warning that The Twenty is frequently more visible on a map than on the ground. It's not so much a trail as an idea, a general direction that links the island's highest peaks.

Jim, just ahead of me, stops, turns, and voices my thoughts. "How can they call this a trail? This is effing crazy." Hmm. Something other than nonchalance from him.

"No idea what to call it." I look up to see the others down on all fours, bottoms in the air, strewn across and crawling up the boulder field to regain the ridge. "But it looks like we have some serious scrambling ahead. Let's not think about it and just do it."

I'm very good at being a cheerleader even while questioning my own enthusiasm.

Up until now, we've tackled the trail upright with both feet on the ground. But in front of us, looping up to an airy col, are nightmarish vertical jumbles of rocks, one on top of the other, daring us to climb.

"Shall we?" I say with a wave, inviting Jim to lead.

"Have to tell you, I'm not a fan of these crawls." But up he goes, mumbling under his breath.

It's now my turn to carefully find footholds and scale the steep rock chimney. I'll need both my hands as well as my legs to scramble up this barricade, so I slip my sticks from my wrists and try to swivel around to put them in the loops on the side of my Osprey. But, ouch! My shoulders scream when I attempt the twist and so I have to take off my pack to store the poles and then hoist it back in place. Damn invader! Leave me alone!

I've lost sight of all but Jim, now well ahead. My emotions are as raw as my palms, scraped red from the coarse granite ledges, and I scold myself for not having put on the gloves buried deep in my bag. I really need a break. Julien said lunch was an hour away, but that was ninety minutes ago. My breathing is labored, and my arm and leg muscles are Jell-O. I pull myself over each successive rock, convinced an evil troll has replaced what's in my pack with lead. This is rock-climbing without ropes.

I'm lost behind my sunglasses, sweat pooling in my eyes, making it difficult to see.

I stop before hauling myself up and over the next ridiculous rock, put my hands on my knees, and lean over to expand my diaphragm. I take a few deep breaths in the thinning air that's left me dizzy. When I look back up, atop the rock is Phil—mountain goat extraordinaire, to my rescue.

"Hey there," he says with a huge smile.

I'm awkward and embarrassed as I grope for Phil's outstretched hand. I should be able to do this on my own. Everyone else did. With no more words and just a grin, Phil's now on his stomach, offering both hands. I take them and then feel someone else grab me under my arms. A firm tug pulls me up and my jaw drops when I see that Joe is there as well.

"Phil pulled me up. Jim too," Joe says. "Our own personal Sherpa."

"Happy to help," says Phil.

"I thought you guys were way ahead."

Joe shakes his head. "Wanted to wait for you. My body and I both. This is really tough going." He comes up behind me and circles my waist. "Love you," he whispers.

"Ditto." It does feel good that he stayed.

"Follow me," Phil says. "I'll show you both right where to put your feet and what to grab onto. We'll get there." Our upbeat mountaineer guides us up to our first set of mountain chains where the others and the rusted metal links bolted to the rock await. Joe and I used them before on very steep inclines on the TMB, those impossible to climb without hanging on and hoisting yourself up.

Although the GR20 is not considered "technical," meaning hikers need no special gear, its steep ascents, descents, and scrambles, many at forty-five-degree angles, sometimes require the help of hardware. Gripping the metal leads as you advance hand over hand, your feet following below on the rock face, guides you up or down particularly steep sections.

I'm usually pretty good on chain-assisted climbs, but will my aching hands hold tight enough and help pull me up this time? Julien prompts us to go up the practically vertical rise, one by one. Kees, Chris, and then Jim go first.

"I will follow Sarah," says Julien, "and then Marianne and Joe will go." Our wise leader has recruited Phil as his assistant and asks him to go up last, right behind Joe—our bumper if we need him.

Jim has some difficulty—he ascends very slowly—and to my surprise, Sarah struggles with her grip on the linked cable, its metallic clanking reverberating across the rock face. She needs Julien's help to place her feet properly. But I have no problem. I ascend steadily despite sore palms, tender wrists, and painful shoulders. I'm so in need of this small victory.

"Vertigo bothering you?" I ask Joe when we're at the top, hoping his poor head for heights that gives him problems even when he's not inching across precipitous rock isn't nagging.

"Not too much. That climb was fine—not too long—but I think

it's just a taste of what's coming. Not looking forward to many more of those, though."

I rub his arm.

"But I'll be fine—long as I don't look down. Just have to keep moving." He takes a deep breath. "You were a champ. Looked like that was a piece of cake for you."

I give him a thumbs-up.

The day is now sweltering, the sun a searing orb. Sweat trickles between my breasts, soaking my bra, my shirt plastered to my back. It drips from my forehead, down my nose, over my upper lip, and, salty, into my mouth. I stop, tilt back my hat to wipe my face.

We continue to climb. Endlessly. I breathe hard as I lean against a broiling boulder, wondering how I'll ever manage to keep doing this.

At long last, on a verdant hillock shaded by a wall of rock, we drop our packs for lunch. My legs are close to collapsing, and I fear that when I sit, I'll never get back up.

"Well, I'm right chuffed with myself," says Sarah, hands on her hips, grinning from ear to ear.

"Is that a good thing or a bad thing?" I ask.

"Oh, it's good all right," she says, face to the sun, arms outstretched.

I mutter, "Chuffed I'm not. Just exhausted."

As Julien unpacks and spreads out lunch goodies, Jim asks, "Hey, Julien. If it's going to be this hot for the next two weeks, why are we carrying extra layers and foul weather gear?" I listen carefully for the response, having thought the same thing.

"Ha," he says, chuckling. "You do not like the extra weight, Jim? Just wait. We have *approximatively* three more days of heat, and then it will change. You will see, and you will be happy about what you carry. When we go above two thousand meters," I do the math in my head—about sixty-five hundred feet, "the weather changes quickly, and it is possible we will have snow and *grèle*—how do you say this, Marianne?"

"Hail," I respond, but can't quite believe him as I wring sweat from my hat.

Conversation dwindles, as we're all ravenous. We do manage, however, to tell Julien how much we love the unique flavor of the wild boar *saucisson* he cuts for us. The lean, chewy chunks are marbled—deep red, herbaceous, and slightly sweet, from the chestnuts. I imagine they would taste even better with some salt.

"I promised you would like it," Julien says, puffing out his chest as if he himself were Corsican. "Do you want more?" We all reach forward for the peppery bites he hands us.

"Who knew feral pigs would taste so good?" says Chris, his long, lean legs stretched in front of him.

"Julien, did you say we have some cheese?" asks Phil. He pops a slice of sausage in his mouth and then takes off his shirt to soak in some sun. Despite his hiking prowess, he's barrel-chested, with the slight swell of a middle-age belly.

"Oh yes, I forgot!" Julien says as he reaches into a plastic sack and then tosses a chunk of cheese to Phil. "I always forget it. I am not a very good Frenchman because I do not like cheese."

"What?" says Sarah. "Unheard of! I thought loving cheese was required if you're French."

"Even Époisses and Saint André?" I ask, naming my favorite French *fromages*.

"Especially Époisses and all those soft, smelly ones. I *déteste* them all."

Jim chimes in as Phil hands him the pungent communal wedge. "Were your parents upset with you about that?"

"Oh no. Not at all. I love charcuterie and I love bread, so it is not a problem for me. Or for *mes parents*."

"You can always give me your share of cheese," says Phil.

"Sure, give your cheese and any other leftovers to Phil," says Joe, "since he's obviously part billy goat and will eat anything."

Phil responds with a quick laugh and broad smile.

"Here's my pasta salad," I say to Phil, handing over the container I took from the hotel this morning. "I have more than enough with everything else there is."

"Looks like I'm her new favorite, Joe," Phil says.

Joe rolls his eyes. "Yeah, yeah."

I try to slow my bites, savor each mouthful, and chew deliberately. I mustn't overfill my empty belly too quickly or weigh myself down before tackling what the afternoon has in store. But it's difficult because with every calorie I consume, my muscles relax, and I can actually feel energy flow back into them. The exhaustion that slayed me only fifteen minutes earlier has been eased by just a few swallows. I hold back the urge to down my entire bowl of tabbouleh in successive gulps.

"So, Julien," I say, taking advantage of our break to learn more from him. "Can you tell us a little about Corsican wine?"

"But of course, Marianne. I cannot tell you about cheese but *oui*, I can tell you about wine." Sarah scoots over closer to make sure she doesn't miss a thing.

"Are there many different grapes on Corsica?" she asks.

"There are three main grapes on the island, and I will tell you their Corsican names. First, the reds. There is *sciaccarellu* and I think it tastes a little like the red wine from Burgundy. From the pinot noir grape. Next is *niellecciu*, a Corsican word that means dry and black and it is like the sangiovese grape in Italy. It is used for more heavy wines. And *vermentinu* is the grape for the white wines."

"Is it like a chardonnay or sauvignon blanc maybe?" I ask.

"I do not drink too much white wine, but my friends tell me it is like sauvignon blanc."

"You're in luck," says Joe. "Your favorite." We high five each other.

"Mine too," says Sarah.

"There are nine AOC zones on Corsica—you know, the *appellation d'origine contrôlée*. But of course, I'm sure you know that the wines we will drink on the trail are *vins de pays* and are mixes of many grapes—even some from Italy and mainland France. You will have to wait until we get back to Bastia to have an AOC wine."

"No problem," says Jim. "As long as there's plenty."

Joe sits next to me, our arms and legs touching, and we say little, too exhausted to speak more. We gaze ahead at mountain after mountain, an endless procession of peaks. Behind us, ridges and valleys extend for miles all the way back to Calvi, now in distant miniature. We've climbed so far already, but my heart races and I feel queasy about how much more we have to go up this afternoon.

Joe finally interrupts our reveries. "Can you believe we're actually here? On Corsica?"

"I know, I know. I've just been trying to take it all in. It's gorgeous, right? All the way back to the beach from way up here. Beautiful but tough."

"Definitely tough. But we're doing it. Finally doing what we trained for. We'll see what this afternoon brings." He puts his arm around my back. I lean over, head on his shoulder. "Body holding up?" he asks. "Any joints swelling?"

"Holding up, yes. All good so far." I flex my feet and hands stretched out in front of me to show him.

Having eaten his meal, Julien stands and says, pointing back to from where we came, "You will all soon become sick of Calvi. For the first three days, when we look back, we will always see it: Calvi, Calvi, Calvi. It will become smaller but you will ask me, 'Julien, when will we finally see something new?' But do not worry. We have a lot more ahead."

A lot more ahead. Please don't remind me of how much more, Julien. But I do think about whether tomorrow's terrain will be much different from today's. Or might it be even harder?

I look around at our group and wonder if they're also speculating about what's to come. We've certainly discovered a lot about each other in a short period of time, but I haven't yet learned to read their minds. We've let down our defenses quickly—all of us but Chris and Kees, that is. Chris will warm up in time, I'm certain, but I have yet to hear Kees say much at all. Why is he so quiet? Is he shy perhaps? I can certainly understand that. Takes one to know one. Or is it because his mother tongue is Dutch and not English? He has a saturnine quality—a bit like Eeyore. There seems to be a sadness under his surface, beneath his long face and dark glasses, which makes me wonder. I mentally note to talk to him before we get back on the trail.

Joe hands me our guidebook so I can see what we'll face this afternoon. I've already learned that Julien tempers descriptions of upcoming terrain, probably because he doesn't want to scare us, so I want to see what the book says. I skim the narrative for our first day until I find where we are and then read aloud to the group when Jim prompts me. "There are a couple rocky notches to cross . . . the scrambling from gap to gap should take about one and a half hours . . . the refuge is then visible across the valley." Julien never mentioned more scrambles.

"Sounds like we should be heading down soon. True, Julien?" I ask.

He confirms my hope. "Yes, we have very little more going up and then it will be all down."

Anything to do with descent is music to my lungs and legs. Downs I can do. But how should we interpret his "very little more going up?"

I know that if I stay in one position too long, I'll stiffen beyond my ability to move.

And so I force myself to stand, stretch my arms, arch my back, and then fold forward in half to reach down to my toes. I stand back up and then pick my way over to sit with Sarah on a patch of flattened grass.

"Do you think there's a gene for wanderlust?" I ask as she runs her fingers through her mop top. "I read the other day that some scientists think so."

"Well," she says, cocking her head. "I guess there must be. How else do you explain the difference in how people feel about traveling and most things international? My parents certainly didn't raise me to be an explorer, so I must have been born with it."

"Totally agree. Of eleven siblings, maybe four of us really love traveling, and only two of us are truly travel-crazy. And even if they hadn't had so many kids, I don't think my parents would have traveled much. My mother always said, 'Going away scares me, especially to another country. I just like being home.'"

"Seems I heard my mother say something similar."

So, given how our mothers felt, how did Sarah and I grow up wanting to explore? In my case, did I want to see the world because I felt so sheltered? Because I grew up apart from anyone not white, middle-class, and Catholic? Going to public school at age twelve was the first time I realized there were families unlike my own.

* * *

What's her name?" my mother asked when I told her a classmate invited me to her house after school.

"Sherry. Sherry Fingerman."

Silence. But I saw the corner of her mouth twitch.

"So can I? Can I go, please? Mom?"

My mother knew how hard finding friends had been for me, especially since we'd moved to New York and I'd started public school. She finally agreed. "I'll ask Dad to pick you up on his way home from work."

"So what did her house look like?" my Mom asked after my afternoon at the Fingermans'.

"I don't know. It was just kind of a regular house. Why?"

"Well, she's Jewish, and I wondered what it was like. I've never been to a Jewish house before."

"My father's family is from Guadalajara, Mexico," I tell Sarah, "and I can't believe he never wanted to visit. Never went to Mexico at all. He wasn't even a little bit interested. I never understood it, and maybe that's part of why I have itchy feet and wanted to go see the world for myself. I always had my nose in a book and I can remember so desperately wanting to visit the places I read about. I was always cutting out maps and pictures of France and other places in Europe from magazines. Pasting them in notebooks and hanging them on my walls."

"So when was your first big trip?"

"I was twenty-one—the summer after junior year in college. My roommate, two friends, and I backpacked around Europe for six weeks. I went with five hundred dollars—almost all my savings—and came home with two hundred. I sure did learn how to travel on a budget!"

"I was about the same age when I was an au pair. Loved living abroad. Wasn't nearly as far from home as you were, but France was definitely not England."

"Don't mean to sound like one of those old people who says everything was better way back when, but I'm nostalgic about how backpacking used to be. You arrived in a new country with no Internet, no cell phone, no texting, and had to fend for yourself. It was a real adventure, totally cut off from everything familiar. It really felt like you were in hiding from everyone back home."

"Definitely agree," says Sarah. "In today's world, it's almost impossible to truly get away from it all."

"I actually feel sorry for young travelers today who, unless they're deep in the Amazon, probably won't feel that sense of isolation and freedom of going somewhere and being totally cut off. Being away from everything really puts home in perspective, but can you actually do that if you're constantly in touch with it?"

"Probably not," Sarah says.

"I remember dreading becoming parochial and insular once I got to college—a Catholic college where everyone looked like and had a background like me. I so wanted to see the wider world to help me understand it. I was just always really curious and felt that if I didn't get out and see the world, I'd end up being dull and boring."

"I like to think that once you taste travel, you're ruined for life. Your appetite never fades," Sarah says, and takes a huge bite of an apple.

"Exactly! Like Pandora's box. Once it's opened, you can't close it up. At least for people like us. It's like that World War One song, 'How Ya Gonna Keep 'Em Down on the Farm? (After They've Seen Paree).'"

Julien interrupts us with an offer of post-lunch tea. "It is not hot, but at least it is warm. Sarah, I am sure you would like some."

She lifts her plastic cup with a huge smile. "I always say yes to tea, no matter the temperature." I take some as well, knowing I'll benefit from a hit of caffeine since I'm feeling pretty sleepy. Julien moves on to make his offer to the guys.

Sarah continues, "I've always thought Americans have such gamblers' souls—you're chipper and hopeful, even when things seem hopeless—while Europeans are so pessimistic. We believe it's nearly impossible to change destiny and nothing ever gets better. I say this because I think optimists make the best travelers. You can't be a good traveler and also a worrywart. You have to believe everything's going to work out, even if you lose your passport, miss the train, or get totally lost. You agree?"

I think for a moment as I bend forward to massage a muscle spasm building in my leg. "Yes. Definitely. Most Americans do tend to have sunny outlooks, but in the case of Joe and me, I'm the eternal optimist and he's the skeptic. I get us to take risks and he keeps us from getting too crazy. The combo seems to work."

"I can already tell you're a risk-taker. A woman who, although she's quite jaunty, knows where she's going and always has it together."

"Ha!" I say, lobbing my last bite of a biscuit over a ledge. "Would that!" Sarah's turn of phrase is rubbing off on me. I jump up suddenly to stretch out the charley horse that's finally cramped my calf and then kneel, easing back into a lunge.

"That's sweet of you to say, Sarah, but that is not, I repeat *not*, how I always feel." What is it about me that makes people think I'm this unflappable presence? If only they knew. . . .

"You have a quiet confidence," she adds. "Not sure I can put it in words."

"And I'd say the same about you, Sarah. But maybe not so quiet!"

"You know me so well already!" We both laugh.

And I wonder, as Sarah gets up for a refill of tea and to grab some cookies, what makes some of us who are so uncertain inside appear so confident to the world. Is it that we look like we have nothing to prove and need no outside validation? Or maybe it comes down to doing what I tried at breakfast this morning— holding my head high, walking in like I belong, acting the part until I believe it.

Sarah returns and I say, "You know, it's funny—I know so many Americans who've gone to another country and swear they'll never leave the US again. It's as if they're allergic to all things 'foreign.' How does that happen?"

"Genetics," says Sarah, "definitely genetics."

"Well, here's to travel-hungry genes." I raise my cup and then gulp down the rest of my tea.

"Pray for your future," said Sister Mary Vincent at the front of Saint Agnes's fifth grade classroom. We all bowed our heads for the end-of-day reflection. My future, I thought, and was off wandering the maze of a medieval French hamlet, exploring a Greek ruin, crossing an Alpine meadow. Someday I'll see the world I've read about, and I'll be adventurous and sexy, mysterious and interesting, not just a goody two-shoes teachers refer to as "a nice girl." Classmates will no longer make fun of my scarlet face when the teacher calls on me, or when my backside wiggles as I walk. I prayed for a future of confidence and style, of exploit and exploration.

Sarah asks about our TMB hike, and so I go on chattering about the week we spent hiking around Mont Blanc. "There were some pretty tough climbs, but it was all much less rocky and more pastoral than this." I pause to massage my neck. "How 'bout you, Sarah? Is the Tour du Mont Blanc on your list for the future?"

When Sarah doesn't respond, I look over and see that she's gone down flat, eyes closed. I fall back and join her for a quick snooze.

The last thing I'd call my upbringing is "adventurous." Picnics at the beach and backyard barbecues were as alfresco as we got. My parents were not camping, hiking, or outdoorsy people; overnighting in a roadside motel was a luxury we couldn't afford, and vacations away were the stuff of imagination.

Eating out was a once-a-year treat in June when we brought home good grades. I learned early on what to order by looking at the price column first. Didn't want to add to my parents' financial stress.

In my girlish fantasies when we lived in New Jersey, Ohio, Massachusetts, and then New York, I was a missionary, a pioneer, an explorer, yearning for distant places. I dreamed and I read, discovering the world through characters and words on the page. When Joe and I met in high school at fourteen, we quickly learned we had much in common: reading, restlessness, and the prospect of foreign lands beyond our youthful reach. He also escaped boring summers devouring piles of library books. Both his parents worked, his mother as a waitress and his father an electrician. Travel would have to wait.

Fed, rested, and reinvigorated, we load up, ready for what Julien says will be two hours to the end for today.

"Just two hours?" I ask him.

"*Alors*, maybe a little bit more."

I wince as I tighten my backpack, the morning's efforts having left nasty welts on my hips and collarbone. I tuck some tissues under the offending straps and head over to Kees, who is getting ready to go.

"Enjoy your lunch, Kees?" I ask as I look up at all six foot five of him.

"Yes," he says. "It was good."

"I just love that *brébis* cheese. I had it at breakfast and was so happy Julien packed some for lunch. But do you believe he hates cheese?" I pause, hoping he'll add a word or two. Silence. I continue chattering with one more attempt to draw him out.

"What's the last big hike you did, Kees?"

"In the Alps. From Chamonix, France to Zermatt, Switzerland," he says concisely, politely but with an almost imperceptible grimace.

"Oh, the Haute Route. It's on our list to do one of these days. It'll probably be our next big hike in Europe. Did you go alone or with a group like ours?"

"With my wife."

"Oh, so why didn't she want to do this one?" I ask with a laugh. "Did she think it would be too much?"

At that very moment, Julien whistles and announces, "*C'est parti, mes amis.* Time to go."

I turn back to Kees for his answer. "No," he says, his affect flat, staring ahead. "She is dead."

I can't move, my mouth hanging open. While he appears not to have minded my questions, he offers no more and turns to follow Julien.

I've always told my children, one of the worst things you can do is hurt someone's feelings. I've just trampled all over my own rule. I think about how he must feel and wonder how much I've upset him.

For the next hour, my heart breaks for Kees. It distracts me from my tight legs and the additional ascent Julien claimed was "very little." When we stop to gaze over the final valley into which we'll descend, I mention the exchange to Joe.

"You couldn't have known, Marianne, and I'm sure Kees appreciates that you reached out to him. Try not to beat yourself up too much about it."

But it's not easy to let it go. When did she die? How did she die? Was it an accident? Did she have cancer? Do they have children?

I finally force my attention away from the conversation to the narrow, steep trail ahead that winds down through the shade of a chestnut forest and then under lofty laricio pines. I lean heavily on my poles to keep pressure off my knees. For the first time today, I keep up with the group and even pass Sarah and Chris when the path widens across a rocky patch. My steps are light and flow with confidence as we drop down the mountain.

Perhaps to ensure I not get too full of myself, my right trekking pole catches between two rocks. I keep stepping forward, not realizing the jam, and my wrist takes the brunt of my error. It snaps back with the pole, my shoulder twisting in its socket. If I'd forgotten about my RA, that move puts it back front and center. My wrist and shoulder throb in pain when I stop to massage them. "Damn," I say, watching my wrist inflate.

"Okay?" asks Sarah as she and Chris slip by.

"All good. Just wish I hadn't been so careless with my pole." *Stay alert*, I caution myself. *Even when things go well, don't get too ahead of yourself.*

I've caught up with Joe so we can be together as we exit the pine wood. In the distance appears nirvana itself: the Réfuge d'Ortu di u Piobbu, like the Emerald City rising from the field of poppies in *The Wizard of Oz*, visible far across the valley, perched high on a dirt plateau. My legs shake—for once, with giddiness rather than fatigue—as

I take in the rough-and-ready wooden hut with pistachio shutters surrounded by terrain dotted with tents. I picture smoke coming from its chimney.

"Oh, my God, we're almost there!" I'm breathless. "Can't be more than fifteen minutes straight ahead." We're both laughing like crazy people having finally caught sight of our destination.

"We might want to wait and see what the terrain ahead actually looks like before we celebrate too much," Joe says. There's that optimism again.

But despite his caution, there's fresh zip in our step as we push forward, like horses to the barn. We pass a lone tent pitched in a copse of trees a ways back from the trail. *Camping sauvage* (wild camping) is illegal on Corsica, but Julien tells us many people do it since nobody enforces the rule. "I guess they were anxious to settle in and couldn't wait the extra minutes it would take to get to the campground," I say. But then we make a sharp turn and catch ourselves abruptly, stopping just short of the lip of an unexpected gorge.

Julien and Phil are perched on a rock, waiting for the group and peering out over the abyss around which we have yet to hike. "Good news," says our guide, tousling his shaggy blond hair. "We have only one more hour and just a little going up to reach the réfuge. It looks very small from here, but there it is."

I can't speak. Joe and I exchange glances, mouths agape. *Another hour? Are you kidding me?* Our bodies and wills are prepared for just a fraction of that, and so I take deep breaths to remain rational. In an instant, I'm dog-tired, as if my muscles have detached from my bones. Any energy I have left bleeds from my still sore shoulders down though my torso and into my thighs. It tumbles over my knees, through my calves, into my feet, dripping through my toes onto the dusty track until I'm a melting Dali clock oozing over the mountain precipice.

Julien and Phil jump up and waste no time taking off. Joe and I hold back to pull ourselves together, my face buried in his chest, our arms dangling poles around each other.

"I feel like we're at the end of a marathon and someone just moved the finish line ahead five miles!" My throat stings as tears threaten from the deadly combination of rage and exhaustion. "It's right across the way but look at how far around we have to go to get there. I know part of it's in my head, but I swear, Joe, I don't know if I can do it. There's absolutely nothing left in my tank."

"I hear you, Babe, I'm totally exhausted too, but we have to do it. Just focus on the glass of wine at the end."

"Honestly, all I want right now is a huge, fizzy Orezza in a frosty mug." I wipe my face with my bandanna. "And since when did you become Mr. Positivity?"

Joe rubs my shoulders hard, and though I wince inside, I don't tell him his affection is causing me pain. We survey what's ahead and see that in contrast to much of what's behind us, there's actually a visible sandy path. It hugs the contour of the ridge, cuts sharply down the mountain to the left, and swings right round the far end of the gorge where it disappears into a stand of birches. It then reappears in the far distance and heads straight up a steep incline to the finish.

We start the descent, and I lose myself in grandiose fantasies of what awaits us at the end: a hot bubble bath, lathery lemon shampoo, and a huge fresh salad with salty ham. But this is the GR20, and anything resembling luxury, including fresh produce, is a remote recollection, so many miles behind us.

After forty-five minutes, we come out of the birch woods, and all that's between my aching body and a bottle of ice-cold mineral water is a half-mile rise. Because what remains is vertical, and I'm once again at the rear. Joe hangs back a bit, the others well ahead. I've gone through all but a few sips of my three liters of water, my lungs burn, I'm unable to take a deep, satisfying breath, my thigh muscles judder, and my tongue sticks to the roof of my mouth. *You will do this, Marianne. You will not fail.*

I count my steps in mindless exertion as they fall slow and heavy up the once again rocky path. Each time I get to fifty, I allow myself a quick break and sip the dregs of my now warm water. I'm in danger of falling asleep on my feet. Keep walking, keep walking, keep walking. My ankle turns on a loose stone, as I have no strength left to put my feet just where I want them. I catch myself with my poles, saving me from a serious twist, but my wrist screams. This time, it's the left one.

Twenty-three, twenty-four, twenty-five. I can't make it to fifty. Stop. Breathe. Sip. And then continue, step after step. Perhaps this time, I'll just count to twenty. I'm getting so close. Eighteen, nineteen, twenty. Stop. I attempt a sip but my water is gone. Pole, pole, step, step; pole, step, pole, step. I switch from steps to counting stones, flowers, lizards. I count whatever's in front of me. I imagine my pretty peach butterfly from the Luberon and revive my Provençal chant: butterfly, *farfalla, mariposa, papillon.*

Interrupting my stupor is the sweetest sound I've heard all day. "Honey, we're home." I look up to the ledge and there's Joe, just ten paces ahead where stage one of The Twenty ends and the Réfuge d'Ortu di u Piobbu plateau begins. "We made it, hiker girl." He walks down to greet me. Relief floods my every pore, and I drop to my knees.

"I am so proud of you for doing this," he says as he bends down and pulls up a corner of my bandanna to wipe my face. "Are those tears or just sweat?" he asks, laughing.

"I don't even know anymore. It's all mixed up together." He pulls me to my feet and envelops me in a sweaty hug. "But let's not get too happy quite yet. I still might crumple, and you'll be stuck throwing me over your shoulder, lugging me the rest of the way."

Joe strides and I stagger toward the rudimentary wooden building, multicolored prayer flags fluttering from the deck. With no appearance of permanence—some of its washed-out wall boards rotten and its stone foundation crumbling—it looks about ready to topple. I shuffle my final steps, bone-tired and brain foggy. We've just done the first nine hours, and I feel like we've been on the trail for a week. I know it's not my Osprey's fault I feel miserable, but I slam it down on the growing pile of discarded gear beside the stairs. "Take that." I turn to Joe. "I really don't think any amount of training could have prepared us for this."

"Definitely don't disagree, but maybe some of what you're feeling is just first day jitters."

"Come on, Joe. Really? Jitters? Stop trying to make me feel better. It only makes me feel worse." Roles have reversed. I'm no longer the conciliator. I'm the provocateur. Maybe it's my swollen wrists and aching shoulders talking. "I feel like crap, and it's only day one. It literally brought me to my knees. Now I just have to figure out how I'll manage to do day two."

"Let's get some cold drinks. I'm sure that'll make you—us—feel better."

"Sure, sure *Monsieur* Pollyanna. . . ."

But Joe's right. Just the thought of a cold Orezza and maybe some of my meds pulls me up the stony stairs to the sun-drenched wooden reception deck strewn with a United Nations of hikers refueling with drinks and snacks. Some from our group—Julien, Chris, and Jim—chat and laugh with others in various states of exhaustion.

Kees sits alone on a length of bench, picking at his fingernails, staring off in the distance. It's difficult for me to even look at our Dutch comrade after our awkward exchange because I'm feeling so sad. But I do catch his eye and he returns my quick smile.

While Joe goes to buy drinks, I find an unoccupied picnic table for myself. I sit heavily on the edge of the seat, my head dropping onto my arms folded in front of me. I'm on the edge of sleep when I feel Joe slip in beside me.

"Mineral water to the rescue," he says, pouring the bubbly liquid into a plastic cup. "Cheers to doing day one," he toasts, willing me to lift my head, trying to get me to smile. He swigs a frosty Pietra from the bottle as I toss back some pills and then guzzle my Orezza.

"Thanks, Joe." I put down my empty cup to pat him on the thigh. "I'm really, really sorry for lashing out before. At you. I shouldn't have. I know how I'm feeling isn't your fault." I can hardly keep my eyes open. "I'm just going to take a little catnap, okay? I swear if I don't, I won't make the hundred yards to a tent. Why don't you go hang with Chris and Julien and have another beer?"

"Sounds like a plan," he says, patting my shoulder and getting up to join the guys at the next table.

I undo my braids, snapping the hair ties around my wrist. My head back on my arms, I analyze the day. I was so slow. I should have been more careful with my poles. I shouldn't have been so nosy with Kees. And I definitely shouldn't look like the wreck of the Hesperus instead of a veteran hiker right now. Before I can berate myself any longer, I lose all thoughts and give in to sleep.

I awaken half an hour later and lift my head, finally able to take in where we've landed. Our destination paradise is even more perfectly sited and with broader vistas than I first thought. It's the sloped highland of a former shepherd's retreat overrun with farm animals at the top of a *transhumance* trail. Angular cows, hairy pigs, bony horses, and bearded goats root around the dilapidated outbuildings—their high-altitude home for the summer. They nibble at phantom grass and roam freely among the scattering of olive green tents punctuating the plateau. Never occurred to me that we'd be sharing our space with these wraithlike creatures.

"Any of those pigs wild?" I call over to Julien.

"*Mais, non!*" he says. "They are from farms, but I told you, they walk free. The *sangliers*—the wild ones, and there are many thousands of them—are too scared to be here. They do not like hikers."

"Well, thank God for that," I say, moving over next to Joe at what's become our group's table. I turn to watch Sarah and Phil walk up on the deck reinvigorated, faces flushed and hair wet after having taken a dip in a mountain lake several hundred yards away. "Where'd you two find the energy to walk all the way over there?" I ask. "I'm having a hard time thinking about dragging myself over to our campsite."

"Totally refreshing," says Sarah. "I never pass up the opportunity for a swim."

"We Brits don't mind the cold water. And that means we don't have to queue up to wash," says Phil, bare-chested in running shorts.

"What are you, a boxer?" Joe asks, pointing to the white towel draped around his neck. "Ready for the ring?"

Phil laughs, taking his best fighting stance, fists in front of his face.

Julien explains that the *bergerie*-style building has a dorm in addition to flat terrain for camping. I force myself up to take a look inside the building with Sarah. It's close to what I imagined, having seen a similar setup on the TMB. But unlike the refuge in the French Alps, this bunkroom could use a good scrubbing or even just a broom. Thirty slim, ratty mattresses march down two lengthy wooden platforms, one over the other, forming elongated bunks with a ladder at each end.

"Thank God we're not sleeping in here. A little too grimy for me," I say.

"And I sure wouldn't want some snoring bloke rolling into me in the middle of the night," Sarah replies.

We walk through the dorm to the kitchen side of the hut. It's equipped with a rusted gas stove and ancient oven, an eating room with rough-hewn tables and benches, and behind a closed door, a bedroom for the *gardien*. Julien told us that while the *gardiens* do not get paid, they are granted the concession franchise and make their money selling supplies to guests: granola, macaroni, cheese, canned beans, freeze-dried meats, chocolate, cookies, and coffee. Prices are high because the cost of transport by either packhorse or infrequent helicopter is significant. And although the kitchen and a trough outside have running water, it's for washing only. Drinking water must be drawn from the spring down the hill.

"Pretty basic," says Sarah.

"Very basic. Even more primitive than I thought. But hey, we can get a hot dinner and cold drinks, so I guess it does its job."

"I suppose room service is out of the question," Sarah says as we rejoin the others. I shake my head and giggle.

Joe points from where we're seated to behind the shower shed across the hilltop. "Shall we go claim our tent?" he asks. "I really want to get set up and do my laundry so it has enough time to dry."

My Orezza and nap have indeed revived me. We grab our packs, my thighs screaming from the reintroduction of the weight, and head toward a grove of trees. We're careful not to tread on the discus-sized cowpats swarming with luminous green flies dotting the hill. I hear Joe groan behind me.

"Where there are farm animals, there is *merde*," I say.

We choose our tent, one of four set in a ring of silvery birches, carefully crawl inside on tender knees, and change into our second set of clothes. My feet practically moan with relief as I pull off mucky, reeking boots and dusty socks to slip on flip-flops. My soles feel like they've walked across hot coals, but although they're sore and red, I see no blisters. I give my trusty Garmont boots a loving pat. With our dirty clothes ringed with white salty sweat lines and smelling of our labors, we head to the long basin next to the showers. A cursory scrub with soggy soap slivers left on the lip of the sink and a quick rinse is all we can muster. The Corsican sun remains well above the horizon, and the rocks surrounding our campsite radiate warmth. Ignoring the lizards skittering across the stones, we spread our clothes to soak up the heat. We unroll our sleeping bags on the mats in our tent, inventory our gear, and grab our toiletries.

"Have your headlamp handy?" says Joe. "Soon as that sun goes down, I'm sure it'll get dark really fast."

Keen to wash off the dust of the day's rigors, we take our towels and head for the showers—just two wooden cubicles for several dozen hikers. We make a stop at the toilets—again, only two—with a porcelain foothold on either side of the drain. The makeshift locking mechanism on the door doesn't hold so I trust that someone saw me enter and won't come barging in. I almost keel over when I bend my knees because there's nothing to grab onto as I squat, and I dare not put my hands on the filthy floor. Having lived in France, I'm accustomed to basic bathrooms, but I've never before had to crouch with thighs trembling after a day on The Twenty. I prefer peeing in the maquis.

"Well, that was interesting," I say when I join Joe at the end of the shower queue.

"Wasn't exactly the Ritz? All part of the experience, right?"

I flex my fingers and do circles with my thumbs and wrists, anxious to get them in warm water.

Seeing my movements, Joe says, "I totally forgot to ask about your joints. You never complain, so I forget about your RA sometimes."

"Actually, so much of me was hurting today that the joint pain was kind of lost in the mix. But now that we've stopped for the day and I think about it, everything's feeling pretty tight." Joe reaches over to massage my hands.

After a twenty-minute wait, we slip into a stall to enjoy a tepid shower together, following the lead of the couples ahead of us. Rinsing in tandem helps move along the growing line more quickly. "Nothing to complain about with this system," says Joe, soaping my back. He gently runs his hands over my sore shoulders and down my back, traces my arms to my hands, and slowly rubs my wrists. My joints, my muscles, my stiffness slacken, loosening in the warm water. I sigh and turn, slowly, easily, closing my eyes as I lift my arms over my head and lean back against the wooden wall.

We return to our tent and in the time we've been gone, the circle of trees has morphed into a motley laundry line of intimate freak flags flying. The dripping dress of a throng of hikers hangs from the branches: shirts, shorts, socks, bras, bandannas, underwear, thongs, and yes, a few jock straps. No such thing as decorum in the wild.

My legs, loose from the soothing shower, tremble on the gentle rise to the canteen for dinner. The sun low in the sky, the early evening temperatures steadily drop, and so we've each added a warm layer. We pass the simple two-burner cooking shelter where the most budget-minded hikers boil pasta and heat soup. I take tight hold of the railing as I mount the stairs to take weight off my throbbing thighs.

Inside, we sit at the table Julien claimed for our group. Chris is on his second Pietra, the first empty in front of him, and Phil drinks a Coke. The rest of us agree to red wine, and so Joe inaugurates what will become our nightly ritual. The wine drinkers—all save Julien who, according to trekker etiquette, never pays for drinks—take turns buying carafes for the table. The red-by-the-barrel is full-bodied and fruity. My very first delicious sip courses down my arms and legs all the way to my fingertips and toes.

Jim reveals that his feet have some hot spots, so Phil launches into hiking mentor mode. "Got to prevent blisters before they bloom. Can't ignore them. Much harder to deal with once they're full of fluid—and make sure your boots aren't too tight or too loose. I'll check them when you put them on tomorrow morning." Phil seems the only one still able to form complete sentences. Maybe it's the caffeine. The rest of us sit quietly, even Sarah, ready to be served. Chris yawns audibly, and it catches round the table. Good to see I'm not the only one this exhausted. We could definitely use some sustenance.

"If anyone needs duct tape for hot spots, just ask," Phil continues.

"We have some too," I say. "We swear by it."

"Duct tape?" asks Jim.

"Sure," says Phil. Best thing for preventing friction, and it almost never comes off. Even when you sweat or get wet."

Julien delivers a tureen of vegetable soup followed by baskets of French bread. Sarah offers a toast. "Here's to twelve more days and no more talk of blisters." We touch our juice glasses, take first sips, and agree that a hearty red in bulbous Bordeaux crystal couldn't taste any better. Slurping and swigging, chewing and chomping—the sounds of enthusiastic eating amid clinking glasses and scraping spoons fill the room. It's family-style, filling fare, and by the time the bowl of spaghetti arrives, I barely have enough energy or belly room to down my second glass of wine and a few forkfuls of pasta.

In the lull before dessert, Sarah says, "Well, if we didn't know before what the GR20 was going to be like, I guess we do now, right?"

"Mm-hmm," we say, nodding, too tired for words. The sun tiptoes away from the plateau and down into the trees until it disappears—losing its fight against the dark, just as I have. Sleep tugs at my eyelids and I can't imagine keeping them open for more than another few minutes.

"I'm going to call it quits for the night." I drain my glass in one gulp. "Phil, you can have my dessert—for being such a great Sherpa."

"Don't mind if I do," he says with a self-satisfied grin, taking my plate of chestnut *fiadone*—a Corsican cross between cheesecake and flan drizzled with honey. Joe smiles and shakes his head.

"Wait, wait," says Julien. "Before you go, we must talk about the weather for tomorrow." His meteorological report, which the refuge receives from the park authorities, will become part of our evening ritual and dictate how we'll dress the next morning. He gives us the temperature and wind details. "Wear what was good for today because tomorrow will be the same. Be at breakfast by six thirty. We must leave at seven fifteen."

Joe wants to stay with the group, so I sleepwalk back to our campsite on my own to the ragged howls of nocturnal animals, the fiery sunset as a backdrop, and my headlamp cutting through purple dusk. I feel the delicious fatigue that promises that the minute I put my head down, I'll instantly dissolve into sleep. I slip into our tent, strip down, and then slither into my cozy Big Agnes, inching down flat on my back with a slow, deep moan. I contemplate rolling over on my stomach, my normal sleeping position, but there's no need to decide. It's eight fifteen and I fall fast asleep.

I'm awakened much later by my screaming bladder and am greeted by the international sound of guttural snoring from neighboring tents. Every inch of my body is sore—it feels like I've been pummeled—and protests any movement. But I really must get up, and so I wrestle into a fleece, shorts, and flip-flops, grab my light, and unzip the tent flap slowly, not wanting to wake Joe. The air is much colder than I expect—frosty even—given the heat of ten hours ago. I find a bush, careful not to step in animal dung, and take care of business.

Before I crawl back in the tent, I stop to gaze up at a starry backdrop unlike any I've ever seen. The full clarity and depth of the night makes the hair on the back of my neck rise. I'm shivering uncontrollably but can't bear to look away from a shooting star. It's the darkest of night skies, so utterly devoid of manmade light, that allows the astral glimmer of the Milky Way to shine. Carl Sagan's "billions upon billions" echoes as I take in the firmament of blue-white stars bowled across the sky. What miracles of life and death, of love and loss, have they watched over as people of the earth come and go? I hold out my hand to cast a shadow in the ethereal light. Surrounded by eternity, I feel suddenly small and reminded of forces much larger than us—what Phil articulated earlier—on this island mesa high above the Mediterranean. For just a moment, I experience the mystery of infinite space, the divine beauty of the night sky, and a profound, overpowering silence, my wondrous world for now.

I return to the warm spot I left in my sleeping bag. I'm next to the man I love, nursing the aches of an aging body, on an adventure of a lifetime, under a ceaseless celestial sky. Not even the insecurities that normally keep me up at night or the terror of tomorrow's climb can diminish these miraculous moments.

Tuesday, August 2
The Hike—Day Two: Réfuge Ortu di u Pobbio to Réfuge de Carrozu

↗ **Ascent:** 2,726 feet

↘ **Descent:** 3,609 feet

→ **Distance:** 7 miles

Guidebook Description: Today's terrain is challenging.

In the shapeless moments before fully waking, I rise from the depths of the sea to the bickering of ravens. I struggle to place where I am until I try to roll over, my sore muscles reminding me of yesterday's miles. My body feels like one big bruise. The caustic solvent of The Twenty's reality has eroded any gauzy notions of the romantic wild.

As I've done since I was a schoolgirl, when faced with a terrifying prospect—an exam, a speech, a difficult conversation—I summon options for escape. I rarely ever use them, but somehow the possibility of flight calms me down. Neither this refuge nor our destination for night two is reachable by car, so the only way I can leave is on foot or in a rescue helicopter. And wouldn't the latter be embarrassing?

But I stop my ridiculous musings cold. I mustn't dwell on the negative. Or the knots in my calves. In the early morning stillness, I lie quiet and do my best to allow gratitude to replace my pain. I'm grateful for Joe, who helped me through our first day; for Sarah, who offered entertaining talk; for Jim, fellow plodder; for Julien, unruffled leader with whom I so enjoy speaking French; and finally, for Phil, selfless teammate. As for Chris and Kees, I appreciate the challenge of cutting through their shells.

Activity on the GR20 begins early, the campground rousing well before first light. As we climb ever higher toward Corsica's core, it's critical to make tracks before the sun crowns the ridge and energy-zapping heat explodes across the valley.

"Rise and shine for the maritime," Joe says, as he did for years with our children whenever the day called for an early start. He leans over and plants a kiss on my forehead. "Let's go, sleepyhead. We've got mountains to climb." He's committed to complying with Julien's directive to be seated for breakfast by 6:30 and not a minute later. Like I am, Joe is very good at following orders—the predictable outcome of twelve years of Catholic school and four years at Kings Point, the US Merchant Marine Academy. Straightaway, he establishes an efficient morning routine for breaking camp. He pulls my sleeping bag down from around my shoulders, but I tug it back up with a grunt.

"Just five more minutes. I swear, I just need five."

"Up to you," he says, a hint of reprimand in his tone. Damn. He knows me too well and has taken a page from what's usually my playbook. Guilt always works to get me to do what I might not otherwise.

"But the sooner you get going, the more time you'll have to get ready." He unzips the tent, adding his waking sounds to those around us: zippers whizzing, latrine doors banging, showers spluttering.

I crawl from the tent, bleary-eyed and tight-muscled, willing myself to stand. "Ow!" I cry as I straighten my knees, my right calf in a knot until I massage it loose. And my left hand is really puffy, my wedding ring digging into my finger.

Just past a line of conifers, I see the earliest risers lift their packs and check their pitch to be sure they've left nothing behind. They must be postponing breakfast to get a jump on the trail, setting off on the next étape in a groggy hush, their winking headlamps dotting the woods.

I glance over at Joe who has all his things neatly rolled, folded, ready to be piled in his pack. But I'm a total disaster. I attempt to take inventory, looking in the tent, surveying the jumble on my side.

"Know where I put my black shirt?" I ask, my bottom in the air as I paw through my stuff.

Joe frowns as I toss things every which way. "Oh no," I say when my hairbrush escapes my grasp in a slow-motion arc. It lands with a splat in a fresh cow patty. Bristles down. Tears are at the brim as Joe chuckles and shakes his head.

"No way I'm cleaning that," I say. My brush will stay where it is. I'll borrow Joe's plastic comb—hardly helpful for my long tangled hair—but I'll have to make do.

"This what you're looking for?" Joe asks, retrieving my black tee from the branch on which I'd hung it the night before.

"Oy—yes. But how about my ChapStick—did I give it to you?"

"You usually put it with your phone. Where's your phone?" He's trying to be patient but can't help a long frustrated exhale.

"Maybe I put it in that inside pocket next to the flap." I duck into the tent, rummaging around.

Joe gathers the other things I'd hung to dry the night before and tosses them in a heap. I grab the crumpled pile.

"Thanks. Appreciate it." My weak smile belies how foolish I feel. I'm not used to being disorganized, but this morning I'm a mess—a sleepy, rumpled, unmade bed. In the Corsican wild, with no dresser drawers or closet shelves for smartly stacking my things, I've fallen apart. Perhaps the altitude has gotten to me.

I struggle to release the plug for my pillow to deflate it, my fingers on fire and my knuckles swollen. "Joe?" I ask, my voice catching. No response. I think he's decided to ignore me.

He pops his head into the tent. "Marianne—you need to get it together," he says. He easily unplugs my pillow and kneels on it, escaping air whistling. "I think I'd better leave you alone—give you some space. I'm heading to the spring to get us water, assuming you can find your bladder."

"Can you just pull it out of my pack?" I ask, amazed that I actually know where it is. I step outside and point. "Over there."

The dutiful Catholic schoolgirl inside me scolded, wagging her finger, "How could you? How could you not have all your supplies? Pencil, pen, black-and-white composition notebook. Homework. Your lunch." I was in first grade, at Saint Clare's, had forgotten my metal Yogi Bear lunch box at home, and was starving.

I doodled with my pencil, surrounded by forty classmates eating at their desks what their mothers had packed for them in brown bags and aluminum boxes: American cheese, bologna, or peanut butter and honey sandwiches on white bread, wrapped neatly like gifts in waxed paper. A piece of fruit. Oreos in aluminum foil. Hunger gnawed.

Sister Mary Irene circulated with baskets of pretzel sticks (two cents), potato chips (five cents), cheese corn (ten cents), and a plastic cup etched with a cross for payment. I never asked my mother for snack money because even at age six, I knew we couldn't afford it. I pulled my hand from my pocket and pretended to drop a dime in the cup. I reached for a bag of cheese corn. "Marianne," said Sister. My face reddened, my eyes lowered as I returned the bag. *How could you have forgotten your lunch?* The shame of not being prepared.

I watch Joe disappear down the trail, take a deep breath, and then gather my things. In the glow of my headlamp, I manage to eventually find all my gear and then lay it across the tent, like an REI photo shoot. Increasingly visual the older I get, I have to actually see the totality of what I'm arranging—each and every item—to make it work. When Joe returns, I'm ready to go.

"Got yourself all set?" he asks, hoisting our water bladders, one in each hand like freshly caught trout.

"Yessir," I point to a neat pile with a cockeyed smile.

We slip our reservoirs filled with cold water into their slots in our packs. I cram in my gear and we head up through the misty mountain dawn to the canteen. Despite my fumbling, it's 6:25. Minutes to spare.

Just as we sit, I accidentally bang my sore hand on the bench and realize I've forgotten my morning meds. I jump back up. *"Merde."* Thank God I remembered them now and not hours into today's climb. If ever I miss a dose, my joints blow up in just a few hours.

"What's up?" asks Joe.

"Forgot my pills," I call as I slip out the door. "Just order me tea. Please?"

You are not going to ruin my day, dear trespasser.

On my way back to the tent, I catastrophize about how a hungry Corsican critter has run off with my pillbox in the dawn light. But there it is, sitting right where I left it atop the tent—my fuchsia-flowered Vera Bradley pill case, purchased in my least favorite color for easy retrieval. As I down my drugs, I hear Sarah call from across the rocky wall, "Sleep well?" She's in exactly the same clothes she had on the day before—khaki shorts and a lime green "Life is Good" tee. I've changed my shirt and shorts per our plan of wearing outfits every other day between washings.

"I did. And you?"

"Slept fine, but now that I'm up, I need an infusion of tea as soon as possible or I'll be back asleep before we even start."

"Well then, let's get you your English Breakfast fix—three cups coming up."

"Where's Joe?" Sarah asks as we head up the hill.

"Already at breakfast. I was up there too but forgot my pills." I hesitate about revealing my RA secret, but affection for Sarah outweighs reluctance and a surprising tinge of embarrassment. I feel the need to share. I explain my recent diagnosis and list my prescriptions when she asks.

"Well, aren't you a brave one tackling this thing given that news. You ever think of backing out? My patients with RA get so tired— fatigue's a real issue."

"No idea how I'll ever find the energy to get through thirteen days of this—but no, once my doctor gave me the go-ahead, I was ready to try. Joe was tentative at first, but we talked about it a lot and decided that if one of us had to quit—and we both assumed it would be me—the other would go on. Unless, of course, he or I got seriously injured." Not wanting undue attention, I sugarcoat my discomfort. "The first day's done, and I'm feeling good, so we'll see. And as I'm sure you know, the meds for RA are amazing."

"They definitely can be, at least on most days. Well, you must let me know if I can help in any way."

"Will do," I say, but then add, "Can we please keep this between us? I didn't tell Julien and don't plan to. Don't want him treating me any differently, you know?"

"Not a problem, Marianne. I understand, and your secret's safe with me. If you're feeling good, there's no reason for a BBC broadcast."

"Thanks, Sarah. Appreciate it. Also want to fill you in about a chat I had with Kees yesterday. I was so beat last night, I forgot to tell you." I give her the details of the conversation. "I felt really bad afterward. My heart was and still is aching for him, even though I don't know any details about what happened."

"That is so sad, but I have to say I can't quite figure him out either. Wouldn't go getting your knickers in a twist about it," Sarah says. "How could you have known? Maybe you can get him to talk about it more later?"

"Maybe." But I can't imagine causing him any more pain. And I wonder if I should have shared my RA intruder with Sarah. Having someone other than Joe know about it makes me feel a little weaker already.

We arrive at our table in the mess hall just in time to hear Phil ask, "Hear about the bedbug invasion?"

"You mean the one in your sleeping bag, Phil?" says Joe. Phil takes a sip of tea and shakes his head, chuckling.

"What about them?" asks Jim.

"I know bedbugs are always a problem," says Phil, "but I heard that last night it was so bad everyone had to evacuate."

"Where did they go?" asks Kees, and I smile. This is the first time I've actually heard him offer a question and not just a quick response.

"Out to the tents, I guess," says Phil. "It was a real infestation." I feel myself itch as I grab a hunk of freshly baked bread from the basket. I fill a spoon from the sticky communal pot of jam and cut a slice of butter from our group's soft slab, breadcrumbs clinging to its corners. I look over at Sarah and say, "Thank God for small blessings. Definitely a good thing we won't be staying in those dorms."

Julien joins us with hot drinks on a tray and says, "Oh, the bed-bugs—*les punaises de lit.* They are always a problem, but they are now a very huge problem. Even if they burn all the buildings and build new ones, the bugs will still come back."

"Why not just make the refuge interiors out of stone?" asks Chris, swigging the first of two cold Pietras sitting in front of him.

"I would not want to sleep on a platform of rocks," says Kees with a smile. Another first. He looks somewhat upbeat.

"Can we please stop discussing *les punaises*?" I say. "Or I won't be able to sit still on this wooden bench."

"Some coffee or tea?" Julien asks Chris, changing the subject.

"Cheers, Julien, but no thanks. My morning brews are reinforcement enough." He raises his bottle and pulls an energy bar from his pocket.

I look across the table at Sarah to see what she's thinking and give a little shrug. The slight rise of her eyebrows says it all.

"So," I say to her, after we've taken our last bites of breakfast and are enjoying our tea, "What do your kids think about you doing this hike?" She's already filled me in on her four children, all in their late twenties and early thirties.

"Oh, they think I'm insane. In fact, they know I'm insane, doing things like this and then going to Africa next month. I'm joining Doctors Without Borders for a year in the Congo."

"Wow, that's so cool! Good for you, Sarah."

"I've been wanting to do it for years, and now that I'm retired, I finally have the time. But I'm not exactly in the bloom of my youth, so the children worry. My youngest daughter asked me before I left to come here, 'Mummy, how many other women go off hiking on Corsica for a fortnight when they're sixty?'"

"Well, now you can tell her there's at least one other one. I turned sixty in March."

"Well, I'm definitely glad you're here. Jolly good company, you are."

"Back at you." I reach over with my cup to clink hers. She gives me a thumbs-up, takes a gulp of tea, and continues. "My offspring put up with my escapades, and I'm sure nothing I do surprises them anymore. They know I'm independent, too independent sometimes. I just like to pave my own way, if you know what I mean. And that's why I often have to go it alone. The children have stopped asking when I'm finally going to grow up."

"I'm not sure I'll ever feel grown up, no matter how much gray hair I have."

Sarah nods. "I'll second that."

"A hiker friend once told me that if people question how far you'll go, go so far that you can't hear them anymore."

"I like that, Marianne! And how about your children? They must think you're mad as well."

"It's about the same with Chris and Caroline. They're used to us traveling and going off to who knows where, but I think how much we're roughing it this time surprised even them. We're definitely hikers, but basic camping for two full weeks is a first for us."

"For me too," Sarah says. "Don't normally spend this many nights in a tent."

Julien gets up from the end of the table and summons us. "*On y va!* It is time for day number two. We will meet by the tents in five minutes."

* * *

I was thirteen and had been sick with the flu for a week when I headed back into junior high. Combined with Christmas break, I'd been away from school for sixteen days. It seemed an eternity. No work I'd missed gave me pause until math—Intro to Honors Algebra. From the moment I stepped in the classroom lorded over by Dr. Smith, a middle-aged woman with skinny white legs in a miniskirt and mad-professor gray hair, I was terrified. I understood nothing that came out of her mouth. Everyone nodded as she scribbled on the blackboard. I concentrated hard, biting my lower lip, but I'd missed so much and would never catch up. I'd never received less than an A in math and could not bear being the dumb kid in a smart class. I could not let myself fail. How many times had I heard, "We need you to be a role model for your siblings?"

I had no friends in the class. I still had no friends in the huge public school. I was lost, and I panicked. I'll fail this class, I know I will. How can you be so stupid? But I couldn't do the problems, gibberish in white chalk. "You'll be fine," I could already hear my mother say, "You'll figure it out." Her words would only make me feel worse. "But, I won't," I'd cry back and want to run. I could not handle not being able to do things. I couldn't handle not being in control. What would my brothers and sisters think? I was the oldest. I was responsible for everyone. For everything. I'd have done anything to make the feeling go away. I raised my hand, escaped to the bathroom, gave in to dry heaves, unable to stem my tears.

Having walked twice around the hallway perimeter to control my crying, I slipped back into math class with just minutes to go. My head was bowed, my hair in my face, so I'd catch no one's eye. Oh God, please let the torture of this class be over. The know-it-all girl sitting in front of me twirled her curly red hair around her finger and raised her other hand, waving it back and forth.

"Marianne, how about you?" Dr. Smith asked, looking past the redhead to me. "How do we solve the equation for X?" I looked up, opened my mouth, but was unable to speak as fresh tears hovered. My cheeks went hot and I froze. Everyone looked at me.

"Marianne?" she asked again. The board was a blur. I couldn't see. I couldn't think. I didn't understand.

"I don't know." Barely a whisper. She held her open palm behind her ear. "I don't know," I repeated, louder this time. I wanted to disappear. I wanted to die. The bell rang and rescued me. Dr. Smith approached, but I slipped out the door, vowing never to return. I refused to go to school the following morning, not until my mother agreed to have me transferred to the on-level math class where I could breathe easy among the "regular" kids. Where no one would pay me any attention.

Late the following morning, I sat on the edge of the leather chair, trying to focus on what my mother and the guidance counselor said but their words tumbled over each other. I was trying so hard to be brave. "Transfer" and "Dr. Smith" cut through the chatter.

"Marianne, will that work?" my mother asked as she touched my forearm gently. "You'll start in a new class tomorrow." I nodded, slid back in the chair, and breathed a sigh of relief. I'd never have to go into that classroom again.

"You know, Marianne," the guidance counselor said, sitting on the corner of his desk, elbows on his knees, leaning forward. "Before you and your mom leave, I just want you to know that I think you're a reflective, sensitive, special young lady to have spoken up." I gave him a halfhearted smile but quickly lowered my head as we left, too timid to say anything at all.

We drove home in silence, nothing more to say. My mother knew she'd done well, agreeing to the transfer and letting me skip school for the rest of the day. I looked out at bare January trees, and inside I smiled. The counselor would never know how I hung on his words. They may not have been what a self-assured grown woman needed, but it helped ease the chaos in my adolescent brain. My insecure self heard that I was worthy.

As we head back into what I now consider the "combat zone," I check in with Joe about our new brand of footwear. "How those Darn Tough socks working out?"

"Darn great," he says. "They're really comfortable, but it's a little strange to be talking about comfort when our feet are actually killing us."

"Mine feel good right now, especially in fresh socks, but I know it won't last long. Pretty soon they'll feel like they've been tenderized with a meat mallet."

"Still, it's hard to believe we don't have any blisters yet. Not even any hot spots."

"Don't jinx it!"

The first hours of any uphill hike are the toughest for me, perhaps because it takes that long for my body to warm, my muscles to loosen, and my joints to be oiled. But Julien's on a mission—to cover the seven difficult miles to our next overnight stop, the Réfuge de Carrozu, by late afternoon—and there's no time for moaning.

The first rocky yards descend to the spring and then immediately reverse direction, climbing a rugged, rocky slope through a glade of delicate birches. On this relatively easy ascent, our group sticks close together, and I manage to relax, simply enjoying our surroundings. Casual conversation flows, but since I find talking and uphill breathing at the same time difficult, I'm content to just listen. Wide-ranging discussions cover favorite hikes, our families, local Corsican politics, and next year's French presidential elections.

But then Sarah raises a topic that disrupts the amity.

"So what do you Americans think about the UK Brexiting the European Union?" And before Joe, Jim, or I can respond, she adds, "I have to say, it's the stupidest thing we Brits have ever voted for. It's time to put the canard to rest that leaving the EU will be good for England. What a heartless little country we've become. Have you seen what's happened to the pound since the vote in June? And just wait 'til we see how far wages and employment fall." She brandishes her trekking poles to emphasize her points. I'm careful to stay out of range.

"Easy now, *Doctor* Sarah," says Chris. Leading the way, he stops and turns around just ahead of her. "Hate to break it to you, but you're looking at a Brexiter. Some of us have had it with handing over jobs to immigrants and caving to what the rest of Europe wants." His declaration hints of practice. He's said this many times before. "It's rubbish. All my mates voted to leave as well."

Conversation skids to a halt, and I flinch. Chris turns on his heel to continue up the trail, and I hear him mutter, "A legend in her own lunch box." He leaves a wake of awkward silence.

"Really know how to stir things up, don't you Sarah?" I ask with a titter as we resume walking.

"What a cock up," she says, turning to Joe and me, the three of us now bringing up the rear. "I shouldn't have mouthed off so quickly."

"Hey, you feel strongly, so why not speak your mind?"

Joe adds, "Had a feeling Chris was a Brexit fan based on things he said about his oil drilling job and taxes."

"Well, I do have a tendency to be Miss Bossy Boots, assuming everyone thinks like I do. I'm doing my best to be sensitive to other opinions, but clearly I have work to do. Didn't mean to cause a kerfuffle."

"But are you ready to respect the decision of the voters?" I ask.

"I just can't forgive such ignorance, at least not for now."

"We have the same issues in the US, as I'm sure you know—people feeling like the country's changing and they're being abandoned—the whole Trump thing."

Joe has stepped up his pace, leaving Sarah and me behind. I know he doesn't dare engage further in the discussion, fearing he'll get too fired up. The possibility of Trump becoming president disturbs him to his core. But I genuinely enjoy political exchanges with Europeans because no matter their beliefs, they're usually well-informed with good breadth and depth of analysis, and cite specifics, while Americans offer sound bites and generalities.

"The way I see it," says Sarah, "Brexit is a perfect example of how to provoke populism. Talk about a grievance shared by lots of people and pick a target to blame—immigrants, minorities, working women, the media, whatever. Paint them in the nastiest possible light, publicly point fingers, and then define the group by its worst members."

I take a while to respond, as I need to stop and catch my breath. Sarah pulls up beside me. When I've finally recovered, I say, "And don't forget to tell people you feel their pain. Use inflammatory rhetoric to tell them you'll protect them from whoever it is that left them behind." I'm now using my poles for emphasis. "Support me because I'll tell you that nothing is really your fault."

"It's going on here in France too with the rise of xenophobia," Sarah says.

"I know." I shake my head. "Farage, Trump, Le Pen . . . they're all using fear for traction. Britain first, American first, France first.

They're spoiling for a fight and are really tapping into people's anger. And to a certain extent, I do understand why people feel that way. But those politicians take it too far and they're just so divisive. Always talking about us and them."

"Well, now that I know where Chris stands, I can hedge what I say. For now though, I do feel a bit stupid."

"Why, Sarah? All you did was express what you think."

Sarah shrugs. She seems to want to let things go.

We carry on in silence for some time, breathing heavily, winding up through a rocky ravine bristling with scrub. My thoughts turn to the inevitability of globalism, the blurring of borders, the consequences of technology, and the anxiety it all arouses, especially among some prominent politicians. I start wondering about religious fundamentalists of any ilk and if they'd cause as much death and destruction if technology hadn't made so visible how others, especially in the West, choose to live.

My world affairs musings peter out as Sarah and I ford a lively stream and approach our group on a water break. I hear Jim ask no one in particular, "Oh come on . . . is this a joke?" I look up at what's ahead as he jabs his pole at the base of a cascade of broad, flat granite boulders piled one atop the other, all angular patterns and geometric shapes, that stretches up and away to the horizon. Wide swaths of lichen in assorted shades of greens, grays, and golds daubed across gray striated rock faces diluting to watercolor. It gives the effect of a massive open-air mural. It's a Goliath climb that would give any David pause. I watch as Jim lets his pack crash to the ground and launches into a diatribe under his breath.

"Yes, this is a hard part, James," says Julien, "because it is very steep and slippery, and today there is wind." There's no playing down what's rising ahead of us. "We will go slow, and you will be very, very careful about where you step. You can put your poles away because you will need your hands. *Allez.*"

As Julien coaches, the sun crests the peak behind us, illuminating the barricade in bright light. Unlike hiking trails that ascend by zigs and zags, this one goes directly up over bare rock. For one of only a few times in my life, I'm grateful for my particular center of gravity: low and broad-beamed, confidently stable as we take on the vertical climb, some of it through tight corridors between boulders. I look up to see tall, wiry Kees, along with Chris and Joe, stooped over, advancing slow and steady, clinging to the precipitous rock face. I fear they'll topple with a stiff gust because of their height.

About a third of the way up, we veer right to follow a diagonal gully cut into and across the wall for a marginally safer ascent. After an hour's climb, we reach the crown and what I thought was the top, but then my heart sinks. There's yet another crest looming, threatening, mocking the feat we've just accomplished. Like Tantalus, destined forever to stand neck-deep in a pool that flows away when he tries to drink, fruit hanging above him just beyond his reach, so do elusive targets tease us with the torture of false hope. I succumb to the reality and acknowledge a key lesson of this hike: You never, ever actually reach the top. And perhaps it's a life lesson as well. There will always be another summit to scale and yet another after that.

Perhaps I need to set more proximate goals—those with more frequent rewards. Ascend to that gigantic pine, round the big boulder, reach the next trail marker. I sigh, having convinced myself no one else needs such psychological coddling.

Above this particular crest, however, the landscape changes markedly. We're well past terrain that can support the maquis or summering farm animals, having reached an area of unadulterated rock. There are no trees and no vegetation to break the infinite stony scene of scree and clusters of gray rock. We negotiate multiple short, steep ascents where we go up sharply only to quickly come back down abrupt descents. There's a spring in my step since we've deviated from interminable climbs.

The punishing sun is now high in the sky, heating the rock of the gorges and gullies like an oven. My skin sizzles, despite slathers of sunblock. The stark, treeless terrain is tremulous with visible waves of heat pressing down like a fever. I take off my bandanna, hoping for a slight breeze to cool my neck.

No longer a mix of chalky greens and pallid tans, the landscape is now redder and a hundred shades of brown—desolate, dry, and silent—dotted with gargantuan rock formations. I recall reading the words of Seneca, the Roman philosopher exiled to the island two thousand years ago: "What can be found so bare, so rugged all around, as this rock?" The panoramas are like nothing I've ever seen in Europe. They remind me of the Grand Canyon and the wilds of Utah: Arches and Canyonlands National Parks—gut-punches of austere beauty.

Corsica's interior is rough and rugged with no rounded edges, at least not what we've seen so far. The Alps are mature and pastoral by contrast, while these young mountains are desolate, dark, bleak, and ever-changing.

We've now reached the highlight of our second day—a precipitous promontory at over sixty-five hundred feet, the Bocca Piccaia, beside which serrated peaks flank Ladroncellu, a deep, constricted gorge with bare stone walls. Astonishing towers of angular rock sprout like successive rows of teeth biting into the sky. Everything about this geological marvel is vertical.

"We will stop here for a long break because these will be the most *spectaculaire* views of the whole GR20," Julien says. "You will enjoy them, I know, and you will see why this part of the hike is used by France to train soldiers who will go to Afghanistan."

I gaze down and catch my breath. The chasm is boundless, its distant bed invisible, its voracious orifices keen to devour us. I grip a natural handhold, just a sliver in the fissured rock, frightened that an errant blast of wind will send me tumbling. My head grows woozy as I contemplate the menacing pinnacles and red peaks, recalling what a trekking companion once cautioned in the Alps: "You must never think otherwise; the mountains will always win." I shudder despite the heat.

I entertain the possibility we're in purgatory since surely these are the gates of hell. I move closer to Joe, knowing that if I'm experiencing an irrational fear of falling, he must be struggling with vertiginous visions as well. "This is awesome terrain, but creepy too."

He nods.

"We're not hiking down into the inferno, are we Julien?" Sarah asks, peering over the edge.

"Do you want to?" he says, winking at me.

"Julien, I'm daft, but not crazy."

"What is this word, *daft*?"

I interpret for him, reminded of how carefully we must choose our words when communicating with nonnative speakers.

"Is that our trail across the way?" asks Sarah. She points to a clearly visible path in the distance that after a sharp decline cuts left, heads down again, and then winds up to and over the next pass.

Julien nods, and I exhale my relief, putting my arm around Joe.

"Thank God we're not going over that precipice," he says. "I'm already feeling dizzy and that definitely would have freaked me out."

"This place is primeval but so magical. Scary and gorgeous at the same time. I swear I feel like we're in *The Princess Bride*. Over there are the Cliffs of Insanity and down there's the Fire Swamp."

The power of the place and the lament of the wind drive me back from the cliff and away from Joe and the group, now all safely seated for a water break. I sit under a rocky overhang and contemplate this natural cathedral, reflecting on the forces that carved these monoliths over millennia.

A few quiet moments are the real reward for all the effort, sweat, and lactic acid it took to get up here, seated in silence with serious thoughts in this curiously eerie setting. It's the sort of place for thinking about big things, important things: mortality and eternal life, the power of good and the forces of evil, deep friendship and all-consuming love. I look down at the cracked, parched path beside me, struggling to grasp the vastness of time, the millions of years gone by since these menacing peaks rose up and were then carved by the elements. They were here long before and will be here long after I pass by with my temporal interest—a mere observer of such grandeur.

I consider all the hikers whose boots passed this way—each but a speck on this commanding canvas. What were they thinking? What were their reasons for taking this challenge? Each of us comes and goes, but the land is always there, and despite man's attempts to hold it off, nature continues to shape the universe, and there is little we can do to stop it. I pull myself from being lost in my head to watch the others, now standing, snapping pictures from one angle and then another.

I catch my breath when I see Phil inch out to the far tip of a rock that juts over the gorge. The sheer drop appears to have been sliced with a butcher's cleaver.

"Joe, take my picture?" he says, having handed over his camera.

"Be careful, Phil!" I call, my voice harsh. "Do *not* move another step or I'll have a stroke." My heart drops to my stomach as I remember Julien telling us that every year, at least one hiker perishes on the GR20 from a fall, lightning strike, or exposure. My imagination takes over, picturing Phil teetering on the edge and then plunging into oblivion.

"He'll be fine," Joe says, well back from the edge as he snaps a couple shots. "Remember, Phil has the DNA of a mountain goat."

"No worries, Marianne. I survived the photo op," says Phil, retreating from the brink. "Thanks, Joe," he adds, reaching for his camera. "I'm sure one of those will be on my Christmas card this year."

My heart floats back to my chest as I return to the group.

On the lunar loneliness of the terrain, there's neither tree cover nor the shade of rock walls as the sun is directly overhead. The tops of Joe's ears are burned ruby red, and sunburn stings the tender, exposed skin on my head. I twist around to grab the hat hanging off my pack. Sarah seems to be struggling, in part because her fair skin is frying despite a visible white layer of sunscreen. I see her tilt the collective thermos of tea to her lips. Finding it empty, she peers in once and then again. I fear she's going to cry.

Hunger claws as we've agreed to a late lunch, holding off for what Julien promises will be a perfect spot. I unwrap an energy chew from my pocket, juicy citrus and a needed glucose burst exploding in my mouth. I hand one to Sarah and one to Joe.

"*C'est parti*," says Julien. "I am afraid we must leave this beautiful place. You must be very careful for this next part. Please."

Our pace, is slow and we make a hang-by-your-fingernails kind of progress that forces our full attention on our surroundings and where we place each step. We inch across the precarious lip of a rocky ledge, our backs to the drop-off, toes bumping against the wall. I lodge my boot into a fissure, afraid to turn around lest the weight of my pack drag me off the cliff, and grip whatever I can, my knuckles white. Joe is in front of me, averting his gaze from the precipice, fear and a cold sweat I see on his forehead forcing him forward. His boot dislodges a handful of pebbles, and I watch them roll and then tumble over the rocky ledge behind him, hundreds of feet to a mossy sill below. Just one false move and any one of us could free-fall into the ravine—*splat* on a stone shelf. I recall the narrow section of our hike down the north rim of the Grand Canyon that showed me the gravity of Joe's vertigo. I hugged close to the wall with him so we didn't have to look down.

After the ten-minute eternity it takes to traverse the narrow protrusion, we step down to a broad, dizzying slope of loose shale. It drops with no pretense of a path, straight down from where we are on the ridge to the valley floor a mile below. It's a swath of nothing but razor-sharp scree—deposits of fist-sized and smaller stone debris for as far as we can see. Over thousands of years, the incessant heating and freezing of moisture in the rock base has broken it apart, releasing chunks that tumble down the slope. As wide as a football field, this is a long-established descent, yet there's no evidence of anyone having passed before us—no boot indentations that pack the talus into identifiable footprints. It would be so easy to misstep, twist an ankle, scrape a shin, break a bone. We're in a confusion of pebbles, cutting our own routes through the real-life scree of my nightmare. But that was a dream conjured in my dark Bethesda bedroom at home, and as with most things, in the light of day it loses some of its menace. And since heading down is my specialty, perhaps this won't be so bad.

Kees and Chris plunge right in, anxious to keep moving, not waiting for tips from Julien. Rocks fly every which way as Kees's long legs and clunky leather clodhoppers kick up rubble like a Clydesdale. Sarah and Jim take a break waiting for Julien to elaborate on his basic instruction: Put your heels down first.

Since it's our first true scree field in the direction I favor, I'm eager to tackle what I envisioned for so long, as is Joe. We follow Chris and Kees with Phil between us in a horizontal line, doing what we know we must to handle this daunting terrain: Never descend a scree slope straight down the fall line. Go across the mountain, switchback style, to keep the person in front of you out of the path of what you push loose.

We make good progress on the long slither to the bottom, just like the rocks that tumble down ahead. But it's tough to get solid footholds in the unpredictable stone river underfoot, even with support from my poles. Each time I deliberately, forcefully, plant my heel in the rubble, it gives way underneath like the sand of a dune. Taking even a small step results in my boot slipping a foot forward in the scree and creating a mini-rockslide, which I then ride down. With movement somewhere between a slide and a jog, I'm skiing through the stones, planting my poles one after the other on either side as I would on a snowy slope.

"Kinda cool, isn't it?" says Phil.

"Took the words right out of my mouth. This is a blast, actually, but the soles of my feet are burning from the friction."

"This stuff is super sharp," says Joe, "but I love how fast we're going. Look at how much ground we've already covered."

I turn to look uphill and see that Julien is just behind us, but Sarah and Jim have barely made progress; they're resisting the natural downward pull, attempting to steady themselves after every step. I insist that Joe continue while I hang back to wait for them.

"Go with the flow," I call up, tunneling my hands around my mouth, "or you'll kill your knees. Just let yourself go." It seems they haven't heard me, as nothing in their strides changes. I sidestep up several yards, hoping it will help my voice carry, and repeat my call.

Sarah waves and I see her loosen up but she's still leading with her toes. Jim has stopped, bending over, hands on his knees, his face tight with pain.

"Need some help, Jim?" I shout.

"Yup. I do."

"Stick your foot out straight. Now flex it and put it down—all your weight in your heel. It'll feel strange, like you're going to fall forward, but as long as your weight's in your heel, you'll stop." I watch them both follow my advice with one successful step each.

"Now stick out your other foot and do it again." Assisting someone else makes my heart swell and reminds me of the joy of my years in front of the classroom. Phil must be euphoric, having helped Joe and me so much.

Once I see they've got the basics, I turn and resume my sliding rhythm: pole, heel, step, slide—pole, heel, step, slide. I catch up with Joe and Phil, Chris and Kees, stopped mid-slope. Julien continues, an unspoken suggestion that we have to keep going.

"Hey, you have good screeing technique. I'm impressed," says Chris, nodding toward me.

"So that's what it's called . . . skiing, screeing. Thanks, Chris."

"Awesome," says Joe with a quick pat to my back. "You're faster than all of us." For the first time in two days, I feel my face flush from something other than the heat. It's not just that I know I've performed well; it's that Joe has acknowledged it too. The fact that he's the one giving me the compliment reminds me that we're not just a married team, we're a hiking team as well, and teammates support each other.

Chris takes off, followed by Kees, and I overhear Joe say to Phil, "Way too much stuff flying up behind Kees. Let's stay clear." They veer left to cut their own path. I decide to follow Kees, just to the right and well behind, leaving plenty of room for his galumphs and turbulent wake. I continue drifting through the talus to my switchback beat.

I sense the peril before it appears, my peripheral vision catching disaster in the making. I stop cold in my tracks, adrenaline surging. Cantaloupe-sized rocks kicked loose by Kees are careening down the hill, straight for Chris.

"Chris, watch out!" I scream. "Rocks behind you! Go left! Now!"

Julien, well ahead, turns and sees the dozens of careening rocks closing in on Chris. Intellectually, I know this slope is unstable, but to see it actually crumble, letting loose deadly cannonballs with unpredictable trajectories, sends my heart to my mouth. Chris veers abruptly—"For fuck's sake!"—the largest of the projectiles just missing him. His abrupt movement dislodges more rock, this time smaller, orange-sized missiles, but equally deadly. Julien dodges the lesser rush and the scree field finally calms, all of us frozen in place.

I'm now a ragdoll, floppy after the terror, but limbs heavy as if I've just stepped from a hot bath. It seems minutes before anyone moves. Perhaps we're all waiting for Kees to say he's sorry? Acknowledge what he put in motion?

But the culprit appears unaware. Where is his head? What is he thinking? No apology materializes as he bends to adjust his boots.

I slip down to Chris to see how badly he's shaken. "I'm fine, Marianne, but goddamn it, that was scary. Appreciate the warning."

"How can you be so calm? You were almost leveled!"

"My mates call me 'Mr. Cool,'" he says, taking a swig from his water bottle. "If staying calm was easy, it wouldn't be a virtue, now would it?" He laughs.

"Very true, Mr. Cool," I shake my head.

"We are all not hurt?" asks Julien, looking shaken, having climbed back up as Kees continued down. Heads nod as Sarah and Jim catch up to us.

"Didn't expect to need helmets for the GR20," says Sarah, stepping in front of me. I see that her hiking uniform is covered in dust, her backside caked in grime from falling back in the scree.

"How'd you manage to get so dirty?" I ask. "I'm hardly clean, but look at you!"

She twists to glance behind and then brushes her bottom. "All part of life on the trail, right?"

Today's tortuous path passed few spaces conducive to a relaxing picnic, but the sheltered ledge Julien promised finally appears. My back is soaked, rivulets of sweat having collected under my pack and so, when I take it off, I enjoy a shiver in the breeze.

Lunch, at last, quiets my angry stomach. At this point, anything that fills the void will satisfy, so I'm delighted when Julien unwraps not only a bulky loaf of bread, but some of my favorites: pungent cheese so strong it makes my eyes water, spicy pork *rillettes*, grainy fig compote, and oily tapenade. Combined with the contents of the plastic containers we took at breakfast—couscous with diced vegetables, pine nuts, and raisins, and cookies and fruit for dessert—it's a spread worthy of Corsican elders. Once again, I try to eat slowly, but today I can't help myself. I shovel sporkfuls of yummy—scrummy—morsels into my mouth, almost forgetting to stop and breathe.

Kees has parked himself to the side, up on a sunny rock. I still can't understand why he has yet to mention the avalanche—the one he caused! Am I the only one still thinking about it? Even Chris seems to have forgotten.

After fifteen minutes, we're full-bellied, sprawled out in the sunshine, awaiting what Julien promised would be a crash course on Corsica's people—what he's learned as a long-term resident.

"Well, first I will tell you that as *un étranger*, someone from outside Corsica, it is very hard to know them," he says, pausing for a few slices of pear. "It is difficult for them to tell their emotions, so they stay closed. It is also because they are afraid of gossip."

"Why would they be afraid of gossip?" asks Jim.

"They love to tell stories about everyone, especially their neighbors. But they don't want outsiders to find out about their families and gossip about them. They will be very nice to you and then use wine and food for you to, *comment dit-on, vendre la mèche?*" He turns to me.

"Spill the beans."

"Yes, spill the beans. It is how they think. Do not allow people to know too much about you because they will use it against you. There are always many stories about families trying to take land from other families or neighbors and if they do, there is *la vendetta*. Do you say that in English? *La vendetta*?

"Oh, yes. A vendetta or a blood feud," says Chris.

"You will hear that Corsican people are stubborn, and since I have lived here, I think it is true."

"I want to hear more about vendettas," says Sarah, leaning forward.

"The code and the tradition of *la vendetta* says if you insult the honor of a family, especially the honor of a female, you must be punished with blood and murder. And sometimes, whole families were killed by people who were normally peaceful. It was because of these men, the ones who never broke the law except to kill for their family—that the *mythologie* of the *bandit d'honneur* developed. The feuds sometimes lasted for generations and hundreds of years."

"Surely that kind of eye-for-an-eye justice isn't still around," says Sarah.

"It's definitely illegal, and the last blood killing was back in the nineteen-fifties," Julien says.

"You mean the last one actually reported," says Chris. "I've always heard that Corsicans make good friends but terrible enemies."

And I remember reading that for thousands of years, the law of rough-and-ready justice was the only one Corsicans trusted. "Better occasional murders than frequent adulteries," wrote James Boswell, the Scottish biographer who traveled to Corsica in the mid-1700s.

Julien goes on to tell us that women usually stayed away from the violence. They were in the background. He shares stories about a man who shot his neighbor's pigs after they destroyed his vegetable garden and another who started a feud about the ownership of a chestnut tree. "You see, Corsicans do not really understand why the police get involved in these private fights," he says. "They believe they are family matters, not ones for the government."

"Do we need to worry about any violence while we're here, Julien? Or that people will steal our things?" asks Jim.

"*Non, non, non.* Definitely not. '*Le problème corse*' almost never affects tourists. You will be safe on La Corse."

"So, have you gotten close to many locals?" I ask. Julien is so open and affable, I can't imagine anyone rejecting his friendship.

"Oh yes, of course, but it took much time. I have a Corsican girl-friend, and I know many people now. But it is hard for them to trust people who are from outside their island. And they do not really appreciate outsiders trying to speak their language. They want to keep it for themselves and are very protective about it. You have to have *de la patience.*"

"I thought you said your girlfriend is in Paris," says Chris, perking up. Seems Julien has touched on a subject of interest.

"I have more than one girlfriend," says Julien, laughing. "I am French, do not forget."

And no wonder, with Julien's smile, bronzed skin, sun-bleached locks, and infectious personality, he must have no trouble attracting women wherever he goes.

"No worries about offending a Corsican family if they find out you're also dating a Parisian?" asks Phil.

Julien just smiles.

"You're a bloody chick magnet," says Chris, who then has to explain the term to Julien.

"I like that," Julien says. "I will tell my friends my new British *copain* says I am a 'chick magnet,' like Don Juan, *non*?" Julien laughs.

I'm back thinking about the Corsican character, adding what I've read to what Julien shared. Devoted to the soil, loyal to family, and rebellious. Their island is rugged, obstinate, and unyielding, populated for centuries by rugged, obstinate, unyielding people: herders, huntsmen, and subsistence farmers. Frequent invasion drove entire clans high in the hills because, for Corsicans, the sea meant conquerors and pirates.

Perhaps I'm a bit like Corsica. Here in these hills—dealing with my own RA invader.

Driven inland, island inhabitants built villages in mountain nooks, crannies, and deep gorges, leaving the shoreline for the occupiers. So Corsicans never fully exploited fishing or maritime pursuits, managing to survive by killing wild boar; breeding cows, sheep, and goats; and gathering chestnuts. Eventually, a small number came down to the eastern lowlands to grow, produce, and cultivate wine.

Wretchedly poor for centuries, most islanders now make good

livings welcoming tourists. They may resent the invasion of summer visitors but can't complain about how it fattens their wallets. Even so, ambitious youth can feel trapped because, other than those in hospitality, employment opportunities are few. There has long been an exodus of young people following economic opportunities that beckon from the continent, leaving Corsica with an inordinately high percentage of elderly citizens stubbornly clinging to traditional lives. Because so many youth have abandoned their island home, the French government has begun to support local artisans to preserve Corsican workmanship and tradition.

Tenacious residents with deep respect for their island helped block the rampant construction along pristine shores, endeavors that turned many Mediterranean coasts into unsightly concrete confusions. They used all means necessary, including bombs and arson, to resist those that saw only dollar signs, including French government agencies responsible for Corsica's economic growth. Designating so much of the island a national park in 1972 helped as well. As a result, the coast remains relatively untouched with few condo complexes, no casinos, and certainly no Disneyland.

Our postprandial roller coaster takes us above wispy clouds as we go through the Bocca Inuminata pass to a confusion of rocks and brambles with once again, no apparent path. We're only two days in, but the leg-trembling reality of what we're doing has sunk its teeth deep into our sweaty behinds. We have yet to encounter a flat stretch of more than twenty feet. We crawl over the tops of boulders, drop to our bottoms to slide down to the next perch, and then squeeze through tight gaps, our backpacks often getting stuck, too wide to easily slip through.

We reach an extended knife-edged ridge with thousand-foot

barren plunges on both sides, and scramble for an hour through a
sequence of rocky notches like secret passageways that send us from
one side of the rim to the other. Thank God Julien knows what he's
doing because it would be so easy to slip down an errant animal pathway and end up miles off the GR20.

At the beginning of our final descent down a rugged, knee-pound-
ing gorge, we glimpse the Réfuge de Carrozu in the distance, at the
base of scintillating gray granite spires. But I'm cautious with elation
given yesterday's end-of-day disappointment. Above the steep path,
stooped, centuries-old pines look down like old crones gawking from
the crest to the east. After an hour and a half in the heat-radiating
couloir, alder trees appear and bring longed-for shade. The sharp
rocky track gradually tempers and softens to sand, and eventually
the refuge appears in a clearing ahead, the white-and-black Corsican
flag flying proudly. Much more solid than last night's Réfuge Ortu di
u Pobbio, the building is made of neat, tidy fieldstone and has dark
green trim, shutters, and doors. It blends in perfectly with its setting.
Four solar panels and a satellite dish sit on the roof, and carefully
lettered chalkboards hanging near the entryway list the snacks and
provisions it sells. While rustic, it is not primitive. It definitely looks
like it's here to stay.

We enter the campground, limp as socks, and pass a weathered hiker leaning against a chestnut tree. His fingertips pinch
a hand-rolled cigarette and he pulls hard, the twisted tip glowing in response and I smell the acrid singe of smoke. He sports a
provocative black tee with the Corsican maxim in white: "*Souvent
conquise, jamais soumise,*" Often conquered, never subjugated. A
loyal Pascal Paoli acolyte. The separatist movement is alive and
well on the trail.

We stop next to the shower shelter while Julien checks in with the refuge staff. Phil sees me struggling with my tangled pack straps. "Can I help you get that off?" he asks.

"Thanks, but no. I'm good." Even as I say it, I know I should take him up on his offer as my shoulders throb and my lower back aches. It's time for my meds. I manage to release my load by myself and then lean forward, pushing up and stretching my lower back like a cat to relieve the strain. I strip off my socks, careful not to take tender white flesh with them. Slipping my feet into flip-flops, I see my tan line is just above my ankles—a hiker's tan to be proud of.

Next to the shelter is a sturdy wooden platform supporting four composting toilets. I carefully go up the stairs, my thighs protesting. I report back to the others with a huge smile when I rejoin them. "We have real toilets with actual plastic seats. No squatting tonight."

Jim returns from inspecting the showers. "Much nicer and newer than last night," he says. "That's the good news. Bad news, the water is cold—bloody freezing cold."

Julien comes back and announces, "Our tents are not together tonight. Phil and Kees, you are over there. Sarah, your tent is up the hill on the right. Christopher and James, you are down by the dining room. Marianne and Joe, you have the honeymoon suite behind the bushes."

"You mean next to the trash," says Joe. "Thanks for taking care of us, Julien."

Julien laughs. "I did my best, *mes amis*. At least you have a romantic place by yourselves."

"Just us and the raccoons," says Joe.

"Where's your tent, Julien?" Sarah asks.

"I do not use a tent. I just put my sleeping bag on the deck or on a picnic table. I like to sleep where I can always see the stars."

"I bet the ladies like that, right, Julien?" says Chris.

* * *

We strip down for arctic ablutions. No showering *en couple* today. When Joe steps into the gushing icy stream with both feet, he can't suppress a shout. I go into the next wooden stall, turn on the water, and avoid the spray. I soak my towel and sponge away the day's grime as fast as I can, shivering madly. I dry, dress quickly, and step out, carrying the things I wore today, stiff with dirt and sweat, crumpled in a tight ball. I head to the trough on the side of the shower hut where I join other hikers doing laundry, brushing teeth, and splashing faces with mountain water.

Two young Frenchmen take the spots next to me and ask where I'm from. "Washington, DC," I say, because most people stare blankly if I say Maryland. *"Ah . . . vous aimez Obama?"* is their first question. Do you like Obama? I nod. *"Oui. Beaucoup."* The extent of Europeans' interest in American politics never ceases to amaze me. I ask if they've ever visited the US. One shakes his head, but says he'd like to hike the Rockies. The other tells me he worked one summer in Orlando. He switches from French to English, "I was a *serveur* at the ESPN restaurant à Disneyworld. I like America. *Beaucoup.*" He laughs.

As I wring out my socks and my new French friends dry their faces, a blood-curdling female scream followed by expletives in a British accent fly from the shower window above us. "Oh fuck, oh fuck-fuck-fuck-fuck! Holy Mother of God! This is fucking freezing!"

We assess the day's exploits over dinner, like Frodo's band of Hobbits discussing their quest around rustic tables, sharing what hurts most—arms, calves, feet, wrists. Enormous servings of stick-to-your-ribs, high-carb, belly-warming lentil soup, *pulenda* (polenta made with chestnut flour), crusty bread, and rice pudding are tonight's fare. But no matter how many calories we burn during the day, I can't help thinking about the calories in what we eat. I wish I could just let it go and enjoy our meals, but fifty years of monitoring every bite that passes my lips is a habit hard to break.

"Why can't I take the junior life-saving test?" I asked my instructor. "I'm a really good swimmer, and I know I can pass."

"You have to be thirteen," she said. "Two more summers and you can go for it."

My younger sister and I stayed at the town pool for the rest of the afternoon in our red tank suits and white rubber swim caps, doing lap after lap, perfecting our strokes, diving off the low board, jumping off the high.

"Just one more from up top," I called. "Then we'll head home."

We climbed the ladder to the upper platform, and as I launched my final cannonball, a boy from my swim class shouted, "Thar she blows—watch her splash!" He and his friend laughed wildly.

I never took another swimming lesson.

From the western-facing wooden deck, we watch evergreen shadows lengthen across the campground. The evening's wine envelops me in a heroic haze, and I picture my lips purple from Corsican red. The balmy evening evokes sweet sensations of summers gone by—insects buzzing, hovering by golden electric bulbs on the porch until I slip down to the lawn, frolicking with my sisters in our baby-doll pajamas, trapping the magic constellation of lightning bugs twinkling in jars. This hike isn't so hard after all, my anxiety about tomorrow's terrain forgotten.

The sky glows with molten fire as the now crimson sun prepares to set behind darkening mountains. I lean my head against Joe's shoulder and yawn. I told him I would stay up for the full sunset tonight, but despite my best intentions, I can't keep my eyes open. I know he'll be equally happy to witness day's end with Phil while I crash.

I kiss him goodnight and then use a few alone-time minutes in our honeymoon space to get organized. I cannot have a repeat of this morning's jumbled disaster. My pile-making is interrupted by a young French couple passing our pitch in search of the trash. "*Là-bas*," I direct them. "Just over there." With my wash hanging to dry overnight and my gear neatly assembled, I ease into Big Agnes in our out-of-the-way tent. I hear no snoring or even murmurings from the terrace and I'm soon fast asleep.

Some hours later I'm roused by a husky, indistinguishable sound. Am I dreaming? Joe snores gently, but the other noise has gone silent. I float back toward sleep when the sound reprises, this time inches from my head. There's a varmint just outside the tent, I'm sure of it, snuffling and rooting around. It's likely a wild boar—a big, ugly, bristly *sanglier*—but do I really want to know? *Don't move*, I tell myself, hoping Joe closed both zippers tight.

But wild pigs have tusks, I think. He'll cut right through the nylon and gore us both. I'm quickly wide awake. Did we leave anything edible outside the tent? Please just take what you want and leave us alone, I think as the snuffling continues. After what seems an eternity, the grunting moves down toward our feet and eventually fades into the bushes. Convinced he's found the trash, my terror releases and I let myself drift off to dreams of friendly pigs, like *The Lion King*'s Pumbaa and Wilbur of *Charlotte's Web*.

Wednesday, August 3
The Hike—Day Three: Réfuge de Carozzu to Ascu Stagnu (Haut Asco)

↗ **Ascent:** 3,077 feet

↘ **Descent:** 2,503 feet

→ **Distance:** 6 miles

Guidebook Description: Today is a strenuous day.

If I roll over and keep both eyes shut, might I return to my dream that has absolutely nothing to do with Corsica?

But such a retreat won't get me any closer to starting the day—so I turn on my side, pull one leg from my sleeping bag, and drape it over Joe to rouse him. He opens one eye, closes it, and then opens the other just as his alarm sounds.

"Hear anything last night?" I ask before saying good morning.

"No. Why?"

"Well, I'm sure I heard a *sanglier* poking around. Like, inches from my head."

"I think you've got an active imagination, Babe." He turns his face away, wrapping his arms around his pillow.

"Maybe." I crawl out of the tent, anxious to see if there's evidence of an overnight caller. But I can't make out anything in the pale early light. No tracks, no droppings, no disturbance. Still, I'm sure something was there. I didn't just imagine it.

Joe joins me in the crisp morning air, stretching and yawning, to take down and fold our laundry. I grab our plastic lunch kits from the tent and head for the shower hut. We never rinsed them out last night, which may be what attracted a hungry critter. I swing by the trash to see if all is in order. The plastic bins are on their sides, their covers astray, and a string of masticated debris trails into the woods.

We inhale the aroma of fresh coffee brewed by Marie, the middle-aged refuge matron. Julien is buddies with all the *guardiens*, but he appears to have a special bond with this one. They share hearty laughs as he makes multiple trips to the kitchen, helping her lay out breakfast on the alfresco picnic tables. Once all are served, Julien sits as Sarah and Chris straggle in.

"*Tu as la patate ce matin, Julien?*" I ask. Are you bright-eyed and bushy-tailed this morning?

He flashes his teeth and grins at my use of the casual expression.

"*Mais, oui!* I am always ready for the morning, Marianne, you should know this by now."

"Well, I'm not," says Sarah, ruffling her bed head with both hands. "My kingdom for a cup of tea." I hand over the mug I fixed for her.

"So, Julien," says Chris, "we'll do just ten klicks today, yes?"

"What is this thing, a klick?" he asks.

"A kilometer," says Phil. "It's a military thing."

"Yes, yes, today we will do ten klicks—just six miles," says Julien. "It is shorter than our other days, but it is *definitivement* going to be very difficult. Today we will do the Spasimata Slabs." There's no making light of today's exertions.

"How'd you sleep?" I ask Phil, sitting next to me, not wanting to think yet about the Slabs.

"Not so well," he says, tilting his head toward me. He lowers his voice and nods to the far end of the table. "In fact, it was awful." I look down and see Kees adjusting his navy blue sweatband. "I'm afraid my tent mate was snoring. I'm surprised you didn't hear him."

"Ha. You forget that Joe and I were way over in the honeymoon suite last night."

"I'm still surprised. I would've used my earplugs but I forgot them in my luggage. I can pull them from my bag tonight, thank God."

"Sounds like Kees makes up for not saying much during the day by making a racket at night."

I learned yesterday's lesson so well, and did such a good job of getting ready this morning, that I'm now at a picnic table with my pack filled and sitting beside me. Having taken my meds, I'm now drumming my fingers, waiting for the others. To all appearances, I'm impatient to tackle the trail, but my tapping just helps calm my nerves. Now that I have time to kill, I have no choice but to think about the infamous rock faces that line the Spasimata Valley just ahead. Joe did his best to prepare us by reading aloud multiple blog entries about what is recognized as one of the most difficult segments of The Twenty. I've read stories about the slippery climb and seen dizzying pictures, one in particular that I can't get out of my head: a hiker with bleeding hands, knees, and elbows struggling to scale the almost vertical rock. It might have been better to leave me in the dark.

It's a beautiful, clear morning, our third on the trail as we descend sharply for fifteen minutes in the shade of towering pines. Sarah's caffeine-fueled talk, normally a welcome diversion, is too much for me right now. I lag behind to avoid conversation, concentrating on moving myself forward. I review what's ahead, underscoring the list with faux-cheery self-talk. Climb the Spasimata Slabs to the Bocca di a Muvrella. If Jim can do it, so can you. Hike across the saddle—never a problem—to a second pass. Begin the long descent to today's destination, Haut Asco. Focus on tonight's accommodations: a former ski lodge with hot showers and actual beds with blankets and pillows.

Unusually fierce snow for New York's Long Island. Almost a foot of powder on our deck. How appropriate for our exchange.

"Please, Mom. Please let me go on the ski trip. It's just one day."

"Marianne, you know I'd love you to go, but we just can't afford it."

"But Mom, I'll pay for it myself. I have babysitting money, and I really, really want to go. Everyone's going. All my friends. Please!"

"Ha, my sister the skier—such an athlete," my brother said as he walked through the kitchen.

There it was again. My family so insistent I was no good at sports.

We go across multiple streams before reaching the Spasimata River and its famous *passerelle*, a one-hundred-and-ten-foot swinging metal footbridge suspended low between cliffs above a waterfall. We can barely hear each other above the deafening roar of falling water. We cross, one by one, what may be the most photographed feature of The Twenty. When it's Sarah's turn, she approaches with eyes wide. "Remember what I told you about my balance?" she asks me. "Let's see how this goes."

"Just go slow and hang tight to the cables," I say as Phil grabs her poles to free her hands. It takes her some minutes to negotiate the span with measured, deliberate steps, but she reaches the far side successfully, greeted by high fives. Phil goes after Sarah and then after squeezing Joe's hand, I start across, leaving him to follow. Wobbly bridges don't usually give me pause, but this one has wide gaps between planks that expose slices of the chasm below and that a foot could easily slip through. The bridge swings back and forth despite my careful steps. I turn to give Joe a wave when I reach the other side. While he starts out tentatively, once he gets going, he quickly crosses to join me. I look at him quizzically and he says, "Not too bad." His vertigo must still be sleeping this morning.

All of us safely across, Julien gives us pointers for our next challenge: a stiff ridge climb scaling the slabs. My stomach is in knots as we look up the steep gorge, white, black, and rust veins running across the rocks. "There are some cables on the most difficult parts," he says, "so you can grab them to pull up. But I do not think you will need them because the rocks are dry today and you will not slip." I take his words as a command.

There's no time to dither. We must come to grips, quite literally, with the Spasimata Slabs. But just before we enter the steep couloir, Phil spies a baby boar, the size of a schnauzer, about five feet down the side of a grassy rim.

"Quiet," Phil whispers, "or he'll go running."

The little *sanglier* has a long face, small black eyes, and a bristly chestnut coat. He stands still, trembling in the undergrowth as we all take turns having a look.

"He's adorable," I say quietly. "Almost like an overgrown chipmunk, except for that snout." How can this sweet little creature grow into such an ugly adult, envisioning the snorting swine that visited last night?

"Careful," says Sarah, "the little guy's mum might be close, and we definitely don't want to upset her."

"*C'est parti*," says Julien, back in charge. "It is time for the slabs."

A natural stone stairway carved by the elements helps us negotiate the beginnings of the steep escarpment. After just a few minutes, we're strung out like a donkey caravan, the strongest among us leading the way. As usual, Jim and I bring up the rear. Despite determined steps, I fall farther and farther behind until I lose sight of my companion. I add to my frustration the niggling fear I'll get lost. My otherwise keen sense of direction has crumbled as I head up this wall.

I lean forward into the rock rib, angled at close to forty-five degrees, and plunge ahead, albeit slowly. I'm able to wedge my feet into slim rock ridges, and on the steepest slabs, find craggy handholds I grip like a vise. At times I'm on all fours, inching along with nothing more than two fingers holding onto a sliver of rock.

"Thank God it's not raining," I say out loud, to keep myself company. "And try to look up and back every once in a while to appreciate the views." I see Joe waiting for me up ahead and give him a quick wave, signaling him to keep going.

My thighs bear the brunt of the ascent and soon feel like they'll give out, lactic acid pooling in my quads, my right one screaming. Why is it giving me so much trouble? Is it you, my assailant? I make a mental note not to push it too hard. At the same time, it seems that whatever mechanism sends strength to my leg muscles has quit. I need a breather, and I spy a horizontal granite shelf a hundred yards ahead. Each step is a struggle and my pace slow, even by my own molasses standard. When I reach the rocky bench, I collapse. I drop my poles and my pack—throw them, in fact—and lie back for five luxurious minutes to recharge, careful not to fall asleep and roll off my perch. I sit up, knowing the climb must continue, but allow myself time to massage my thighs, the soreness in my right quad quickly cinching into a cramp. How am I ever going to make it to the top of this gorge? I'm not even halfway there yet.

Two young hikers approach from below, and I can't take my eyes off them. How can they be climbing so quickly? I remind myself not to be bothered by other hikers overtaking me.

"*Hé, dis-donc, Americaine,*" one calls. "*Hé, Washington, bon courage!*" says the other. With waves of their poles, my French buddies from the laundry trough pass by me.

"*Et bon courage à vous deux aussi!*" I yell back with sudden energy. Same to you.

Their smiles and good luck greetings recharge me and remind me that since we arrived on Corsica almost a week ago, we have yet to meet an American, other than Jim. Europeans have long been familiar with Corsica's beauty, but the island remains unknown to most from the States.

After more than an hour testing my resolve, I send periodic I'm-doing-fine waves to Joe ahead, continue to be careful with my right quad, and rejoice when the shaded gorge opens to a broad slope in bright sunlight. I see our group, spread across the rocks, basking in the sun. They're munching snacks and guzzling liquids, presumably waiting for me.

Joe is there with a happy greeting, but my head hangs low.

"You made it!" he says with a quick hug and the offer of an apricot as I collapse to my knees, pack still on my back.

"I did. Just barely." I need some time to catch my breath. "Those steep parts are just so . . . so hard for me. My lungs aren't as strong . . . as they used to be. You know . . . before. They feel like they're going to burst . . . and my thighs are really killing me."

"You kept waving me ahead. I would have stayed back, but. . . . Do you want some Tylenol? Anything else I can do?" he asks, crouching down to look me in the eye.

I shrug my shoulders but then nod. "Sure, I'll take two." He hands me the pills, I swallow them with a swig of water, and then bite into the ripe orange fruit. I'm grateful for the natural sugar rush as juice runs down my chin.

"I know you have to climb at your own pace, but I think Julien was worried when he couldn't see you. You have to be sure he knows where you are."

Something snaps deep inside, unleashing hot, incandescent anger. My face is on fire, and my reaction is swift as I stand.

"Excuse me, Joe. Really? Really?" I spit my words. "Listen, we paid good money to go on this hike, and it's not *my* job to let Julien know where I am. It's *his* job to keep track of me!" I pound my chest and then shift my hands to my hips.

Joe steps back, as if I'd unexpectedly pushed him. He turns to see if anyone is listening, but they're too far away.

"Marianne," he says, but I interrupt.

"Let's get this straight." My finger pokes his chest. "We have ten more days on this trail, and we need to be clear on how it's going to work. I'll walk at my pace and do what I can, and if Julien has a problem with it, he can tell me himself." I turn to walk away but then turn back. "You know, I don't see Jim breaking any speed records, and I don't see you *or Julien* concerned when Sarah is way behind on the descents." I jam my poles in the ground, upright like two exclamation marks. I pivot and hurl the apricot pit in front of me, watching it skip across a slab and go over the edge. I loosen my pack, drop it at Joe's feet, and disappear behind a bush to heed nature's call.

"I'm really sorry," he says, sitting on a rock when I return. He reaches for my hand but averts my eyes. "You're right. Totally right. It's Julien's job to know where you are, not the other way around."

"Good. I'm glad you get it." I look down at the ground and then up at him. "You know I don't like you worrying about *me*, but I *really* don't like it when you worry about *Julien*. Just remember—he's working for *us*."

"Got it," he says, and then looks me in the eye. "You and I good?"

"Yes, Joe—we're good. I just need a few minutes to think about all this." I stand on my tippy toes to give him a quick kiss. "And I guess I'll just have to keep doing my best to keep up."

We rejoin the group, suiting up to move on. They've been sitting and snacking for almost half an hour and all I've had is a five-minute break. Doesn't seem fair.

"*Ça va, Marianne?*" asks Julien, coming over to see if I'm ready to go. He says nothing about my pace.

"*Mais ouais, ça va.*" I make an effort to smile. "*On y va.*" Yeah, of course. Let's go. My obsequious smile belies the tightness in my stomach.

We're now climbing a chopped-up, stony section, even more difficult for me than the slabs. Perhaps it's the late morning heat. I look up to our destination pass in the hazy distance, the Bocca di a Muvrella at sixty-five hundred feet, where the distinctive jagged stone outline of what appears to be the profile of a colossal Native American in a feathered headdress watches over the pass. The face, formed by a series of granite ledges, is one of the most recognizable rock formations on The Twenty. It seems miles away.

This is wicked tough, wicked hot, wicked exhausting—words from the two years of my childhood spent in the suburbs of Boston, Massachusetts. Today's terrain may not be as wild as yesterday's hellish pinnacles, but it's undeniably wicked steep, and I can't help being wicked slow. I bend down to loosen my boots and see that my leg is oozing red. It looks like I passed too close to a cheese grater, scraping my shin badly. I take my bandanna from around my neck, wet it, and tie it tightly round my calf. It works just fine to stem the bleeding.

Joe hangs back from the group, maybe only fifty yards ahead, but I feel all by my lonesome, left in the dust yet again. I'm lost in the rabbit warren of my thoughts, playing games of distraction. I look for shapes in the stones: a girl's profile, a fist, the outline of Corsica, Pac-Man.

My every blood vessel is engorged, my heart pounding in my ears. I'm woozy, my head lava hot, my face burning, sizzling like bacon. Is this what heat stroke feels like? I suddenly rage with thirst, my mouth a dustpan. I plop down on a rock to suck down water from my bladder straw and fumble with an energy square from my pocket. And just like that, I'm again in a blur of panic, my heart racing, my hands trembling. My elbows on my knees, my face in my hands, I press on my eyes to stave off tears.

Why am I doing this pointless, expletive-inducing walk across Corsica? Despite the difficulty of the last two and a half days, Joe remains enthusiastic—in it body and soul—but I'm depleted, in so much pain. It's taken me over two hours to advance a mile, and the temperature's made me delirious. What am I trying to prove? Whatever it is, I'm failing, and I question why I ever thought this bloody walk was a good idea in the first place. I slump over, breathing hard, my head between my knees. I cannot let this feeling faze me.

The memory washes over me like a wave, its undertow pulling me down. *You're no athlete, Marianne.* Considering this early version of myself is like conjuring someone I knew long ago. A fevered, childhood ghost. But the pains of the past don't remain there—they live on in our present and force us to deal with them.

* * *

Three months into the school year and I was still the new kid. We were in PE class, something we never had in Catholic school. The gymnasium was clammy with the smell of pubescent sweat. I'd dreaded the morning for weeks, knowing we'd be tested on climbing a rope, a physical feat beyond my ken. I had yet to succeed, so why would I have been able to do it then? I grabbed hold, lifted myself up, and pinched the twisted cable between my Keds. I reached higher to pull myself up, but my feet lost their grip. I fell hard on the floor, shellacked to a gloss. Everyone laughed at me. The clumsy new girl.

At last I lift my eyes to see what's ahead but it's like I'm squinting through the wrong end of binoculars. All I see are pinpricks of light that shoot far into the distance, never ending. But my eyes soon adjust when I find myself in shadow, looking up at Sarah's silhouette with Joe's looming behind her.

"Hey, Marianne. Had to go to the loo and then saw you over here. You look really, really overheated." She squats down to look at me directly. "Are you feeling all right?"

I nod but think, great, now everyone's worrying about me.

"You know, Julien can carry your pack if you want," she says, sitting down next to me, patting my knee. Her words threaten to burst my dam of emotion as tears sting and my throat constricts. "Or, we can each take a share of your load."

Let my fellow hikers share my load? Did Julien tell her to suggest it? I dare not ask because I know I'll dissolve into tears if the answer is yes. Sometimes simple statements can uncover a lifetime of past hurts.

I know she's my new friend and I know she's just trying to help, but I take something in her tone as patronizing. I don't want to be talked down to, and I don't want anyone feeling bad for me. I want to tell her to bugger off and leave me alone. But I don't, swallowing the bile that's risen in my throat. As usual, I'm more concerned about someone else's feelings than I am my own.

I shake my head and respond through clenched teeth. "Don't think it's quite come to that."

What I don't say is that I know they're laughing at me. All of them. Laughing at the pudgy girl who can't keep up. Something rises in my chest, and I'm not sure if it's a laugh or a sob. I ignore it.

Sarah stands, and Joe now squats, handing me his bandanna, soaked in cold water from his CamelBak. I douse my face as he says, "That should help cool you down."

I wipe my face, letting water drip down my shirt. "Thanks, Joe. Definitely needed that."

While my emotions remain raw, physically, I'm revived by a cold cloth, a few minutes of rest, water, and an energy square. My fury about Sarah's comments dissipates as I see her rejoin the group. I know she meant no harm. Joe hangs back until I'm ready to go, and we make the long, slow slog over loose rock to the base of the Native American profile together. Forward movement stops abruptly as clots of trekkers from both directions negotiate the tight squeeze through the boulder-congested pass.

"I'm not sure we saw this many people the entire way up," Joe says, "but whoever's on this mountain seems to be right here, right now." He leans over, wipes a line of sweat from my face, and pulls me aside. With that, I can't hold back. Hot tears stream down my cheeks and I'm afraid to look up at him.

"I feel like I'm on a treadmill . . . at its steepest angle," is all I can muster.

"Marianne," Joe says, his voice soothing. "That's how I felt too. It was super tough and you're doing fine. Really. You're actually doing great. We knew this was going to be tough. And you can't forget that you have an illness no one else in the group is dealing with. Right?"

I tell him what Sarah said about Julien carrying my pack, and add, "You know I love Sarah, but she said I'm holding everyone back." I stop to wipe my eyes and catch my breath. "I don't know if it was her or Julien talking but I feel really bad about it."

Joe immediately shifts from reassuring coach to defensive spouse, his hands clenching. "Who is *Sarah* to talk down to you? I know she's your buddy, and I'm sure she wanted to help, but I know exactly how you feel. As if you need rescuing. And we both know that doesn't work very well with you. Look, you and she just arrived up here at the same time, not that long after the rest of us."

"But, Joe. I know you and she were going slow for me. And by the way, did you see how many people passed me since we started climbing this morning?

"And did you see how young they are? They're twenty-five-year-olds, some of them even younger—teenagers! What did you expect? You've got at least thirty-five years on them, and I'll say it again, you're doing great."

"My head knows how old I am, but my heart doesn't want to believe it. It's just so hard to accept that my body is breaking down and getting in the way of something I love."

"Listen. Look at me. You're a sixty-year-old woman, just like Sarah, and you're both terrific hikers."

He's calmed me down, as no one else can.

"You're going to be fine. We're done with most of the hard part for today. From now until we reach the hotel—remember, a hotel!—it's almost all along a ridge and then downhill, and you'll be a champ at that."

I nod and take a deep breath. He's given me the shot of adrenaline I need.

"Please don't make me go, Mom," I said, shaking my head.

"I'm not making you, just encouraging. It's the seventh-grade sock hop. You don't want to miss it, do you? You might meet someone new." Agreeing to let her drive me was easier than further protest.

The gym was dark. I sat at the bottom of the bleachers in the shadows at the far end, self-conscious about my budding chest in my too-tight poor boy sweater. I checked my watch. One more hour until my father picked me up. I was on the outside looking in, watching the crowd slow dance to Procol Harum's "Whiter Shade of Pale"—the popular kids, the athletes, and even the geeks. All of them. I was one of several wallflowers, but the only one alone. Even the boy with thick black glasses from my science class was with a friend. Everyone but me.

"Oh, she's that new girl," I overheard a tall, slim golden-haired girl in my homeroom say as she and her look-alike walked by. I'd been in this school for nine months. Would that label ever disappear?

It's finally our group's turn to wedge ourselves through the choked pass, and we're rewarded with expansive vistas on the other side. A serrated mountain string stretches south like bony knuckles, and we can see past red granite cliffs to the island's west coast and the sea. The south side of the pass is nothing like the stark rock from which we've come. It's gently sloped, dotted with soft tufts of grass. Julien says we'll descend through the field ahead, cross the saddle, and then climb to the day's second pass, the Bocca a i Stagnu. "There will be a little more up, but then there will be no more for the rest of today."

As Joe predicted, crossing the long ridge is not a problem for me, no matter how tricky and rocky the path. We reach the Bocca, looking over a verdant valley just begging to be photographed. Julien takes our camera and positions Joe behind me to maximize the view. "You need some pictures of you two together," he says. *"Fromage!"* Cheese!

"Time for *your* Christmas picture!" calls Phil, poised on a rock.

"You always have to be climbing, don't you? Just can't help yourself," I say.

And then comes the moment that transforms our day.

I can't see Kees's face with the sun blazing behind him, but I can tell something's up. At first I think he's laughing, his shoulders shaking, but then see that his breathing is hitched. He's in tears. Serious tears. I'm the only one who realizes he's crying, sobbing, in fact. Did he fall? Is he injured?

"Kees, are you all right?" I ask, moving over, touching his arm. "Can I help?" I offer him a paper towel.

He shakes his head, pulls a bandanna from his pocket, and wipes his eyes.

"Please forgive me. I am sorry but you remind me . . . of someone I love. You remind me of my wife," and with that, his face crumples and he dissolves into more tears. There's a rawness to his pain—that of a still open wound. He's so much taller than I am, so I go up on my tippy toes, reaching way up to give him a hug just above his waist.

He squeezes me back for a moment and then quickly lets go. I step back but keep my hand on his arm. "I'm so, so sorry, Kees."

"You and Joe. You remind me of the two of us. Of me and my wife, Liese. We hiked a lot, always together." He refolds his bandanna to find a dry spot and blows his nose. Sarah joins us, having recognized the situation. She gently puts her arm on his back. "I have a photo of us on my desk," Kees continues, "just like the picture Julien took of you two."

The enormity of his grief hits me in my gut, and it feels as if my heart is in a vise.

"How long ago did you lose Liese, Kees?" Sarah asks, now rubbing his back.

"Two years ago. Two years ago next month." His tears have stopped, and he's able to speak more easily, but his face remains a cloud. Joe and Phil have now come over and listen as Kees tells us about Liese. She and he loved the outdoors, and he mentions the last hike they did together, the Haute Route in the Alps.

"I really did not know if I could do the GR20 without her," he says, "and I still do not know if I can finish. Since we began, all I can think about is her. But I thought she would want me to do it. She knew hiking made me happy."

"You're very brave to do this without Liese." Kees nods, but I know my words are inadequate even as they leave my mouth. And I now understand your reserve and your reticence. Masks for your grief.

We've all gathered close around him, now sitting on a rock, with unexpected intimacy and quietly ask a few questions. Liese was diagnosed with Creutzfeldt-Jakob Disease (CJD), a rare, degenerative, always fatal brain disorder. Symptoms usually first appear at about age sixty: failing memory, personality changes, severe weight loss, and lack of balance. The illness progresses rapidly and its hallmarks, dementia and involuntary muscle spasms, take over.

Quiet sets in, all of us at a loss for further words until Kees finally says, kicking at the dirt, "I still do not believe she is gone, sometimes."

"I'm sure," says Sarah.

"I can't even imagine," I add.

Kees catches a shuddering breath and then shakes his head when

Julien asks if he needs more time before continuing. "No, Julien. We can go on."

At today's lunch spot, I sit next to Sarah, and when I ask, she says that perhaps one person in a million is afflicted with CJD. "Yes, I have seen cases," she says, "and it's heartbreaking. It comes on so quickly and before you know it, families no longer recognize their loved ones."

"Isn't it related to mad cow disease?" I ask, recalling the UK outbreak in the nineties.

"It is. When transmitted to humans, the variant becomes CJD, and it's very, very sad."

Our group is subdued as we eat the midday meal *gardien* Marie packed in our plastic kits this morning. My stomach growls, but I find it hard to focus on food, unable to stop thinking about Kees and his pain. I remember something my aunt told me a few years back, just after she lost her husband of fifty years. "When you lose someone dear, nothing is as valuable as an old friend—someone who knew the person you lost well and was part of your younger days—because shared memories are such a comfort." I look over at Kees and hope he has that kind of support at home.

Sarah digs into the wedge of white sheep cheese Chris passes to her. As she tries to cut a piece with her orange spork, the utensil breaks in two, leaving its tines in the chunk. And with that, any resentment I harbor from our earlier exchange disappears as I burst into giggles.

"Guess you should have bought the titanium version," says Joe.

"Hey, once again, I win," she says, brandishing a piece of her broken utensil in each hand. "I was the first to break a pole and now I'm the first to break a spork."

Without even trying, Sarah has managed to lighten things up.

I reiterate to Kees, just before we get back on the trail, how sorry I am. "It's so obvious to anyone you speak to about Liese, that you loved her—love her—very much. I hope thinking about her and talking about your memories help," My eyes fill.

"I do my best," he says, his eyes still glassy even though he told us his story over an hour ago. "I would like to give you some advice, Marianne. You must not take any day with Joe for granted." He shakes his head. "Life can be very, very cruel." He turns and takes off after Julien down the stony path.

Joe is tightening the straps of his pack, and I cross over to him, grab both cheeks with my palms, and plant a long kiss on his mouth.

"I'm not sure what that was for," he says, "but will you do it again?"

Lest Sarah and her spork get full credit for the day's comic relief, Phil, just ahead of us, audibly passes gas. And then again.

"Phil!" says Joe. "Have you no shame?"

And with no shred of embarrassment, Phil calls back, "It's high-altitude flatus expulsion—HAFE—makes me fart like an ox."

"What?" I ask, laughing.

Phil stops and turns around. "Really guys, it's actually a thing. At high altitudes, the atmospheric pressure outside the body is lower than what's inside, and passing gas relieves the differential."

"You sure it doesn't have to do with what we're eating? All those lentils and legumes?" asks Chris.

"And I thought it was just me," says Sarah. "That meal last night turned my guts a bit runny. My stomach is definitely not its normal iron self."

"Nor is mine," says Jim. "Happens whenever I climb."

"See," says Phil, smiling. And with that, he turns and prances ahead like a mountain goat, tooting down the trail.

We spend the rest of the afternoon in abrupt descent—a precipitous sixteen-hundred-foot plunge over dangerous, unruly boulders to our hotel. My sticks help keep the pressure from my knees. My right thigh throbs from this morning's exertion, and my wrists are sore, but I do my best to ignore the pain. There's a fresh agility in my step as Haut Asco's rooftops are now visible a few miles below. I spy a rescue helicopter hover and then land down in the valley. I wonder who the hiker is and what led to his or her evacuation. Should I be paying more attention to my nagging thigh?

We come to the edge of a soaring laricio pine forest and its welcome shade, the kind we've grown accustomed to at lower elevations. I tell Joe to go ahead as I'll wait for Sarah, in obvious knee pain, behind us. She's leaning hard on her pole, and her steps are decidedly lopsided. I want to enjoy the last leg together, wishing I hadn't been so angry at her earlier. Talking with Kees has put things in perspective. Being slow on a challenging hike is *not* the end of the world. Losing your beloved *is*.

The drop remains severe, but it's now shaded by tall trees and padded with years' worth of slippery pine needles. We inhale the evergreen scent, the aroma sharp, for the hours it takes to reach the small former *station de ski*, the Hôtel Le Chalet.

Despite the nightmarish appearance of the grounds—rusted ski lifts, denuded slopes, and decrepit, abandoned machinery clanking in the wind—nothing can dampen the enthusiasm of long-distance trekkers arriving at a proper lodge, no matter how shabby. Joe takes our duffels, delivered to reception that morning, up to our room and then joins Julien and Chris in the bar.

I'm not usually prone to running down hotel hallways, but today I make an exception. With all the energy I have left, I sprint up the stairs and down the corridor into our room. I drop my pack and fall face down, spread-eagled on the bed. I'm a marionette whose strings have been cut. I'm soaked with sweat but am soon shivering in the air-conditioning. Yes, our room has worn-down green carpet with cigarette burns and red wine stains, but I find it luxurious. I peel off my clothes, turn on the shower full-blast, and hop in, flinching as the scalding water hits my sunburned shoulders and scraped calf. I watch the grime rinse from my limbs, circle the drain, and disappear. This is heaven, I am sure, as I remain in the spray, steam fogging the glass door. I can't remember hot water ever feeling so good.

After fifteen minutes, I finally turn off the water, dry myself with a clean white towel, and then slip on my navy sundress, the soft polyester like butter on my skin. My hair is washed and shiny, but my scraped, scabbed shin rather spoils the effect.

Joe comes in for his turn in the shower, another long, fifteen-minute affair. On our way down to dinner, we meet Sarah in the stairwell, freshly scrubbed, smelling of soap, glowing in an olive knit dress.

"Well, don't you clean up nicely," I say.

"Amazing what a hot shower and a couple clean frocks can do for us. We look brilliant. You too, Joe."

Julien swirls his pastis, an aniseed liqueur compliments of Chris, adds water, and watches his drink of choice turn milky in the low-ceilinged dining room. Its fieldstone walls and padded chairs are welcome changes from the primitive refuge decor. Dinner served, Julien turns our attention from our duck *cassoulet* to day four. "You saw today, I know, that we did not need any equipment. There were cables, but we did not really need them, because even though it was steep, the rocks were dry. But I will tell you that tomorrow we will *definitivement* use the chains."

"Are there a lot of them, Julien?" Chris asks. "As many as on the Cirque?"

And for the first time since we started, someone has mentioned the Cirque. The infamous stone chasm known as the Cirque de la Solitude and the toughest part of the standard GR20 route, is closed, to the chagrin of many trekkers. In 2015, on the tenth of June, seven hikers were killed in one of the trail's most serious accidents ever when a sudden violent storm triggered mudflows and rockslides. Geologists have deemed the Cirque unstable, and so the hike now circumvents this section.

"About the same number," says Julien. "You all know, I am sure, that the Cirque is closed." We all nod. "We have to take a *variante*—a different path—because the normal route is not safe. I will tell you, I actually prefer the new way. It is more interesting and more *panoramique*, with very good views of Monte Cinto, the highest mountain on Corsica. In the morning, there will be some very steep parts that go straight up the rock, and you will need to hold the chains to pull yourself up. There will also be some for going down, and we will go backward."

I look across to see how the mention of chains is affecting Joe and his vertigo. He tilts his head, shrugs, and gives me a halfhearted smile.

Julien continues, "Other parts have no chains, but they are still steep, and we will have to scramble on our hands and knees. Believe me, tomorrow you will get to know the granite very, very well." We're now all ears, leaning in as he closes his eyes, brings his fingers to his lips, kisses them lightly, and releases them in the air. In his delicious French accent, he says, "Yes, tomorrow I tell you, you will make love to the granite."

I glance at Joe. We can only speculate about what this will entail.

The sun is orange as fire this evening. It disappears quickly behind trees atop a rock face, but its warmth lingers as we walk outside to the wooden deck. Joe buys Julien a second drink and he offers me my first ever sip of pastis—liquid licorice. Not bad.

Despite the painful crick in my neck from straining to look uphill all morning, Hôtel Le Chalet with its modern conveniences has managed to soothe my body. I'm limp as I move to the railing, my dress fluttering in the breeze. It's a fairytale setting as long as I don't look too closely at the dusty parking lot and abandoned snowplow below, the mud-caked boots lining the wall, and the grimy gear draped over the benches. The moon rises in the now dark sweep of the sky, leaving the pines in sharp outline, defining the jagged rim of the peaks we'll scale tomorrow. Once again, the end of the day gives me hope for the next. It blunts the pain of a difficult morning and how I feel about my performance.

Joe comes over to keep me company. I'm dog-tired but manage to raise my arms, clasping my fingers behind his neck. He reaches back to take my hands, loosen them, and bring them to his chest. I lean in. "Thanks for understanding this morning. I was really upset and just felt so vulnerable being behind everyone. And then when Sarah said. . . ."

"Shh," he says, stroking my hair, a gesture I'm so fond of, especially when I'm down. I've felt it a thousand times since we were teens. "What's important is that you did it. Think about what you always tell Chris and Caroline—everything will look better after a good night's sleep." I look up at him and nod, knowing he's right.

"We'll sleep like babies after that meal and those drinks," I say as we head up to our room.

"I feel like I'm asleep already," Joe says, giving in to a yawn.

I collapse under the covers. I stroke Joe's back gently, stem to stern, as he would say, tailbone to neck, making whirls with my fingers. Back and forth, up and down. In a matter of minutes, his breathing is rhythmic, and small twitches tell me he's asleep. But the pain in my thigh pesters. Even so, I'm soon off in my dreams, tumbling from a mountain, lost in the woods, bedbugs scattering in the wake of my step.

Thursday, August 4
The Hike–Day Four: Ascu Stagnu (Haut Asco) to l'Auberge U Vallone

↗ **Ascent:** 4,478 feet

↘ **Descent:** 4,377 feet

→ **Distance:** 8 miles

Guidebook Description: Today, we head toward Corsica's highest peak, Monte Cinto.

I roll over in bed to the sounds of Joe in the shower. He's singing, as he often does when excited about the day ahead. After yesterday's emotional highs and lows, I'm pleased to simply be feeling good. The tables downstairs, set with jam, butter, and baskets of freshly baked croissants, and not just chunks of bread, on checkered tablecloths are a comforting display. The pastry's papery layers and moist, buttery heart distract me from my sore leg. I turn my attention to the morning's pleasures: the cool breeze, the warmth of the tea, the friendly hum in the room. The morning brightens further when Joe puts a plastic salt shaker from the inn's gift shop in front of me.

"Thought you'd appreciate this. I know you've been going through sodium withdrawal for the past few days," he says.

"Oh, my God, you wonderful man! I swear, this might be the sweetest—or should I say saltiest—gift you've ever given me. I love it!" I jump up, kiss his cheek, and rip off the cellophane wrapping. He does know the way to my heart.

The others at our table stare until Phil finally asks, "Joe, is that all it takes to make a woman happy? Some salt?"

"Oh, I can think of a few other things, but salt's a good start," Joe says, winking at me. "You should try it with your next date, Phil."

"Maybe that's where I go wrong. I take women to the mountains but forget the salt."

I say to Phil, sitting next to me, "I hope I'm not being too nosy, but have you had any serious girlfriends?"

"Oh, there were a couple."

"But no one that really blew your hair back?" I ask with a smile.

"What hair? He's Mr. High and Tight," says Joe.

"There was a day, Joe. I know you can't believe it but you should have seen my locks when I was a young man."

"I'm sure you were a regular Fabio."

"Don't let him get to you, Phil. You'll always be a salt-and-pepper Fabio in my eyes." I pause and then ask, "So what happened with those women?"

"They weren't very happy that I always put the mountains first. Didn't like the competition, I guess."

"Well, it sounds like you made the choice that's right for you."

Today's *variante* includes the hike's steepest ascent and descent. "Not the longest ones, but *definitivement* the steepest," Julien says, his hands tilted at sharp angles.

The skies are brilliant blue as we disappear into dense ever-green woods. The shadowed trail is crisscrossed repeatedly with gnarled, exposed roots and begins with a gentle rise that allows me to keep up with Sarah and chat. We've talked about her children but she's never mentioned their father. Fearful I'll put my foot in my mouth as I did with Kees, I haven't pried, but this morning, when we discuss where each of our children is living, she mentions that one is with her ex-husband on his farm. I have the opening I need.

"Sarah, do you mind telling me a bit about your ex?"

"Well, we were married for over twenty years, and it's a familiar story. We just drifted apart—like the continents," she says with a laugh. "I was so busy with my medical practice and the children that I didn't realize what was happening until there was an ocean between us. I also discovered there was another woman, which knocked me for six. I know it sounds crazy, but I blamed myself. I actually went a bit dotty for a time—really did think it was all my fault."

This supremely confident physician admitting vulnerability is a surprise. It's the first time I've seen a dent in her armor. Perhaps none of us is as self-assured as we appear.

"But I eventually realized he wasn't just hiding the cheating. There were other things, including some financial, he never told me about."

"Are you happier now that you're on your own?"

"Oh, definitely. After the hurt faded, the children and I settled into a new life. It's actually been brilliant. And now that the kids are grown and I'm retired, I love the freedom I have to travel and do things like this hike."

Sarah does a hiker's jig down the trail, arms raised, poles swinging. She breaks into song, belting out a spontaneous celebratory jingle only she could have written. I giggle as her impromptu refrains morph into show tunes and then classic rock, anything referring to climbs: "The Sound of Music," "Rocky Mountain High," "Ain't No

Mountain High Enough." Ah, to be such a free spirit. I'm forever hesitant to sing in front of others.

When she finally pauses, I ask, "Do you miss your medical practice?"

"I do, actually. But I've managed to fill my days volunteering and traveling. And you, do you miss teaching?"

"Very much. Mostly, I miss my students and getting to know them. They're so awkward in middle school, and they just need someone to listen. I always had an open door for them. But I'm quite happy to have all the piles of paperwork behind me."

I promise myself, once again, that teaching young people in one way or another will be part of my retirement—as long as I can still fill most of my days with writing, traveling, and seeing Chris and Caroline.

During a water stop, I ask, looking up into the trees, "What's that beautiful sound?"

"A nuthatch," says Phil, pointing. "A male. See that tiny blue-gray bird?"

"You really did your *oiseaux* homework, Phil," says Julien. Phil beams with the compliment as Julien continues, "It's unique to Corsica and we call it a *sittelle corse*."

"It's delightful," says Sarah, and I agree, hoping the sweet guy and its song follow us.

Our mellow morning ends abruptly the minute we leave the woods. The sun hits hard, and a rocky climb up to the Bocca Crucetta col and then to the base of Monte Cinto's nine-thousand-foot summit rises before us. Bright red-and-white stripes have been painted over the yellow blazes of what used to be a wayside variant to the Cirque de la Solitude but is now a permanent part of The Twenty.

We cross a fifteen-foot iron bridge, rusted but sturdy, over the tumultuous Tighjettu torrent. It's time for the day's real climbing to begin, the tree line now behind us, save a few stunted, wind-wracked pines sculpted into goblin shapes. I've lost Sarah to the front of the line, Julien wanting her close as we tackle the initial chained inclines. He knows she's a bit wobbly when it comes to mountain hardware.

We crowd together and then go up one by one, each of us careful about where we place each step, preoccupied with holding tight and not tumbling back down the ravine. It's finally my turn, and I grip the chains, hand over hand, forcing my feet to follow up the incline.

"Your wrists hurting?" Joe asks from just below me.

"A little, but I'm working through it. You? Staying calm?" I can tell from his strained voice and the fact that he won't look at me that his vertigo's needling.

"Just have to keep moving."

On a narrow stretch between chained ascents, I grab a stone rim with both hands so I can look back at our progress. I'm standing still but it appears the valley, miles below, is being pulled away in the distance, receding as I watch. I twist my head back around and see both of Julien's hands on Sarah's bum, boosting her up the final section of chain. She struggles to catch her footing, but then up and over the final rock she goes. Each of us follows, leaving the hardware behind. Joe leans over, hands on his knees. I say nothing because I know he'll need a few minutes to recover before he speaks.

Endless zigzagging switchbacks continue up. For a time, the chains allowed my arms to bear most of my weight, taking pressure off my legs. But now, my right quad is back to straining with every step. Every few feet, I feel I might tumble, my pack's weight dragging me backward, but I hang tight, remembering Julien's words in his accent: "You will make love to the granite." I lean forward as I sidle around an outcropping, my arms hugging the rock, thighs scraping, toes pressing hard. Make love to the granite. I must lean in and make love to the granite.

Joe remains silent, his concentration complete.

We continue to climb and Julien points out huge, cavernous hollows in the rock walls, some of them several yards in width. "They are called *tafoni,*" he says. "And they are sometimes even bigger inside than the hole you can see. The wind and water cut them into very strange shapes in the rock, especially the steep rock. They are very beautiful, *non?*"

"Looks like you can live in some of them," says Chris.

"*En fait,* Christopher, some people did live in them hundreds of years ago."

"Maybe we can take a quick rest in one?" Joe says to me. Back on a trail and away from the edges, he's finally able to speak.

"I wish. My legs are on fire."

Hours pass, the air thins, and the heat in my thighs shifts to my heaving chest and then back again. My legs have gone from Gumby to Jell-O by the time we reach La Tour Penchée, the Leaning Tower, an enormous rock eminence the size of an eighteen-wheeler thrusting out over the trail at a precarious angle.

"Looks like that baby might fall at any minute," says Jim.

"Yeah, right on us," says Joe.

"*Mais non, mais non,*" says Julien. "It has been there, just like that, for hundreds of years. Thousands."

"Just like the Cirque de Solitude. . . ." Joe does always conjure the worst.

The terrain at long last levels, and we cross a drift of old snow that's managed to outlast the summer heat and then stop at a small glacial lake. Its clear green water reflects both the soot-colored rocks surrounding it and a mirror image of the needle-like peaks above. Hikers recovering from the tough rise behind us are scattered along the shore, sunning, snacking, snoozing.

"Here, try this," says Phil when he sees me leaning on a rock, methodically rubbing my thighs. He pulls what looks like a red plastic rolling pin from his pack. "It's a deep tissue massager for kneading out the knots."

"Phil, you're my Sherpa *and* my medic." I jump up to hug him, careful to put my weight on my left leg.

"It'll hurt, but it's one of those hurts-so-good kinds of things. You know, after the pain comes the pleasure, and all that. In the end, it'll loosen your muscles, and you'll be happy for it." He shows me how to position the massager but leaves the rolling to me. I move the device back and forth, up and down, over my quads, grimacing as my sore muscles give way beneath the ridged surface.

Phil, Sarah, and Kees wade into the lake's freezing water, and Julien calls from the water's edge, pointing to the bluff on the far side. "*Voyez!* Look! We have visitors. *A muvra.*" A trio of Corsica's wild sheep—the mouflon (*a muvra* in Corsican)—a red-brown ram with white facial blazes and beautifully coiled helix-shaped horns, a smaller brown ewe with short, straight horns, and a tawny lamb scamper on the rocks, pausing to look at us before continuing across the scree.

We gather around Julien as he fills us in on the notoriously reclusive mouflon. They were once close to extinction but since the mid-fifties have been a protected species. Still, there are fewer than eight hundred on the island. During the winter months, the sheep descend to warm, south-facing hollows, but at this time of year, one of their favorite haunts is where we are, atop the Asco valley.

Back on the trail, we're at the foot of a scree field of shale shards rising to the ridgeline.

"You sure we're not on the moon, Julien?" asks Chris, in a rare commentary on the terrain.

Julien smiles. "It is beautiful, *non*?"

An overly fit couple of indeterminate age, both sun-scorched to a leathery brown in matchy-matchy outfits of frayed denim short shorts, white midriff tees, and reflective sunglasses, barrel down the last stretch of the slope. How in God's name can they go so fast without poles? The rawboned man with a handlebar mustache wears a goofy straw hat, the kind tourists buy off cruise ships, and munches the end of a long cylinder of *saucisson*. The woman tears bite-sized pieces from a baguette and puts one in her mouth and then one in his, all the while sliding down the scree. He greets us with, "*Allez, allez!*" Come on, let's go! And she wishes us, "*Bon appétit!*" as they roar by, a bit ironic since they're the only ones eating. Takes all kinds on The Twenty.

"My God, this is scree on steroids," Jim says to me and Joe, shaking his head as the rest of our group forges ahead. "For fuck's sake, we're supposed to go up this thing? This is insane!" He kicks at a pile of stones with his boot.

Jim has hiked the Annapurna Circuit in Nepal more than once, and so I wonder why he's surprised by what we're facing on Corsica.

"Well, we had some serious downhill scree on day two but now we'll just have to deal with it going uphill," I say. "Time to dig in our toes." I'm outwardly cheery but although I can scree down a mountain, can I scree up?

While Jim takes some water Joe asks, "Was the Annapurna Circuit hard? As hard as this?"

"Was Annapurna as hard?" Jim repeats. "I'll say one thing for sure. All this loose crap we're about to go up? There's none of it on the Circuit. There's an actual track, usually a pretty wide one, and even though there's a lot of up, it's much more gradual. There's nothing as steep as what we've done so far."

"So it's harder than what you did in the Himalayas, but is it harder than you thought it would be? You seem pretty frustrated."

"Absolutely harder. I hiked Annapurna with a girl who'd done the GR20 and she said it was no more difficult than the Nepal hike. We had to deal with the high-altitude thing, but that was the only *really* hard part. She said I could handle Corsica. But I realized two days ago that her idea of difficult isn't the same as mine. She'll get an earful when I get home, that's for sure."

"But how are you doing, Jim? Joints hurting?" I ask.

"My knees are giving me hell, especially going down those knee-crunchers, and I'm definitely taking more painkillers than I should."

Maybe if I'd asked earlier, I'd have realized I'm not the only one struggling.

Joe plants his pole and starts to climb.

"Our turn," I say to Jim. "The sooner we start, the sooner it'll be over."

I take a giant, determined step, thinking I can outsmart this death trap of stone marbles, but can't get a foothold. My toes slip and I go down hard on my knees, opening the scabs on my shin. Jim falls next to me with a loud, "Shit!" Joe turns, but I wave him on. After several tries, we're back on our feet. I look down at my leg, blood trickling, and dab it with my sweat-soaked bandanna. Sanitary first aid will have to wait for lunch.

Jim and I continue in silence after finally figuring out an uphill scree technique that works. We lean in toward the slope, jabbing the tips of our toes first, but progress is like quicksilver, hard to grasp and even harder to hold.

My heart jackhammering, Jim and I stop to watch a trio of runners dressed only in Speedos whiz by us at a suicidal pace on their way downhill.

"Did you know the French Foreign Legion trains here?" Jim asks.

"I read that. And now that we're on this terrain, I can see why. You think those guys were part of the elite forces or just some crazy skyrunners?"

"You mean those people who run up and down ridiculous inclines at absurd altitudes?"

"Exactly. And all we have to do is walk. Whoever they are, they're amazing athletes."

The balance of the ascent is a blur punctuated by Jim spewing expletives. While in the distance we can see the dark profile of the GR20's highest point—the Pointe des Éboulis on Monte Cinto's shoulder—I'm once again feeling low, my feet on fire, thigh screaming. I vow out loud—never again. I'll never, ever do another hike like this. I become Scarlett O'Hara: *As God is my witness, I'll never climb a mountain again.*

We catch up with Joe and then rejoin our group at the Bocca Crucetta pass at 8,045 feet. After just a few dozen steps on level ground, my legs loosen, feet cool, and breathing moderates. I decide that this mountain misery is akin to childbirth. The pain comes in torturous waves, you vow never to do it again, and then in a whoosh there's success, relief, euphoria. You hold your baby and labor is forgotten; you reach the summit and suffering is behind you.

"We may not have done the Cirque de la Solitude but that was a bloody tough climb," says Sarah, plopping down to take off her boots. "Look at these feet!"

"Think I'll pass," says Chris.

I look over to see that Sarah's extremities are swollen and red, nails torn, toes covered in blisters.

"That was definitely the hardest climb so far," says Phil, and Kees chimes in, "Yes. It was the worst."

"Please tell me this is where we stop for lunch, Julien." I let my pack fall with a thud.

"*Oui*, Marianne. *C'est l'heure de déjeuner*, time to eat, but first, everyone look." Julien points to a brick-hued silhouette in the distance. "We can see Paglia Orba there—the big red mountain like a shark fin."

"Looks like a shark's tooth to me," says Sarah. "A massive shark's tooth."

"Shark's tooth or shark's fin—I love this mountain," says Julien. "And the Corsican people love it too. It is very important to them because they can see its special shape from very far away. It is a *porte-bonheur*, and they are so proud of it."

"A good luck charm," I say. We gaze across the sweeping valley, a solitude of stone, taking in the peak. It does cut a distinctive profile.

"We are very lucky with the weather," Julien continues, looking up and around. It is pure sunshine with not a cloud in the sky. "Monte Cinto has its own *microclimat*—how do you say that, Marianne?"

"The same—microclimate."

"So Monte Cinto has its own microclimate, and even if everywhere else has sun, it can be very cold and have snow. It was maybe twenty years ago when seven hikers died in the middle of the summer on the summit. Because of a *tempête*, a very bad one with very bad snow. But today, we can hike it. It will take maybe an hour for both ways. We must go soon because good weather on Monte Cinto is never for very long."

Julien unfolds his map on a flat rock and traces the path to the summit with a pink highlighter. "If you want to go up, you can have a short lunch and then come with me. If you don't want to go, you can just have a longer break here."

I glance over at Jim. He takes off his hat and shakes his head "No way. Ain't going up."

"Gee," I say, turning to Joe, "can't imagine what I'll choose, especially with my quad acting up."

"Yeah, this morning was a killer. I'm not up for more climbing either. But what's going on with your thigh? Which one?"

"My right one. Ever since yesterday it feels like I've been working it too hard. Kind of like I pulled a muscle."

Joe looks down at my leg and then gives it a gentle pat. "Doesn't *look* bad but be careful and go easy. Look at me, Marianne. Don't want you getting injured."

I nod but think, too late. All I can do now is keep it from getting worse. Joe pulls over his pack and takes out his baggie of pain meds in what has become a lunchtime ritual. "Aleve or Tylenol?"

"How about two of each today?"

He takes out four pills for me and two for himself.

The large boulders around the Bocca offer plenty of shade, so our team joins a dozen other hikers who've found cool spots to refuel. Julien, Phil, Chris, and Kees down sandwiches before the rest of us have even started, and then they're off for more uphill torture. Sarah, Jim, Joe, and I take the opportunity to eat leisurely and nap as golden eagles ride the thermals high above.

The group is back together, and the balance of the afternoon is spent descending to tonight's accommodations, l'Auberge U Vallone. I hang back with Sarah, anxious to resume our morning conversation on the trip down.

"How about you and Joe?" she asks. "How'd you meet and how long have you been married?"

"Well, we met in high school and have been married thirty-five years. We're doing this for our anniversary, actually. That and our birthdays."

"I can think of more relaxing ways to celebrate!"

"Did those things too. A night at a country inn, a nice dinner. Those kinds of celebrations have always been important to us—shared experiences rather than gifts. But we also wanted to do something really challenging together and something we'd always remember."

"Oh, you'll never forget this, that's for sure."

"Yup. I'll never forget how much my body hurts! You in as much pain as I am?"

"Definitely, but I can't even think of doing this with RA. How're you feeling, by the way?"

"My joints are sore, they always are, but it seems to be my lungs and leg muscles that are letting me down."

"So tell me about your family. It'll keep my mind off my swollen knees. I overheard you say you're from a big one."

"Eleven children, and I'm the oldest—or first born, as I say these days. I was sixteen when my youngest brother was born, so we're all pretty close in age."

"How about your Mum and Dad—did you get along?"

My small frame tenses at their mention. I wish it weren't so, but the girl who fought an internal battle about being the perfect child rages still. "Oh, that's a complicated one. How long do we have?"

The eldest two, my sister and I, were perfect children: respectful and obedient, studious and submissive, resourceful and polite. We brought home stellar report cards and were responsible for much around the house. Like the little red hen in the children's fable, we planted and harvested, working hard while those around us played. But constant acquiescence to others' wishes, especially in the formative years, can corrode. Perform a role long enough and it either becomes who you are, or you revolt. We were flawless players, toning down our voices and fitting in until our adolescent years. And then the fault lines appeared.

After multiple moves, we settled into a four-bedroom colonial where I would live until I graduated from college, in Smithtown, on New York's Long Island. I was twelve. By my sixteenth birthday, our house was bursting at the seams—three bedrooms for eleven children. But somehow, it was only when I was restless that it felt cramped.

When I entered Holy Family High School in Huntington, NY, our mother developed ulcerative colitis and was bedridden for most of her last two pregnancies. My younger sister was twelve and I fourteen. We became surrogate moms for our younger siblings and took on even more household duties: cooking, cleaning, diapering, dishwashing, dusting, folding, grocery shopping, laundering, packing school lunches, putting little ones to bed, scouring, sweeping, and vacuuming.

The added obligations soon took their toll. Initial feelings of being happy to help twisted into tight cords of resentment after weeks turned into months and beyond. On the surface, I did what was required, but inside, I seethed.

A chasm opened between my parents and me, and what became a key motivator in my life bubbled up. As much as I loved her, I would not become my mother, her life taken up with a list of domestic gerunds. I didn't want what she wanted, and I didn't want her life. I imagined travel, adventure, and possibility, a life far different from the one I was born into.

I had finally made friends, and it became increasingly difficult to move back and forth between my two opposing worlds: hormone-driven high school hallways and the duty-driven world of a thirteen-person household. I worked hard around the house and resented it when my parents told me it wasn't enough, was enraged when they said I was selfish because I asked to stay after school to watch a basketball game, and defiant when I questioned why my brothers didn't have the responsibilities my sister and I did.

"You're the ones who had all these children," I once said, pounding my fist, perhaps too hard, on our yellow speckled Formica counter. "Not me." And I thought about what had bothered me so much lately. Being part of such a big family means that sometimes you're not nurtured as you need to be. I could see it in my younger brothers and sisters and did what I could.

Thus, from the bitter broth of my adolescence flowed a lifelong determination to find a path unlike my mother's. I swore when I was sixteen, my hands chapped from folding yet another pile of bleached cloth diapers, that I would never have children. Ever. I'd had enough taking care of my mother's babies.

In a large family, routine was key—unremitting attention to chores, mealtimes, and overarching religious ritual. And money, or its absence, was a constant stressor. I was the dutiful daughter, meeting obligations and going beyond. Yet, much of what I had to say was dismissed. Having an opinion—at least one that differed from my parents'—was not welcome. The few times I spoke up to question their beliefs, it was like red rags to a bull. "Do you really believe babies go to hell if they're not baptized?" "There's no difference between birth control pills and the rhythm method. Intent's the same." "Divorced people are *not* bad." "Priests used to be married, right? The apostles were."

In the wake of my candor, my father glowered, his eyes narrowing. And though my mother might waver, my father brooked no dissent. He told me I lacked the intellectual capacity to understand. Resistance was futile when there was no common ground. And so I learned to tuck my tail between my legs and keep my opinions to myself, my backbone softened by duty and then surrender. I became skilled at living—at least to all appearances—according to my parents' principles. I sequestered myself in my bedroom, hot tears of resentment dampening the pages of the books into which I disappeared.

"I take it you were raised Catholic," says Sarah.

"Oh yes—we were a good Irish-Mexican-Catholic family."

"Did you and Joe bring up your children Catholic?"

"We did. Until confirmation. We wanted to raise them in a religious tradition so they could choose whether to continue as adults. I know they rarely go to church now, but I'm not sure they've fully decided yet. Maybe when they have children of their own. . . ."

We stop for some water, and I continue, "There was also a huge part of me that just didn't want to deal with my parents' anger and disappointment if we didn't raise our kids Catholic. Being the oldest and the first to have children, I had to go through things before my siblings did, and there was lots of pressure to conform. Growing up, we all just knew what was expected."

"Like what?"

"Go to church on Sunday, go to confession often, go to a *Catholic* college, meet and marry a *Catholic*, get married with a *Catholic* mass, never question *Catholic* teachings, baptize our children within weeks of being born. I could go on and on."

"You all married Catholics? That's incredible!"

"Actually, my youngest brother went rogue and married a

non-Catholic. And thank God he did. She's wonderful. But I can't help but wonder whether faith forced on children might make them turn away."

A long day of household chores. I smelled like Pine Sol after scrubbing the sinks, floors, and toilets of three bathrooms. I kept frustration to myself until my teenage bravado found a voice. Suddenly, I was rebellious—a defiant fifteen-year-old needing to say exactly what was on her mind. I wanted to curse and be angry and talk about sex. I wanted to be a badass. I wanted to be a bitch.

"I named you for my two favorite saints: Mary and Anne," my mother said from her sickbed, rosary in hand.

"That's a lot to live up to, Mom. I'll never be as perfect as they were. Especially Mary. The Immaculate Conception, born without sin."

No reply.

"You know the way you spell my name is French, right?"

"No, I didn't realize."

"Well, it is. And I'm going to live in France one day." Again, no reaction. She wouldn't take the bait.

"And I really don't understand your whole devotion to Mary. Because you have her name and she was a mother too? But she had just one and you have eleven." I was on a roll and couldn't stop. "She wasn't so special, you know. If I'd been born without sin, I'd be a saint too. God just made her special—she didn't do a damn thing to deserve it."

She managed to get out of bed and I anticipated her slap. But she stopped just short. I imagined the red welt that would have appeared on my cheek, felt the sting of the blow never delivered. My short-lived rebellion was dead. Knowing I'd disappointed her hurt more than my sentence: grounded for a week.

* * *

"You still consider yourself Catholic?" asks Sarah.

"Ha! Only in the sense that I'm recovering, as the expression goes. Around the time the kids were confirmed, my already tentative tie to the church just snapped. I didn't believe most of what I'd been taught, especially about birth control, divorce, and end-of-life stuff. I was so tired of the obsession with sex, the abuse of power, and the disregard for women—misogyny in the name of religion. One of my best friends would be an excellent priest, but the church won't have her, even though they're desperate for vocations. I felt like every time I sat through mass, I was endorsing something I didn't believe in, so I just stopped going."

"I took a similar approach and now it's up to the children to decide—the Church of England or whatever. You ever try going back?"

"I took a several-year break. And on the one random Sunday I tried one more time, the priest's sermon was about how homosexuals are dangerous to our children."

"You're not serious."

"Afraid I am. It was years ago, and I just walked out and never went back. I have much better ways to spend my spiritual time than listening to that crap. I get really angry about it sometimes—can you tell? Especially when I think about a bunch of old guys in Rome with their gilded slippers coming up with rules for lives they know nothing about."

"How about the new guy, Francis? Seems a good chap."

"Oh, he's a good start, and I think someone Jesus would be happy with. But he has a lot of catching up to do and years of damage to fix. I guess we'll see."

* * *

The Catholic Church wielded profound power over our household. I was forbidden from attending the wedding of my boyfriend's aunt. ("She's divorced.") When I was caught hiding *Our Bodies, Ourselves* under my mattress like pornography ("Sex is not something you read about.") and admitted that yes, a friend and I had actually seen *The Last Picture Show* (condemned by the Catholic Church) instead of *Willy Wonka*, there was hell to pay. I tried to explain but was dismissed with a stiff-arm. The message was, "You'll never be good enough (and maybe not loved), unless you think as we do."

As the eldest, I was the pioneer for pushing back. When I summoned the courage to look my father in the eye and disagree with church teachings, it helped tame my fury. But I discovered early on that questioning led to ridicule and hurt, so I kept defiance to myself. The child–parent chasm widened.

The descent to the valley basin is interminable with no shade to mitigate the heat. We're all together as we start down a spill of boulders whose sharp drops from one rock to the next require sitting and then slipping down. A loop on my shorts catches a craggy stone corner and Phil unhitches me, lest I lose my pants. Julien calls this, "grabby granite," great for crossing in boots, not so good for sliding on your bottom.

We pass multiple ponds, and Sarah asks, "Can we stop for a dip soon, Julien?" I follow her plea with one of my own. "*S'il te plaît?* I really need to extinguish my feet."

He leads us to the ideal stopover, a noisy stream with a large rock pool just off the trail. Joe and I break free of our boots and socks and collapse with backs flat and legs stretched across a warm stone. Our sore feet dangle and splash in the water, kicking up a cool spray that drenches our thighs and shorts. I stretch down my toes and feel the stones slick with algae and then sit up to splash my face. Corsican perfection.

Sarah in her swimsuit, and Kees, Chris, and Julien in their underwear jump into the frigid black pool, shrieking at the cold. I'm perfectly happy to just soak my extremities in the frosty rush until they're numb, watch them dry in the sun, and then plunge back in again.

Jim comes over to join us. "Your poor feet!" I say before he dunks them in the water. It looks like he's peeled off not only his socks but also a layer of skin. His heels, the sides of his big toes, and the tops of all his other toes are rubbed raw and red.

"And I thought *my* feet were in pain. Need some moleskin or duct tape?" Joe asks.

"Thanks, but no. Got plenty. Just took off what I had on. Figured the spring water would do me good. I'll just rewrap them before we go."

There's no way I could even pull on my socks if my feet looked like that.

"You really do enjoy freezing water," I say to Sarah as she sits down next to us, dripping wet.

"The most refreshing thing in the world," she says as she towels her face and hair, "and it's good for you—a real endorphin rush."

"Better you than me." I shake my head. "I think I'll keep getting my highs from a glass of wine."

I look over and see Julien—a tanned sight for sore eyes—sunning in his black briefs and sunglasses. He runs his hands through his wet blond hair, and then lies back, his stomach taut, arms above his head. Our very own French Adonis.

The invigorating effects of our stopover are fleeting. It's already been our longest day on the trail, and we still have a ways to go. Wooden buildings appear through the pines in the distance, and my adrenaline rises. We're almost there. . . .

But Julien dashes my delight and tells us it's just the Réfuge de Tighjettu. "I will tell you it is ugly with no protection from wind and rain. We are not stopping there. We have one more half hour to our destination, l'Auberge U Vallone. It is owned by a local shepherd and his family, and it is very pleasant with better food," he says. "You will be happy for the extra walking."

I don't know about that. Right now, all I want is some dinner and a tent. I don't much care about their quality.

The balance of the descent is not difficult, dried mud holding sheep's hoof prints, but I hold out hope that our destination will appear just beyond the next turn, or maybe the next. My muscles rebel from exhaustion. I'm out of water. My face and arms are scorched crimson, and the heat of the late afternoon sun makes them feel they're ablaze. I'm suddenly light-headed, my brain addled, eyes blurred. All in front of me becomes gray, save the backs of Joe's hiking boots and the red-and-white trail blazes. Early in the day they smiled at me, urging me on, but as I've no more energy, their candy cane stripes scowl, mocking me with their stares. They drip down the stones, red oozing like blood, running, muddying the white, melting to pools of pink.

I'm nauseated and feel I'm about to pass out when from what seems a distance, I hear my name. "Marianne." And then again, closer. "Babe." Joe's voice cuts through my delirium and then suddenly he's there in front of me. "Look," he says, pointing ahead. "We made it." I slump to a sit, gulp some of Joe's water, and then look down the trail to the sheepfolds of Vallone—wood and cinderblock huts with corrugated metal roofs—spilling across a rocky flat. The structures are pieced together with whatever material was available, each a rickety one-off work of art.

"It's just a little farther, okay?" asks Joe. Once I give him a reluctant nod and a thumbs-up, in his best French accent he says, "*Allez.*"

We swat at fat, noisy flies and dodge what draws them—all manner of scat dotting the track. While Julien checks in with the shepherd-in-chief—a gaunt, weathered man with a beard like the tufts on the chins of his goats—the rest of us sit on plastic chairs with cold drinks to rehydrate. With every frosty sip of my Orezza, my bout of hallucination recedes. Braying donkeys, bleating goats, molting sheep, and cows with bulging ribs wander past us on the concrete terrace. This is not just a hiker's shelter but a working farm as well. I'm content to sit and sip my water, watching the beasts go by, but Julien points uphill. "It is time to claim our tents." We share a group groan realizing we have to climb back up part of the rise we've come down—all except Phil, ever excited for more ascent. I so admire you, Phil, but where do you find your energy?

We set up camp and then join the line for the single shower next to the single toilet. A tall, fine-featured man in his twenties steps dripping wet from behind the wooden door pockmarked with see-through knotholes. He says to his equally tall girlfriend, next in line, "The water is hot but be careful. The floor is cracked and slippery. Leave your sandals on."

They're both blond, blue-eyed, and lean and speak perfect English with pleasing Scandinavian lilts. In a white towel that hugs his hipbones and contrasts with his tan, he turns to us sitting on a bench. "The floor has only a few tiles and the rest is mud. Don't expect to get your feet clean." We look down at his mud-splattered sandals, his toes and heels covered in blisters, some of them bleeding. Yes, we'll keep our flip-flops on.

I look over at Joe and know what he's thinking: Are we really that desperate for a shower? But my joints are screaming for warm water and we're already invested in a long wait. We're next in line, and so we stick it out to brave the grimy stall.

Rinsed and refreshed, we do our laundry in cold mountain water gushing from a rubber hose beside the kitchen. We head back up the hill, hang our clothes next to our tent on a tree, slip on our sandals, and head to the canteen for dinner. Just ten steps down the steep pebbled path, my feet skid out from under me and I fall hard on my bottom. "Ow!" My eyes water from the jolt. I twist around to warn Joe, but before I open my mouth, he slips and falls with a cry.

"I swear, I was about to say my ass was the only part of me that doesn't hurt," he says. "Not true anymore. . . ."

I'm unable to muster a response, still stunned by the pain. I roll to my side and push myself up but my leg screams as I move. It's that damned right quad again, and my God, it hurts. I gasp, sit back down, and carefully roll to my other side. This time, I put all my weight on my left leg, manage to stand, and let Joe go ahead so he won't see me limp the rest of the way down. No need to worry him for now. And maybe if he can't see my limp, I can pretend it doesn't exist.

It's my turn to buy wine for dinner. I go to the bar, my sore bottom and quad slowing my steps. I order a large *pichet*—a pitcher—of house red from the shepherd turned bustling bartender. I reach deep in my pocket for a twenty-euro note to cover the eleven-euro tab. But all I come up with is a ten. I turn back to our table. "Joe?"

Armed with my new driver's license, I jumped at every chance to run family errands with my sister. We picked up our mother's myriad prescriptions at Rexall and went to the Dairy Barn drive-through for four dozen eggs. They were on sale. It would be breakfast for dinner that night. Final stop: Waldbaum's.

We unloaded the cart, carefully checking off each item on the grocery list: Saltines, American cheese, two boxes of powdered milk, Velveeta, frozen orange juice, margarine, grape jelly, cake mix, brown sugar, three loaves of bread, spaghetti, milk, Jell-O. We looked at each other and shrugged as I added the box of Cap'n Crunch—the one thing not on the list—its bright blue, red, and yellow artwork in vivid contrast to the black-and-white packaging of the generic brands on the conveyor belt. "Let's just try," I said. We avoided looking at the register tally. Magical thinking that it wouldn't add up too fast. But the total was more than what we had. "Not enough," said the cashier, cracking her gum, our insufficient cash flat on her palm. I turned and saw the line build behind us. Our faces flushed red, like the cereal box. My sister took away the Cap'n Crunch and a loaf of bread. Still too high. I handed her the Jell-O. Thirteen cents to spare.

After four days on the trail, we've learned to appreciate simple, hearty evening meals. Tonight we eat our fill of solid peasant cooking—*sauté de veau aux olives*, sautéed veal with olives atop healthy mounds of pasta—on a wooden deck against a hazy sunset. I try to rub my tender thigh, but it's out of the question; even a gentle touch makes me wince.

"This is very traditional Corsican food," says Julien. "*La recette*"—the recipe—"has not changed over very many years. They like to make things *exactement* like their family always has."

"I get the feeling that the market for veal in England or America is not the same as on Corsica," says Sarah, turning to me for confirmation.

"You mean that a lot of people don't eat it because of how calves are raised?"

"Quite! The whole confinement thing and taking the young ones away from their mums so early. That isn't how Corsicans raise baby cows, is it, Julien?"

"*Non, non, non,*" he says, taking a second helping of stew. "All the cows just walk around the island as you have seen. They are always out eating on the grasslands—how do you say it in English?"

"Free range," says Sarah.

"Yes," says Julien. "Free range. And they are always with their mothers, eating the maquis herbs."

"Well, I feel better knowing that," says Sarah, digging into her bowl of dark brown Corsican veal, so different from the pale American variety.

The rapidly sinking sun is an orange yolk over the mountain saddle. It's been a difficult day—the most difficult so far—but memory of the rough edges is smoothed by a chatty meal and a couple glasses of restorative wine. Eventual darkness helps me hide my hobble as we climb to our campsite. I'm increasingly distracted by my thigh and terrified by the specter of a white flag flying over my head. The thought can't keep me from the oblivion of sleep, however, and I'm soon lost in dreams of red-and-white stripes: red round my neck, twisting tighter the more I struggle, and white around my ankles, making me trip and fall.

From troubled sleep, I awaken suddenly with a sense of dread, my chest tight. I'm restless, unable to settle. A shaft of summer moonlight streams through the tent window as donkeys sound off down the hill. I can't lie still; I find it difficult to breathe; I must find fresh air. Joe sleeps soundly as I crawl from the tent, my right leg so stiff I need my hands to pull its knee forward. The open sky calms my breathing as I see and count my exhalations in the cold. I physically shake off the foreboding—my hands, my arms, my torso, my legs—all doing twists in the breeze. I slip back into the tent, gulp back three painkillers, and inch my way back into Big Agnes, drawing myself up into a question mark.

Friday, August 5
The Hike—Day Five: l'Auberge U Vallone to Castel di Vergio

↗ **Ascent:** 2,369 feet
↘ **Descent:** 2,483 feet
→ **Distance:** 9 miles
Guidebook Description: The path pulls very steeply up to the col above. There is a lot of ascent today.

Sunrise paints the morning a palette of vivid reds as tentative fingers of light reach through spindly pines. For the first time since we left Calenzana, we're buffeted by the sawtooth edge of a cold wind. But as I slip on my warmest layer and wrap my arms across my chest, my wrists and knuckles are sore, and I see that they're swollen. *Damn you, RA.*

I say as Joe and I head down to breakfast, "You know what they say: Red sky at morning, sailors take warning."

"Definitely something brewing." He zips up his jacket.

Just as surely as the sun sets only to rise again, so my hiking aches and pains of last evening have mellowed. Despite my attacker flaring, the nippy air refreshes my spirits. "It's going to be a great day, no matter the weather adage. My quads are cooperating, and my right one actually feels better." I decide not to mention my puffy hands.

"Excellent!" Joe says, putting his arm around me. "Just try to go a little easy today."

"Ha! Like that's possible. Ain't happening."

"Just go slow if you need to. Remember, Julien told you your pace isn't an issue."

"Yeah, yeah."

Despite gauzy views of the surrounding valley from the deck, we eat inside to stay warm. Each time someone opens the door, we grab our napkins to keep them from flying away in the wind. I pull my hands up into the sleeves of my fleece to keep them warm. One of the house dogs, a beagle mutt, his coat a dirty doormat, rubs against my legs and then plops down on my feet. His attention is cozy comfort for my popsicle-cold toes, still in flip-flops.

"Got yourself a little buddy," says Phil with a chuckle, glancing under the table.

"Indeed I do—lucky me."

"*Il s'appelle Roger,*" Julien says. Ro-zhay. "He is the owner's dog, and he has been here a very long time."

The comely Danish couple from the shower queue arrives, door banging behind them. We pounce on our napkins. Their blond hair is perfectly coifed, muscled legs bronzed and rising endlessly out of their hiking boots. I've decided to name them Lovely Liv and Lissome Lars. They sit at the table next to ours and give us a collegial wave.

I turn around and ask Lars, "How're your feet this morning? Better than yesterday?"

"Yes, definitely. I put on new bandages, and they should be fine. At least until I take them off tonight."

I'm charmed by his accent. "Awesome," I say with a quick smile.

"Julien," says Chris, only loud enough for those near him to hear. "Can you make sure we're right behind them on the trail?" His one-track mind makes me giggle as I pour myself a second cup of tea. I ask Kees to pass the milk.

I hate to disturb my personal foot-warmer but it's time to get going. My new furry friend leads us out the door. As I knot my bandanna, I hear Phil. "Oh no!" He points to the end of our lineup of gear. "How does he know that one's yours?"

Roger is peeing on my pack.

The sun shines a false promise as the cold leads to multiple layers. The gusts calm to whispers as we do a gentle climb through protective woods. But once we emerge, the sun goes behind the clouds, and all is in shadow under a fine, soft mist, promptly followed by thin drizzle. The gradient pulls up sharply to the col above, and after a short stretch we're buffeted by fierce winds and pelleted with rain. Phil lifts his arms and tilts back his head, mouth open. "Our first GR20 rain!" Everything about his stance screams delight.

"And why is this good, Phil?" I ask, laughing. How does he manage to put a happy face on *everything*?

"Come on, Marianne," he says with a laugh. "I like the rain."

"You like everything in the mountains, Phil." I roll my eyes but feel his childlike enthusiasm rub off on me.

"At least we won't be complaining about the heat."

"It is time to put rain covers on our packs," says Julien, swinging his to the ground.

"Also time for foul weather gear?" I ask.

"It is your decision. If you are cold, you should wear it, but the rain will be light until later."

I'm already shivering, so I dig out my slightly damp black slicker that reeks of dog urine. Roger will be with me until I figure out how to fumigate this pack.

Everyone else has advanced up the immediate and crushing incline, since I'm the only one who took the time to don an extra layer. Joe hangs back but is still ahead. Clad in my rubber suit, I hear my backpack squeak against it with every step. I'm a packhorse with my load chafing, a pioneer crossing the Rockies, an explorer braving the wilds, until a greeting from behind pulls me back to reality. I'm a middle-aged woman struggling to catch up with her crew.

"Hi there," says Lovely Liv, out of breath. "These rocks are really hard!"

Lissome Lars wipes raindrops from his forehead. "Your group is very hard on you, I think. Too hard, yes?"

I manage to wheeze, "Maybe." I shrug as if it's unimportant.

"They shouldn't leave you so far behind," says Liv.

"I really don't mind. It's all right." I point. "And look. My husband's right there waiting for me."

"Maybe you should stay with us," says Lars, a twinkle in his gorgeous blue eyes. "We're going a little slower than they are."

"You are, but you're not as slow as I am. Don't want to hold you back, but I'll stick with you as long as I can."

"Great," says Liv, her smile revealing flawless white teeth.

Do they actually want to hike with me, or are they just being kind? Right now I feel like a knock-kneed novice impersonating a seasoned hiker, and the time has come to show what she can do.

We're back to advancing without a trail, white-over-red blazes painted on rocks leading the way. I follow close behind them, each of us taking our time climbing up, over, and around boulders. I chuckle thinking about what Chris would give to trade places with me right now. A six-pack of Pietras? He'd think just this one close-up of Liv's tan legs stretching up this stone stairway would be worth at least two.

I concentrate on every step, on every touch of my poles, trying to keep up. But despite pushing myself hard, my new friends outdo me. Several times they wait when stopping to hydrate, but finally, I wave them on since I've now reached Joe.

"Good luck," they call. "We'll see you at the top. At the refuge."

Joe and I hike in tandem for about a mile, and I do my best to match his step. But my energy lags, and the distance between us grows. I know he can only go so slow.

The wind kicks up further, and my pack cover fills, billowing out like a sail. Just what I need, more resistance to forward motion. I tremble to my core, my bones quaking, as I look up at blackening clouds, the squall and potential lightning hanging dark above the green line of peaks, threatening to descend. Doom lurks. I must catch up as the storm is about to explode. I focus on the ground, calibrating every step. When I finally look up, I see Joe on a rock just fifty yards ahead, calling something I can't hear. He's putting on his own rubber suit and waves to me to catch up.

Fleeting anger flashes. Don't you think I would move faster if I could? Aren't you the one who told me to go easy? But I also know he's probably terrified of this storm and the havoc it will wreak if lightning lets loose.

But between us, a gargantuan outcropping blocks the way. A lack of foresight and dwindling visibility have me in a face-off. Too much looking at my feet. If I'd just planned ahead and picked a better hiking line, I could have avoided this impasse. Following the long, gradual way to the left, where I'll have to hike down and then go back up through some scrub, will take more time and leave me even farther behind. Continuing straight up and finding my own footing will be tougher but more direct and decidedly faster. I want to join Joe as quickly as possible, especially given his primal fear of electrical storms, the single biggest cause of fatalities on The Twenty. And since I've become obsessed with never, ever losing altitude, refusing to put my foot even inches below any elevation I've gained, I decide to tackle the barricade head-on.

I reach behind and stash my poles between my pack and my back, freeing me to grip the granite with both hands. Thank you, Phil, for suggesting I wear gloves this morning. I grab a handhold. My toe finds an indent in the boulder. But my feet slip the first time I put my full weight on them and I fall back down, just a few feet, scraping my knees. Crap. My heart pounds, my pulse races, my legs bloody. I can see Joe calling again, but the wind whips his words away.

On my second try, I lift myself high enough so each foot finds a solid toehold. My right thigh strains as I push hard and lean into the rock. Make love to the granite, Marianne. You must make love to the granite. There's a vestigial soreness deep in the muscle of my right thigh, but despite the ache, it's functioning fine. I lift my left foot, find another niche, lift my right, and then again my left in a nice, slow hand-over-hand, foot-over-foot climb. It brings me just below the lip of the ledge.

Just one more step and I'll be king of this shelf. My hand hoists my knee and I lift my right foot high into a notch, covering what I should probably tackle in two steps. But I'm feeling good. Seeing Joe approach me and Julien's lime green shirt fluttering in the wind on the ridge with our team give me a burst of adrenaline. My right quad bears my full weight, tenses, strains, and then pushes hard to throw me over the top.

But mid-thrust, a thunderbolt shoots through the front of my thigh as if to rend it in two. My quad cramps—it's on fire—searing pain radiating from my pelvis to my knee.

Oh, Lord, what have I done?

My thigh collapses like the liquid pop of a flashbulb. The red-hot bolt of pain cuts off my breath, reducing consciousness to a sliver. I wait for it to swallow me whole. I fall forward on my stomach and force myself to breathe, slowly, deeply through my nose. This cannot be happening, I think, as I curse myself with a stream of fiery invective and grit my teeth. The depth of the pain has me dissociating from my body as I look down at myself from high above and hear the hiking gods laughing at me from behind the boulders.

Joe's voice cuts through. "Marianne! I'm coming. . . ." This time I hear him.

I lie still for several seconds, willing my heart to slow, afraid to confirm the damage my heroic push produced. I feel that if I move I just might splinter into a million pieces. Young bodies forgive, but your body holds grudges. I'm the poster child for a middle-aged striver who pushes past her ken and drives her body past its breaking point.

The mewing call of a gull, followed by its throaty, scolding bark, nags above my head. Panic pounds in my throat; my head throbs; my vision blurs. Thoughts tumble in a fog of pain as I slowly raise my head to rest my chin on the rock. I try to steady my shaky limbs and wonder what's more fragile right now: my body or my ego? I consider that maybe I'm in shock, all blood rushing to my thigh. A lizard slinks in front of me, stops to take a look, and then heads up the trail. If I manage to get myself upright, at least I'll have a path to follow.

I straighten my arms, push up my torso, and attempt to stand but am nauseous with the effort. The pain knocks me back to my knees and makes my eyes water. Oh, God, have I torn something? But then my inner voices line up like soldiers ready for battle. *Easy*, they say, *just let the hurt ride and then try again.* I manage to slip off my pack and roll over on my back, stiff like a starfish.

At that moment, Joe jumps down onto the rock to kneel next to me. His words are a jumble, gibberish under the fog of pain. "Marianne. Pain? Thigh?" I try to speak, but all I manage is, "It hurts."

"I'm sure it does. I saw you go down," he says as he pushes my pack out of the way.

He wipes my face, puts his cool hand on the back of my neck, and the pain subsides, finally bearable. "I'm okay," I say nodding. "Really."

"Lie back, Babe. Not the time to be a hero. I got here as soon as I could, but it was so slippery. Please just rest. Julien will be here in a minute."

"But the lightning. . . ."

"It's still far away. Don't worry about it right now."

I feel the beat of my heart thrum in my throat and a suffocating pressure tighten my chest. For the first time on the trail, I'm afraid. Truly afraid. It's my fault. I didn't listen hard enough to my damn leg for the past two days. I pound my fists on the rock. The minute I pushed too hard, it fell apart. The red morning sky, my invader swelling my wrists, Roger peeing on my pack, rain. Bad omens all. I'm usually the last one to give up even when a situation is hopeless, but today seems cursed. My muscles, my hair, my teeth, my heart—they all ache from the inside out, pain hurtling back and forth. Everyone saw me collapse. Embarrassment and frustration fuse to trigger tears that erupt and spill over the corners of my eyes.

The searing pain has dulled to a throb, and I insist that Joe help me roll to my left side. With his help, I manage to push myself to sitting, and then upright with my poles. An ache radiates through my thigh and like the sky after an electrical storm, it remains charged. But the longer I stand, miraculously, inexplicably, the more the pain dissipates. Is it possible my lunge didn't produce a tear? I lean on Joe, put my hands beneath my knee, and carefully lift it. My thigh is sore to its core, but it and my knee can still move. I stand on my own and step forward.

"Look. Now that I'm up, I can walk. I've just got a little limp, that's all. I do *not* want to hold us up any more. I know Julien will take my pack, and that'll make a huge difference."

Joe raises his eyebrows, looking skeptical. "But—"

"It's not like we have a choice, Joe. I *have* to keep going. There's a storm about to explode and they're not going to evacuate me because of a bruised thigh, no matter how much it hurts."

"We'll talk more at the refuge, okay? It's not too far ahead. Let's see how you do getting there, and then we'll talk about next steps."

I nod, wiping my eyes.

As I try a couple more baby steps, pain surges with each move, but I'm making progress. Julien arrives, having practically sprinted down from the ridge. Joe takes me by one arm, and my French white knight grabs my other. Julien turns and looks me in the eye, hesitating before he speaks. He gently asks, *"Marianne, tu peux continuer?"* Can you keep going?

I nod slowly and then gently touch my thigh before trying more steps. If I use my trekking poles like crutches, taking pressure from my leg, I'm able to walk. Julien picks up my pack. *"Je vais prendre ça."* My reflex is to protest—it's so hard for me to relinquish control—but as Joe said, this is not the time for being a hero. I'm beyond thankful, physically and emotionally, to lose those twenty-eight pounds.

I tell Julien, *"C'est difficile, mais je peux le faire, surtout sans mon sac."* It's difficult, but I can do it, especially without my pack.

"Alors," he says. *"C'est parti.* We must beat the storm."

The three of us head up, Joe at my back, Julien with my bag, and I with a hobble.

The ascent is excruciating, not just because of the pressure on my leg but because I know all eyes are on me. Pay no attention, I think as I push toward the ridge. Pain. Push. Step. Please, just pretend you don't see me. Pain. Push. Step. I lean heavily on my poles, and my already swollen wrists swell further from bearing so much of my weight. I banish all thoughts but the opportune fact that tonight, once again, we'll be in a skier's lodge—the second of two over two weeks. My inner positivity applauds, telling me I'm lucky to have been injured when I was. A good night's rest perfectly timed.

On the crest the rain and wind are now a squall. Big juicy raindrops splash on the ground, and wind gusts kick up further, our slickers flapping. The weather demands our full attention, and so I rejoin the group without fanfare. Ciottulu a i Mori, the loftiest refuge at sixty-six hundred feet, is still twenty minutes ahead. We must reach it before the heavens open in full. I'm soaked with sweat from the climb, but now that I'm still, I'm freezing, my teeth a-chatter. No one speaks, as we'd be unable to hear each other in the wind, all intent on adding gloves and hats and fastening jackets. I can't zip my layers high and tight enough to ward off the cold. We lean hard into the teeth of the gale that stings our eyes and sends hats flying. The path has become a swelling stream, and we're barely moving forward, blindly following Julien through the rain that smacks our faces, now coming down in sheets. I tip back my head, open my mouth, and let the rainwater rinse my face, wishing it would wash away the pain.

The rough-hewn stone tavern miraculously emerges from the fog. It's a heavenly haven for recharging and downing hot drinks. We spread our soaking clothes on the benches and hang them from wall hooks next to those of hikers who arrived before us. I spy Liv and

Lars, hands holding steaming mugs, huddling in a corner. Sarah puts her arm around me and offers to buy me tea so I can park myself at the close end of a bench straightaway. She hurries over to be first in line, and I try to stay calm as my thigh cramps with a spasm. After assuring Joe that Doc Sarah will take care of me, he goes to wait with the others in line for drinks. Sarah sits down and passes me a steaming paper cup along with one filled with cold water. She asks, "What in God's name did you do? Tell me. I didn't see what happened. Exactly where does it hurt? Is there a bruise? Any swelling? Does it hurt when you touch it? Did you take any painkillers yet?"

I stir my steaming infusion with endless circles, doing my best to spit out answers as quickly as she asks a question but my words are hesitant, coming out in fits and starts. I painstakingly pull my leg from my pants for her inspection.

"Okay if I touch your thigh? I'll be gentle, I promise."

I nod.

"That hurt?" she asks, pushing a bit.

"Oh, God." I wince.

"You have a visible bruise along with a good amount of swelling. Look, right there." I gently run my fingers over the bulge. "An immediate surface bruise often indicates something more serious underneath. My guess is that you have a bad quadriceps pull, likely of the *rectus femoris*. The muscle was already stressed—I remember you saying it hurt—and then when you pushed so hard, you put it under more pressure than it could take and it said, 'Enough.'"

I nod like a good patient, but my mind races. Will this be the end of the line for me?

Sarah says as I sip my tea, "Do *not*, do you hear me? Do *not* use Phil's massager any more. It may have helped loosen your knots before you were hurt, but now it'll just make it worse. We need to get you some ice as soon as we reach the inn tonight. Already checked and they don't have any here. And I think you could do with another couple Aleve. Right now. Doctor's orders."

I pull the pills from my pack, down them with a gulp of water, and ask, "So you don't think it's a tear?"

"If you'd torn your muscle, there's no way you could even stand on it. So no, I don't. But a serious muscle pull can be excruciating." Sarah takes a long sip of her tea and continues, "By the end of the day, we'll be able to tell how bad this is, based on how much pain you're feeling and if it gets worse this afternoon."

Can it get much worse?

I wrap my hands around my warm cup as Joe slips in next to me, his arm circling my waist. Julien passes out goodies for an early lunch as we hear the wind rattle the windows and rain and now hail pound.

I think about what I said earlier to Joe. I wasn't totally honest with him. Or myself. About my leg. I was just trying to be a trooper. I gently press my fingers to my thigh and flinch.

After an hour respite, the wintery mix dwindles, and a streak of pale, watery light cuts through the otherwise leaden sky. The fog lifts, the wind calms, patches of blue appear next to clouds edged in gold, and slivers of bright sun reflect off puddles. What we couldn't see in the literal fog of arrival is now apparent. The rocky cabin is dramatically sited and, while solidly anchored, is hanging off the side of the mountain cliff.

We can no longer delay our drop into the Golo Valley. Julien checks in to be sure I can start the descent and continues to shoulder my pack along with his. We wave goodbye to Liv and Lars, still eating lunch. "Good luck," they call.

The afternoon passes in a blurry haze of pain and purpose as with every single step, I gasp, my wrists ache, and my pulse throbs in my palms from gripping my poles so tightly.

"Hanging in there?" Joe asks every few minutes, sticking close, never more than several strides behind me. He looks awfully worried, so each and every time I respond, "So far, so good." I'm a good little actress when I need to be.

We stop for a brief water break beside a derelict dry-stone *bergerie*, until recently still in use for milking and overnighting flocks. It's now near collapse. The structure has long lost any angular shape as its stones have disintegrated into piles of rubble—a fitting representation of how I feel. But unlike the *bergerie,* and except for the expanding bruise hidden by my pants, I look no worse for wear. Julien has us quickly back on the descent because I know he wants to get me off my feet.

After zigzagging downward for three more agonizing hours, my limp ever more pronounced, we arrive at a road lined by giant, bristly gray hogs with extra-long pink snouts noisily rooting along the shoulder. A wooden sign on a fence says, *"Charcuterie Corse Traditionelle,"* with an arrow pointing down the road and a crudely drawn pig— Traditional Corsican Cold Cuts. Thank God hogs can't read.

We're at the end of today's stage at the Castel di Vergio, a concrete, Soviet-style structure that was formerly a small *station de ski*. It's a charmless building, but it will give us a bed. Joe takes our bags to our room and, despite his protests, I insist he take a shower first and wait for me there. I remain in the lobby to talk to Julien right away as I know he'll need time to make arrangements.

"I'm so sorry, Julien, but I should probably tell you that besides hurting my leg, I've been struggling with something else. Rheumatoid arthritis. RA. Maybe I should have told you before we started. . . ." I'm afraid to look him in the eye.

He pauses for a moment shaking his head, but finally says, *"Je comprends, Marianne."* I understand. But his tone contradicts his words. He's definitely not happy with me.

While he steps outside to make some calls, I sit sideways on a bench in the foyer, my legs extended in front of me. I reach out successively to touch my toes, each time stretching my thigh a little more. The extensions actually feel good.

After just a few minutes, Julien returns with a bag of ice and to tell me the particulars of how things will work for the next few days. *"Tout sera organisé."* All will be arranged. *"Ne t'inquiète pas."* Don't worry. I'm not up to speaking to anyone but Joe yet, so Julien assures me he'll inform the others.

"Merci," I say, holding back tears. *"Désolée."* I'm so sorry.

I swing my legs around to sit for a minute, my head hanging, eyes focused on the weight of the ice I've placed on my thigh. I feel the prickle of a rash, but on the inside, creep from my toes to the top of my head. We planned everything so well: the celebration of our birthdays; the tribute to our marriage; hiking together; sharing the challenge. Nothing was supposed to get in the way, least of all our age. Does it all no longer mean anything? Disappointment stirs, and I surrender: I'm now going to be a statistic—part of the 50 percent who don't complete The Twenty. I'll hold off on telling Joe for just a few more minutes while I head outside to commiserate with the swine.

"Do you really think I'll think less of you because you're injured? You've been doing really well, and I'm so proud of you. It's not your fault you got hurt." Joe sits freshly showered in a clean pair of shorts and a tee. I'm still a filthy mess.

"But I just wanted to be able to do this *whole* hike. *With* you." I crook my arm over my face as Joe pulls me to his chest, his hand on the back of my head.

"Marianne, are you sure you don't want me to stay with you? What if your leg gets worse?"

My voice rises, my words rushed. "Joe, how many times do we have to talk about this? We always knew one or both of us might get hurt and—"

"But I never thought it would actually happen."

"Listen. Sarah—Dr. Sarah—looked at my leg and said I just need a break. If my leg gets better, I'll rejoin you in a couple days." Easy to say, so hard to accept.

Joe shakes his head.

"No, Joe. You are *not* leaving the trail for me. I won't let you. We promised each other: If one of us couldn't do the whole thing for anything other than being *really* sick or *really* hurt, the other would go on and do it for both of us. Right?"

"But you *are* injured, and—"

"But not *seriously*. I don't have a broken leg, and I don't have a head wound. I mean, look. I can walk!" I get up from my chair and totter across the room. "It's definitely not pretty, but I can do it."

Joe's eyes are now glassy as he pulls me next to him on the bed. "Come here," he says, pulling me to his chest. "I don't want to leave you, but I'll do whatever you want." We're quiet for a minute until he gets up, walks to the window, and looks out. He finally turns, leaning back on the sill. "Why won't you ever let me help you?"

I look at him for a long time and start to unlace my boots before I risk saying, "You know, it really would have helped me, would have been nice, if you'd stayed back with me sometimes—"

"Marianne." Almost a shout. His nostrils flare and his voice has an edge. "You kept waving me on." He gestures. "Told me to keep going. If that's not what you wanted, how was I supposed to know?"

I pull off my boots. "You know I don't want you fussing over me— and you don't—but I guess I just hoped you'd want to hang with me."

He's now pacing. "I can't read your mind, dammit, much as I'd like to. You've trained me not to coddle you. And like I told you before, this hike is a bear, and I really don't know if I can do it at your pace. I don't know if I can do it at all. I'm serious! I'm going through my own doubts about whether I can finish this thing. You do know that, right?"

I shake my head, peel off my mud-caked socks, and then look toward the mountains through the window. "I didn't know, Joe. And I just don't know about anything right now." I look back at him. "This isn't the way I imagined things would be, and I need some time to sort it all out. And lucky me." I raise my arms as if rejoicing, twirling my socks in my hands. "Woohoo! I'll have three long days all by myself to do just that." I toss my socks across the room. We sit in silence for what seems ages, listening to hikers drinking and laughing on the terrace below. The early evening light casts shadows, and the room slowly dims.

"So what did Julien say when you told him?" Joe finally asks.

I take a deep breath. "That the next three days are long and tough and remote, and he agrees I should sit them out. I'm sure he doesn't really want to have to deal with getting me airlifted off a mountain if my leg gets worse." I pause, letting that sink in with both of us. "Listen, it's just two nights and three days and then we'll be together again in Vizzavona. Where a taxi's going to drop me. There's a *gîte* there, and you'll all meet me. Fingers crossed I'll be able to keep going with you after that."

And by voicing our new reality, I've exhausted the extent of my pluck. My voice breaks, my chin trembles, and hot tears spill. I bite my knuckle as my spirit knots. And when Joe crosses the room to the bed and puts his arm around me, I sense a shift, as if a key is turning from "on" to "off" inside my chest. *Do not feel this way*, I tell myself, but I can't help it. It's all gone askew like an uneven seesaw, and I'm left dangling in the air. Something's been taken from me, and even though he's not the cause, I'm resentful.

I'm back in the grammar school gym. I've let go of the rope and fallen on my face.

It isn't the mountains ahead to climb that wear you out; it's the pebble in your shoe."

—Muhammad Ali

PART III: CORSICA
DAYS SIX THROUGH EIGHT

Saturday, August 6
The Hike–Day Six: Castel di Verghio to Réfuge de Manganu

↗ **Ascent:** 2,444 feet
↘ **Descent:** 1,841 feet
→ **Distance:** 11 miles

Guidebook Description: We climb uphill through beech woods and then enjoy an airy ridge walk to Lac de Nino, a glacial lake surrounded by spongy peat.

My Plan: Cry away the day. Figure out what went wrong. Beat myself up for being injured.

I awaken early, restless, on my stomach in the dark, eyes closed. Sleep is always fitful when things are unresolved between Joe and me. I tossed and turned painfully all night, trying to keep ice on my thigh and haunted by questions with no answers. How is it possible I'm not joining Joe today, leaving him and his own misgivings to go it alone? How long will it take me to heal? Will I be able to rejoin him after a few days?

Try to be positive. Rest your thigh, double your miraculous meds because maybe, just maybe, your attacker has played a role. Trust that you can hike again after a few days of rest. I've actually started to anticipate the daily routine of waking early with sore muscles, getting dressed in the morning cool, anticipating the day's challenges. And so this feels all wrong. Sadness is a sludge churning in my stomach. I push myself up to start my ablutions, only to collapse back down.

"Ouch!" But this time, it's not just my thigh. My upper arms are screaming, and my shoulders can't bear my weight. I turn myself over with difficulty and look at my puffy hands and wrists. I stifle further moans so they won't awaken Joe. He's conflicted enough about leaving me behind, and I don't want him changing his mind.

I down my pills and get into the hot shower. I stretch and massage my hands, my arms, my shoulders. For five days now I've repeated over and over, *Never, ever stop walking. Just do it, no matter what, one foot in front of the other. Keep going.* But now my playbook has a new page, and it tells me I must stop. I look down at my now purple eggplant of a thigh, suitably swollen, its skin tight and shiny. I dry myself, gingerly patting my bruise. I slip on my sundress and sandals, but my gnawing guilt mars their comfort. I shove my hiking gear in my pack, cursing under my breath.

"I'm just really sore, pretty much all over. And I'm sure you are too," I tell Joe when he gets out of bed and asks how I'm feeling. "Like Sarah said, my leg just needs some rest."

We stand over the sink brushing our teeth, taking turns to spit. Tonight, I'll be brushing by myself. Joe gets himself ready, and we're soon down with the gang in the bright breakfast room, its picture windows overlooking Monte Cinto and Paglia Orba. But I'm in an invisible bubble that separates me from them. What are they thinking and how do they see me? As a weakling? A wet noodle? A quitter?

There's a nice spread of breakfast goodies, but all I manage is a nibble of croissant.

"No wonder you're so slim," says Sarah, eagerly cleaning her second plate of food as I push my first away.

Slim? Me?

Julien interrupts my question with a fresh bag of ice and a logistics review so that Joe can hear. "A driver will get you at nine fifteen. In an hour and a half. He must stop in Albertacce village for a few hours—I do not know why—but then he will drop you at the *gîte* in Vizzavona, which is on the GR20 route. Today is Saturday, and we will meet you there on Monday in the middle of the afternoon. You will have three days to rest, and then we will see how you feel. *D'accord, Marianne?*"

I nod. Whatever you say, Julien. But the village's name, Albertacce, teases. I know I've heard it before.

He gives me two *bisous*, kisses on my cheeks. "À bientôt et bon courage."

"*On y va*," he says to the others. Let's go.

Leave-takings are painful and best dispensed with quickly. "Let's just get this over with," I tell Joe, "or you know I'll start crying." I hold his stare, unwavering.

"You're sure you want to do this? You can still change your mind."

"I am. You know me—Little Miss Independence." I give a half smile, not opening my lips. "I'll do a little walking and get myself all better. Right?"

"Sure."

"Maybe I'll meet some nice people—some Corsicans, finally. I'll get to speak French and time'll fly."

His eyes fill as he pulls me in and holds me in a hug. I don't want to let go.

"Just be safe," I say, as I pull away after a long kiss. "Miss you already."

"Miss you too, Babe."

We share I love yous. We wave goodbye. I feign a smile.

He's a stocky, middle-aged bear of a man—all fuzzy with big paws, his thick body set on short, bowed legs, his ears too small for his face. He has a well-defined rural look in baggy black work pants, leather sandals, and a cotton Chinese-style blue de chine jacket, the official uniform of the working Corsican. He marches up the hotel stairs, cigarette dangling from his lips, and greets me with a quick but firm handshake, a grumble, and no smile. Without pause, he begins shoveling the pile of our group's bags from the hotel stoop into the back of his station wagon. He throws my duffel and backpack on top.

On a mission to return to the road, he waves me into the sagging front seat next to him. Having been in the wild for five days, it feels peculiar to be in a car. He hunches forward, grabs the steering wheel with his fat, furry fingers, and as the car lurches into reverse, my bag of ice slips from my thigh to the floor when I grab the seat on either side of me. We then pop forward, my back against the tatty seat, and disappear down the mountain, bouncing along the rutted road at high speed. I double-check my seatbelt. I sense the pavement just beneath my feet, and my tender backside tells me the shocks should have been replaced long ago. My ursine driver has yet to say a word.

We reach an easy stretch, and I muster the courage to tell him my name. He replies, *"Ouais, je sais."* Yeah, I know. Not the talkative type.

Just as I recoup my ice pack and open my mouth to ask his name, he jams on the brakes to round a sharp curve, just missing a wild pig on the road's shoulder, and then accelerates until the next hairpin. My head snaps back, and I find it hard to breathe. He's actually handling the blind bends with the confidence of one who knows them well, but then I see there's a jagged hole where the right-side mirror should be. Not as expert a driver as I'd hoped. I picture us smoldering in a ditch beside the road.

Julien warned me that Corsican drivers are always keen to get where they're going, forever overtaking others even in perilous places, passing with an impatient flick of the hand. I'm convinced he's trying to kill us both. My stomach clenches as we zoom past a slowpoke Fiat 500, obviously not a local, and I close my eyes as I'm tossed side to side and then twist to hang tight to the door handle with both hands. We swerve to avoid a pothole as big as a bathtub and this time, my ice spills from its Ziplock bag and splatters on the floor.

Internally, I seethe, but all I say is, *"Désolée!"* I'm sorry. My driver acknowledges neither me nor his sopping mat. I so want to shout, "Slow down! I need that ice!" but dare not. I fear rousing fabled Corsican vengeance and wonder if there's a gun in the glove compartment.

Well down the mountain and finally on a straightaway, we hug the side of a valley and roar past a road sign riddled with bullets. I can just make out the letters of our interim destination: Albertacce. Where have I heard that name? I make another attempt at conversation and ask how long we'll be in the village.

"Jusqu'à seize heures," he says. Until four o'clock. It's now 9:30 in

the morning, and the light is already white hot. What am I going to do for over six hours in this heat?

We pull into a small clearing across from a church where he jumps out of the car. I assume I'm to follow.

"La rivière est par là, et le resto est tout droit." He points in one direction and then another to show me where I'll find the river and the restaurant.

"On va se rejoindre à seize heures. Ici. À plus tard." We'll meet here at four. See you later. He jumps in the car, does a quick U-turn that leaves me in a cloud of dust, and disappears down the road. I imagine my ice melting on his floor.

Rocky Albertacce is closed up, tight as an infant's fist. All is shuttered, and the streets are empty, save a few untethered pigs snuffling in the brush beside the road. Perhaps this is what villages on this island are like on Saturday mornings. I take a deep breath and survey my surroundings, leaning on my trekking poles for support. I gently stretch my thighs and then walk carefully, babying my right leg, to the door of the church in search of cool sanctuary. But Sainte Marie's is barred and locked.

So much for quiet contemplation.

I sit in the shade by the wooden door of the simple white facade and ball the bottom of my dress in my hands. There's something about this unforeseen detour that makes me feel I deserve it. Rather than tackling the next stage of the journey, I'm a mendicant on the stoop of a shuttered church that hasn't the time or the place for me. I'm suddenly very tired, very alone, and very sad. The futility of the whole thing—the trip to this island, the challenge of the hike, and the attempt to actually finish it—overwhelms me.

Under the daunting Corsican sun, the distinction between the parched air and dusty earth is seamless. I squint up at the church's freestanding bell tower and then over at the cloudless horizon. Sweat trickles between my breasts. I stick my bandanna down the front of my dress to absorb the moisture and then drape it around my neck. I kick the dirt with the toe of my sandal, wondering where Joe and the group are right now. I picture them stopping for midmorning dates and granola. My stomach growls, and I realize I have little with me to eat—nothing but a bottle of warm water and half a bag of crackers reduced to crumbs in my daypack.

Please let the restaurant be open for lunch. I have hours of time to fill, and my morning mouthful of croissant is not going to last me until my nameless driver returns.

In silence, I think about the past twenty-four hours and how I got to this dusty, deserted hamlet, miles from Joe, far from the trail, nursing a throbbing thigh. I cringe as I draw up my right leg, grasp my knee, and pull my injured quad close to try to stretch out the ache. I straighten my left leg, toes pointed, then flexed, tracing circles in the air. I've been relying on it since yesterday, but sharp, intermittent pains have been shooting from my knee into my hip. I fear it's starting to rebel. I put my hands on my upright knee and rest my forehead on them.

I search to put words to how I feel, but they elude me, floating just above my head. Like the attempt to recall a dream, the more I reach, the further they recede. I tuck myself into a ball in the narrowing slice of shade, my cheeks damp, tears mixing with sweat. I dissolve into helpless sobbing, unable to stop.

Without warning, an ear-splitting explosion of gunfire from across the valley brings me to my feet. Bam! As if in response, a second deafening row of shots discharges from somewhere downhill, followed by successive bursts that reverberate from every corner of the basin. Bam, bam, bam!

Ugh, I think, just what I need. Intrusive macho aggression—noise pollution at its worst.

I'm now even more on edge than when my driver dumped me. But then I recall Julien saying, "Corsican people like to celebrate almost anything with explosions." And so, I change my tune. Someone must be very happy about something. For hundreds of years, they've rejoiced with things that go *boom*. Who am I to criticize?

And then suddenly I remember about Albertacce. It's the setting for a short story by French writer Guy de Maupassant, about a timid young man who, after years, eventually takes up arms to avenge his father and becomes a *bandit d'honneur* in the Corsican countryside. I knew the name was familiar. I'm in a village from literature.

I take the elastic from my wrist and pull my hair back into a ponytail, wipe my face with the hem of my dress, and grab my pack. Time to find that river.

Respite from the stifling heat is a mile's limp down the road from sealed Sainte Marie. The Golo River runs low but fast among boulders, their pallor in sharp contrast to the water's icy blue. There are a few morning visitors along the banks—a little girl and her father wading with a dog, an old man asleep under a tree, a teenage couple jumping from a ledge into a river pool. I cross over to a broad horizontal rock in the middle of the stream, slip off my sandals, dangle my legs. My toes swing back and forth in the flow, and I watch the swirling eddy I've created, my feet interrupting the current. I settle down, drop to my back, and think about the three days to come. They stretch ahead like forever.

Fury simmers beneath my surface. Making things happen is who I've always been. Let's have Marianne do it. She'll get it done. But feeling as I do right now, I'll never get anything accomplished. And that includes The Twenty.

I sit back up, pull my dress over my head, slide down the rock in my underthings, easing my bottom into the frosty Golo. I initially catch my breath at the cold, but then relax in the river, my legs outstretched, the water tickling around my waist. I douse my face, make splashes with my hands, and allow the icy stream to toss them about. The ache in my leg deadens in the cold and my sore wrists soothe as I recline, light filtering through leafy boughs. I'm exhausted, feeling boneless and loose as I pull myself up to lie back on the warm rock, sedated by the sun.

The bells of Sainte Marie ring noon across the valley and jolt me from my nap. I'm suddenly ravenously hungry.

Chez Jojo is Albertacce's only restaurant, and it is indeed open for lunch, its chalkboard menu announcing the daily plat-du-jour. But more family dining room than restaurant, the simple establishment is packed and bustling with loquacious locals. Where did all these people come from? What happened to the ghost town of my arrival?

I sit at the last available spot, a corner sidewalk table set with a bright pink tablecloth. I'm out of place among the chummy regulars, as it's not easy to be ignored when you're a stranger in a remote village. They look at me with the curiosity of stares that last too long and that I first interpret as disdain, but then I see hints of smiles, and one older woman gives me a quick wave. My seat is in the sun, hot but helpful for drying my still damp bra and underwear that have left dark, wet outlines on my dress.

The server is twenty years my junior, but right now I need a comforting, maternal figure, and she fits the bill. Pale-complexioned, sunburned, and corpulent, she hustles from the kitchen tightly encased in a floral housedress that pulls at the buttons across her bosom. Her arms balance multiple plates until she sets them down carefully in front of each diner and then wipes her hands on her faded apron. She claps, steeples her fingers, and practically sings, "Bon appétit!" She's a Corsican Julia Child. She looks over at me and raises a finger to signal, "I'll be there soon." And back into the kitchen she goes, for another load of lunch.

The gentlemen next to me extinguish their cigarettes and become quiet as they dig into heaping, steaming mounds of roasted goat, chicken, and veal served family style with a huge bowl of small potatoes. Yes, I'm hungry, but there's no way I can handle what they're having.

I've read that Corsicans have a reputation for being brusque with visitors, but my waitress is nothing but patiently kind. Despite the lunchtime rush and the perspiration on her brow, she takes time to carefully explain the menu of the day: three courses for sixteen dollars. She details the ingredients and the preparation of each dish and tells me that no, the portions are not mountain-sized like those of my neighbors. The men are her husband's cousins, and their meal is not on the menu.

"*Mon mari, Jojo, a fait le plat, et moi, j'ai fait les beignets et le dessert,*" she says proudly, her body erect, hands on her waist, shoulders back. My husband prepared the main course, and I made the fritters and the dessert.

"*Vous prenez la formule?*" she asks. Would you like the set menu? "*Mais oui. Je prends la formule.*" But of course, yes.

From the moment she turns and leaves, I miss her presence. I follow her every step as she disappears behind the muslin curtain into the kitchen, from which waft the savory smells of meat roasted with herbs. So much of travel is about big, important details: transportation schedules and connections, finding your hotel, and getting places on time. But here I am, the beneficiary of the other kind of detail—the little things that so often count more than big ones: a wave from a fellow diner, smiles from the locals, a kind, easy exchange with a chatty server. All of them missing from my cab driver, Monsieur Misanthrope.

The waitress, whose name I learn is Annie, brings me my appetizer—*beignets de courgettes* with a tangy fruit coulis for dipping. I bite into my first real food of the day: golden zucchini fritters made with chestnut flour—lightly crisp on the outside and filled with fresh *brocciu*, a soft, mild Corsican ewe's-cheese, similar to Italian ricotta and a staple of the island's cuisine. The creamy filling oozes out the side of the *beignet* and drips down the side of my mouth. I catch every bit with my finger and lick it clean. In no time, I've polished off three. I could eat another dozen.

"You are very hungry," Annie says, her eyes twinkling as she clears my plate.

I continue our exchange in French, oohing and aahing about her culinary talents.

"Would you like more *beignets?*" she asks. "I have many. You're too thin. You need to put on some weight."

For the second time today, someone has commented on my weight, but not in a way that matches my self-image.

"*Non, merci.*" I pat my midsection. "I need to leave room."

"Your dress is a good color blue," Annie says. "Very good for Corsica." She touches a cobalt amulet that hangs next to a crucifix on the chain around her neck. "It will protect you from *l'occhju*, the evil eye, and keep away the jinx." She smiles and scurries off. The woman at a neighboring table smiles at me and makes horns with her clenched fist, pointing her index and little fingers down. Good luck to you and good riddance evil eye.

I think about what Julien told us about the easy coexistence of traditional religious orthodoxy with superstition on this island. Predominantly Roman Catholic, Corsicans seem to have no problem also believing in the power of spirits and magic and their influence over every aspect of life.

My thoughts are diverted by the tinkle of an empty bottle rolling in the gutter. I turn to see a cow approach, making sluggish progress down the middle of the road. Her tail and distended udder swing back and forth in unison until she stops just feet from my table. Has she somehow strayed from the *transhumance* trail? No one but me is paying our bovine visitor any attention, my mouth hanging open. But then Annie's agitated husband, master of his eponymous restaurant, darts from the kitchen with his white butcher's apron tight over his pot belly and out to the road. He gesticulates with a stainless-steel ladle dripping with juices, a collie at his heels. Lassie nips at Bessie's hind legs as Jojo smacks her haunches to hasten her retreat from in front of his eatery. *Is that ladle going right back into the sauce?* I wonder, as *le patron* stomps back into his kitchen.

I giggle as the collie comes over, rests her head in my lap, and nudges me to pet her. Roger at the refuge and now this one—the dogs do seem to love me these days. Annie returns with my *plat: sauté de veau aux petits légumes.* Sautéed veal with little vegetables. The rosemary-infused dish smells delicious.

"Jojo roasted the meat," Annie says, "but I grew the peas, carrots, and green beans." She points through the kitchen to her garden, thrusts out her ample chest, and then waits for me to take my first bite. I raise my fork and take a mouthful, thinking, *Who could have guessed I'd eat veal twice in two days after avoiding it back home all those years?* But then, the past few days have been full of surprises.

"This is excellent, Madame. The veal is very good, but your vegetables are even better." I'm rewarded with a huge smile.

Annie brings me a basket of baguette slices to soak up every last drop of sauce. Jojo comes out of the kitchen, takes off his apron, and comes over to say hello. He has a smiling, weather-beaten face with bulgy eyes and an obstinate nose, front and center.

"Do you like it?" he asks.

"Oh yes," I say, my hand in front of my mouth as I chew. "*C'est très bon.*" He gives me a friendly wave before turning to sit and chat with his cousins. I sneak a morsel of veal down to Lassie.

I down every bite on my plate, and then Annie brings me a wide, shallow crock of *crème brûlée aux châtaignes*. I poke through the perfect, brittle shell to reach the creamy chestnut flavors of the dessert. Though I'm already quite full, I find room to polish off Annie's masterpiece. The restaurant may bear Jojo's name, but Annie is its heart. How lucky I am to have finally chatted with some Corsicans, and this couple in particular.

I put down my spoon, and a glass plate of sweet *canistrelli*—chestnut biscuits dredged in powdered sugar—appears. As if to herald their arrival, from down in the valley comes a reprise of the noisy blasts I'd heard earlier. One of Maupassant's bandits?

"The wedding must be starting," Annie says as she helps herself to a cookie from the plate. She bites into it, powdered sugar dusting her upper lip and the shelf of her bustline, and goes on to explain that a local farmer's daughter is getting married this afternoon. "All Corsicans love making big noises, especially farmers, and especially when they marry off their daughters." Mystery solved.

This midday meal, firmly rooted in the land from which it sprang, is exactly what I needed. For over an hour, I haven't thought about being injured, about quitting, about being a disappointment. This simple restaurant and the warmth of its owners have touched and calmed me. And not since my muscle-numbing siesta in the Golo have I thought about my thigh.

The station wagon pulls up next to the church with a sandy skid at exactly four o'clock. I'm barely in the car and we're off. I dare not ask what my cantankerous driver's been doing since this morning but can't help but wonder. Taking a nap? Tending to farm animals? Meeting up with his mistress? I tell him I had lunch at Chez Jojo, thinking that perhaps he's not a morning guy but will open up in the afternoon. But all he does is nod. We have well more than an hour's ride ahead of us—a long stretch of silent miles.

We race around tortuous turns on woefully neglected roads carved through villages clinging to cliffs. Everywhere is evidence of the work of FLNC separatists and their fight for independence. Signs bear both the French and Corsican names for places and the former is routinely scratched out. All across the island, slogans like, *"Fuor i Francesi"* (Frenchies get lost) are spray-painted on roadside boulders in a language unfamiliar to most French. We narrowly miss an elderly pedestrian weighed down by plastic bags of produce as my driver refuses to brake. He speeds through village after village. It's surprisingly time-consuming to get from one commune to the next, a mile away as the crow flies, but significantly more distant on roads that twist and turn through thick forest and around ravines. Julien told us it's why most residents never travel farther than the neighboring town.

The trees thin, and we whiz by yet another pockmarked red-and-white sign, this one indicating a hill town poised across a deep gorge. And for the first time, Corsican hometown pride overcomes reserve, and my driver finds his voice. "That is my village," he says as he sits up straight and smiles such that I can actually see his teeth. "It is

Corte. We were the capital when we were independent. It makes us very proud."

I look across the Restonica River and see the Corte citadel defiantly lording over the town's tumble of red and orange tile rooftops. Although Ajaccio is technically the island's capital, Corte is undeniably its cultural and spiritual heart, its geographical center, home to its parliament, and the epicenter of the independence movement. My driver—the chest-puffing rebel.

At long last we pull up to the red iron gate of a pleasant pocket of Corsica: a compact, wooded compound that includes a rustic hotel, bar, restaurant, and a simple two-story *gîte*. I step from the car and my driver jumps out, grabs my duffle and pack from the tailgate, and tosses them at my feet. I reach into my rucksack and turn to offer a thank-you and a tip. But he's already pulling away, a trail of dust behind him.

It's only much later that I wonder what he's done with everyone else's bags.

At three thousand feet, Vizzavona village is hidden in a sylvan valley of chestnut and hazelnut trees in the shadow of bald Monte D'Oro. It marks the halfway point of The Twenty, delineates the boundary between north and south Corsica (Haute-Corse and Corse-du-Sud), and is serviced by a station on the Corsican Railway. Thus, unlike other stopovers along the trail, there are many visitors who have come off the rails and are not hikers at all.

I've arrived on a busy summer Saturday and must wait in a line that goes out the hotel reception door to check in at the Col de Vizzavona *gîte*. It suddenly occurs to me that I have nothing in writing to assure me of a bed, only Julien's promise that it would be "*organisé*." Annie's embrace of an hour ago evaporates. Am I at the right place? Where will I go if they turn me away? My breath quickens and my chest rises and falls visibly as I hear couples and families around me chatting and laughing.

I normally relish my time alone, crave to be hidden where the world can't reach me, but right now, in the middle of a thick Corsican forest, I miss Joe, I miss Julien, I miss our group. I imagine them all approaching the beautiful blue glacial lake, Lac de Nino, petting wild horses and then resting on thick green grass. It's one of the most photographed sights on the trail, and I'm so frustrated to have missed it.

I distract myself by focusing on the incongruity of my surroundings. From the breezy, vine-covered terrace, I step into the foyer, a stale salon, its wooden floor covered with overlapping, threadbare Persian rugs. This is not an establishment distinguished by careful arrangement. Like the interior of a Balzac boarding house, the original color of the painted walls is long forgotten under dingy smoke stains. Behind the registration counter is faded toile wallpaper, so out of place in this rural outpost, peeling and rolling back onto itself. On mismatched pieces of dark, heavy furniture, which appear not to have been touched by a dust cloth in months, various vessels hold desiccated flowers. Heavy burgundy drapes shield the room from natural light, leaving it in shadow.

A matron, her former looks hidden beneath too many pounds and a dull fatigue, oversees check-in. Her messy gray curls, likely a source of vanity when she was young, are adorned with pink pins in the shape of flowers and fall well below her shoulders. Glassy green eyes peek from a puffy, fair complexion. She does all she can to remain seated in her upholstered chair on wheels, accessing her phone, files, and keys with quick pushes. When she's forced to stand to summon a colleague from a back room, her tight, pinched pumps leave her with an apparently painful gait. Much like mine.

All this I observe as I await my turn to see if I have a place to sleep for the next three nights.

The woman stabs me with a stare from her rolling throne. "Just you, yes?" she finally asks in French with a thick Corsican accent after consulting a list.

I start to respond but my throat catches as I swallow a thick sob. I fear she'll turn me away. She says, "I'm sorry?"

"*Oui*," I manage, the second time around. She rifles through her basket of keys, tosses one across the counter, and points out the door.

"À gauche," she says, pushing over her chair to help the next person in line. To the left.

In the burgundy-shuttered dormitory across the way, I find my room halfway down the first-floor hallway. It's clean and odor-free—the most you can ask of such humble lodgings and certainly more than I expected. Just inside the door against a mottled beige wall is a heavy wooden chest of drawers that appears to be part of the Balzac reception collection. There are two simple twin beds, cheek by jowl, and perpendicular to a steel-framed bunk. Over the tall window hang two ragged lengths of yellow-and-blue Provençal fabric stapled over a wooden rod, unhemmed and not quite wide enough to fully cover the opening. There's a nail on one side of the window frame and I tuck the curtain behind it to let in the breeze. I'll have this space for four to myself until Joe and the group arrive.

I try to let the calm simplicity of the space sink deep into my bones. A monastic setting perfect for recuperation—exactly what I need—but from nowhere the blues hit. Sadness invades the room, making its way into every tidy corner. There's a sudden commotion down the hall, male voices arguing. I attempt to lock the door but no matter how I fiddle, the mechanism won't move, the latch dangling uselessly. I drag the dresser to block the way.

I wander the room touching things—the windowsill, the bunk bed frame, the pilled blankets at the end of the beds, the scarred top of the dresser—hoping they'll ground me to this place in the middle of nowhere. I open what I think is a closet and smile. I've hit a hiker's jackpot: my very own bathroom with a toilet and shower all to myself. I turn on the water—it's hot!—and decide to take advantage right away.

I try to dig my towel and shampoo from my overstuffed backpack but they won't budge, my inflamed wrists unable to pull them out. I upend my pack, my things falling on the bed. A square blue card flutters to the floor—a note from a friend I'd stuck in my pack. I've read it so many times, I know just what it says: "Good luck on Corsica. I could never do what you are doing. You guys are amazing."

Amazing, I think. So damned amazing. Rage boils over my blues.

As I lean over to pick up the card, I bang my forehead hard on the dresser and with that, I detonate. "Shit, goddamn it, motherfucker!" I scream as I kick the chest. Inevitable pain shoots up my right leg and I repeat my litany, this time even louder, as I rub my poor thigh. I reach down again, grab the card, rip it in half and then in half again and again until I'm left with miniature pieces.

"Amazing," I cry out loud. "Just amazing!" I throw the shards in the air and watch them float to the floor. I take my sandals from the pile on the bed, one in each hand, and smack them against the dresser one after the other. "Take, that GR20! And take that, taxi man! And here's one for you, check-in lady! And this one's for you, you damned mountains!" I slap the things I've just touched gently—the window, the bunk, the bedding. I pick up a hiking boot and hurl it at the door. "And here's to you hiking mates, for leaving me behind!"

I slouch down against the wall, my bottom hitting the floor, my other boot in my hand.

I hear a knock and a woman's voice at the door. *"Ça va? Tout va bien?"*

"Oui, ça va!" I scream and add in English, "Everything's fine! It's all just perfect!" I throw my boot at the door.

Footsteps retreat down the hall.

I sit on the floor for many minutes, carefully pulling up my legs to make myself small, bowing my head to my knees. I've come undone, a shaken can of soda now exploded.

I stand in the jet of hot water until my ugly purple thigh loosens and muscle pain melts. And there I stay for ten minutes longer. I dry myself in the now murky room, the sun having fallen below the treetops. I press the wall switch and a light sputters reluctantly, an ugly naked bulb hanging on a wire from the ceiling. I immediately shut it off. My headlamp will do if I need to see.

I sit on the bed next to the screenless window and push the outer shutters wide open. The relief I felt after my emotional eruption and a hot shower is short-lived. Being able to express my emotions is easier said than done. I'm up against a lifetime of holding back my anger and I'm going to have to work at letting it out sometimes.

I grasp the wooden sill and look out over the pebbled pathway that passes between reception and the *gîte*. It's active with purposeful people and sounds: vacationers on their way to the café, couples strolling arm in arm, the *tick-tick-tick* of trekking poles, and the squeals of toddlers waddling too fast, their parents trailing behind them. They're all having normal days while I definitely am not. I should be out on the trail, having dinner with Joe and my group, not just observing from a wooden window. How did you let this happen?

The hour is early, but I'm in for the night, ready to sleep away disappointment. I sink back on the bed, my head on the pillow, fragile, like delicate glass that will shatter if touched carelessly, but make no attempt to shake my mood, preferring to wallow in the isolation of the solo traveler. Despite my fatigue, however, when life is in flux, I'm wired to stay awake, tossing, turning, struggling with all that ricochets inside my head. I try hard to let my feelings run their course, hoping they'll dissipate. Letdown. Disappointment. Failure. How could I have planned so carefully, only to have it all unravel? It wasn't supposed to be like this. Despite my best efforts to take things as they come, the standards I set for myself are harsh, buzzing round my ears like a mosquito in the dark.

I force myself up to look back out the window, across the now dark passageway. Candles flicker and glasses and silverware tinkle from the restaurant behind the stone wall. I'm now weeping, my entire body racked by sobs from the depths, and I fear I'll never stop. I'm stuck, peering up from the bottom of a deep, dark well.

I lie back down, tears falling into my ears. I mindlessly pull on a loose blue string from the fabric above me. It gives way easily as I unravel the colorful cotton curtain.

Sunday, August 7
The Hike–Day Seven: Réfuge de Manganu to Réfuge Petra Piana

↗ **Ascent:** 2,822 feet

↘ **Descent:** 2,008 feet

→ **Distance:** 7 miles

Guidebook Description: A steep rocky ascent leads up to a high mountain gap where we have splendid views of the lakes below and the imposing summits surrounding us.

My Plan: Stay in bed feeling sorry for myself and, if I'm up to it, find something to eat.

My head pounds as I wake up in a daze, my fist full of blue thread. If feeling my eyes have been scrubbed with steel wool isn't evidence enough, the scattering of tissue snowballs beside my bed attests to my torrent of tears and fitful night's sleep. I force myself out of bed, my thigh cramping when I apply pressure. I hobble to the bathroom and scowl at my puffy eyes and blotched cheeks in the mirror over the sink. My hair hangs in my face, lifeless and ratty in just-got-out-of-bed clumps. What a disaster.

I slip back under the covers, sleep elusive as I think about the interminable day ahead. There's no refuge in routine because all I have are endless hours of blank space ahead. Enforced idleness is not a good state for me, and right now I have no energy, no motivation, no will to do anything. I scour my psyche for a sign of optimism, some ray of hope. But all I find are setbacks. Why even bother thinking about completing the hike? I can't do it. The jig is up. I roll to my side and curl up my sore leg.

A hazy brightness and the sounds of a Vizzavona morning come from outside: gentle birdsong, bonjours, easy laughter, a dog barking, and the ubiquitous clipped sound of hikers passing my window. The click of their poles, ordinarily a sound I love, reminds me I'm a pretender. I should be heading out, as real trekkers are. Real athletes.

I roll over on my stomach, close my eyes, and will my sore body and taut emotions to relax. *Tick-tick-tick.* A child cries. *Non, Maman. Non.* A motorbike whizzes. Hushed conversation. The distant bleat of goats. *Tick-tick-tick.* The curtain's fringe I've released blows in the breeze. The rhythmic call of a *sittelle corse* lulls me back to sleep.

The window is shut tight. A throb of light from beyond briefly brightens the room. I attempt to sit, but the sheet is tucked tight, my arms trapped at my sides. *Tick-tick-tick.* I hear Joe, his words indistinct. It's now Julien. *"On y va."* They don't know I'm here. I thrash about, the sheet finally giving way. I push on the casement, but it won't budge, painted shut. *Tick-tick-tick.* They're passing me by. "I'm here!" I shout. "Joe. Over here. Julien. Sarah. It's me!" I pound on the pane but they're deaf to my cries. They leave me behind. Once more, "Joe!" An owl hoots. Neon pulses, leaving me dizzy.

I awaken flailing in a tangle of bedding, sweat trickling, heart pounding, mind soft from sleep. Bright sunshine through the glass. That dream was the final affront. I must find my way from under this fever of woe. Be the straight A student just handed the reprieve of a B. I kick off the covers and order the pressure to release. There must be more to Vizzavona than this narrow bed and Spartan room. It's lunchtime, and my stomach rumbles. Time to explore this outpost in the woods.

I tug socks over pale feet. They're stiff as cardboard despite repeated sink washings—nettles, grime, and sweat refusing to let go until they get into a machine. I pull on my hiking boots, rigid and foreign after just a day's rest, wash up, and pop my morning pills. I cross the dirt road to the Monte D'Oro restaurant which, despite its simple exterior, serves traditional French food on white tablecloths: *confit de canard, steak au poivre, escalope à la crème.* But my attire falls short, and so I find a map in reception. Leaning on my poles to protect my thigh, I head down the road, my day pack over my shoulders. Surely there's a café near the Vizzavona train station and just maybe this day holds some promise.

Wild roses burst pink along fences, and purple wisteria covers the wooden trellis of the Restaurant-Bar L'Altagna's outdoor patio, providing cool cover from the noonday sun. Four soaring chestnuts deepen the shade, and planters overflowing with flowers line the terrace border. Yes, I'm alone for my second meal in a row, and I'm taking pleasure in the privacy. I huddle over my notebook at a corner table, the international signal for "please don't disturb me," and write a dozen pages.

My salad, crowned with rounds of goat cheese on toasted slices of baguette, calms my complaining hunger, and I delight in the crunch of fresh produce. I'm actually pretty happy not to be eating ham hocks and lentils with a spork. A small vegetable garden next to the café—the obvious source of my lettuce and tomatoes—thrives, heavy with ripe fruit despite the blistering heat.

An Old English sheepdog, eyes barely visible under shaggy bangs, wanders in, sidles over, and sniffs at my knees. He digs his wet nose into my lap while I pet his head, and then settles at my feet. Why have I attracted so many of man's best friends on Corsica—Roger, Lassie, and this shaggy fellow. Is he ignoring my body language, sensing I need a friend? I stroke him for a bit and then turn my attention back to my salad and my writing.

She's sturdy, yet delicate, her bearing graceful despite the walking stick she leans on. Her royal blue blouse is tucked into slim-fitting khaki pants, and her dangly gold earrings are the kind I love to wear. They give her elegance a hippy touch. Soft white hair is pulled back and knotted at her neck. Her pink skin is downy, translucent almost, crow's feet pinch around the eyes of her fine-boned face, and I see the gentle beauty that remains. She must be in her early eighties, a fragile flower pressed inside the many leaves of her life. All this I take in as I watch her approach.

"Bonjour," she says, and continues in French, "I hope Bernard isn't disturbing you."

Bernard? Who is Bernard? And then I remember my furry companion.

"*Mais non.*" I look down. "He's actually keeping me company."

"I saw you check in at Monte D'Oro yesterday when I was sitting on the *véranda*. You're a hiker, aren't you? By yourself?"

"Yes and yes. For now. Since yesterday." And then my words tumble out unbidden. "My husband and I were doing the GR20 with a group, but I hurt my leg and had to stop."

"Oh, I am so sorry. I can only imagine how upsetting that must be for you."

There's something about this woman, with her lovely French and friendly dog, that intrigues me. I wonder about the secrets hidden behind her eyes, surprisingly bright, not pale and watery, for a woman her age. She listened carefully to what I said, and I sense a connection. Inviting conversation with a stranger is not my usual way, but on a whim, I ask, "Would you like to join me?" I sit up straight and point to the chair across the table.

"That would be lovely," she says, her face crinkling into a smile. "Especially because Bernard doesn't seem to want to leave." I look down and see he's fallen asleep, belly on my boots.

She grips the table as she slowly sits. Her hand trembles as she brushes a wisp of hair from her forehead, and I catch a whiff of lavender.

"I had lunch at the restaurant up the hill, but I always come to this café for tea right before I leave. A taxi brings me down. Would you join me?"

Despite the heat, a warm cup of tea appeals, reminding me of Sarah. "Sounds perfect." I down my last bite of *chèvre*. "You said you *always* come here. . . ."

"Every year, the first week in August."

I see she's wearing a platinum wedding band.

"By yourself?" I ask carefully.

As she pauses to reply, the waiter arrives and we order our tea.

It takes her a moment, her blue eyes brimming as she looks at her lap to smooth her pants. Finally she replies, "For forty-six years, I came with my husband. But since he died, I've come by myself. So, like you, I'm here alone."

I quickly touch her arm without considering how she might receive my intimate gesture. I'm relieved when she returns my smile. "I'm Marianne, by the way."

"And I'm Céline. My husband's name was Jim." My grin reaches my ears at her French pronunciation: *Geem*.

"Jim. That sounds American."

"Yes, he was American. You are American too, *non*? Your accent is just like his."

"Yes, I'm American and hard as I try, I can't quite erase my accent."

"Oh, I like to hear Americans speak French. It reminds me of Jim, of course."

"And you're not from Corsica." I place her accent from somewhere in the South of France.

"No, I'm from Montpelier. I take the ferry from Toulon to Ajaccio and then the Micheline train up to Vizzavona. A very bumpy train, I will say. Jim used to call it a 'bone-shaking ride.'"

I laugh. "But why Corsica and why Vizzavona?" My questions make her smile.

Céline switches from French to English. "Do you mind if we speak English? I almost never get the chance and, as I said, it reminds me of Jim."

"Of course not. I totally understand. *Alors, nous parlons anglais.*"

Céline recounts her story with quiet melancholy as she laces and unlaces her delicate fingers on the table in front of her. She seems to take pleasure in sharing the details of her love affair with her husband. He was a US army engineer and she a translator. They met in Marseille working on the Marshall Plan and married six months later. Her sadness is clear, but she punctuates her story with gentle smiles.

"He was no Cary Grant, but *mon Dieu*, he did look *beau* in his uniform," she says, lifting her head and looking off to the side as if picturing him standing there.

"My mother refused to call him Jim. He was Jacques to her and she always called him 'Jacques-the-American.' She was very unhappy that I did not marry a French man."

"And your father?"

"He died right after the war so he never met Jim. But I know he would have loved him. My father's *devise* was '*Bien faire et laisser dire*,' which means something like 'Do well and let others talk about it.'"

"I love that."

"And Jim always said, 'Follow your heart's compass.'"

"I love that too!"

Our tea arrives, and we stir in some milk. Céline adds two cubes of sugar.

"So tell me about your connection to Vizzavona," I say as I lift my cup to blow across the top.

"Forgot to explain that, haven't I?" She continues stirring. "Jim always found things for us to do outdoors because we both enjoyed being in nature. 'I have an idea,' he always said in that enthusiastic American way. We used to hike in Les Alpilles, kayak in les Calanques, and take long walks in le Luberon. He turned me into a real explorer.

"About four months after we met, he 'had an idea' for a sunrise picnic in the mountains above Nice. An army buddy told him you could see Corsica on a clear day first thing in the morning from there. My mother said it was a mirage but we wanted to see for ourselves."

"And?" I put down my tea, eyes glued to her.

"It was true," she says with choked emotion as she looks down and turns her wedding band. She looks back up. "First there was a shimmer of lavender—the beginning of sunrise—and then when the sky turned pink, Corsica appeared across the sea. And right then, Jim asked me to marry him."

"That is sooo romantic." I'm dewy-eyed.

"From then on, Corsica was special for us. We decided to come here on our honeymoon, especially once Jim heard that the stars above Corsica are like nowhere else."

"Well, I have to agree with you about that."

"We married two months later. We went to Ajaccio and then came to Vizzavona to hike. Of course, the GR20 was not here then. We stayed in the Monte D'Oro."

"The hotel and not the *gîte*, right? It was your honeymoon, after all."

"Yes, the hotel. I would have been fine in the *gîte*, but Jim insisted. My mother, of course, couldn't understand why we didn't just go to Paris. 'Hiking is for men,' she said."

"My mother never understood its appeal either." I shake my head. "And so now you come by yourself?"

"Every August. I stay in a *pensione* on Ajaccio's marina and then come to Vizzavona for a few nights. When Jim became ill, we visited every couple of years, but since I lost him, I come every summer."

"Is it terribly painful? Coming alone?"

Céline twists her napkin. "Sometimes. But mostly it's a comfort." She looks up and smiles. "I have so many happy memories, but I do miss Jim. Every day."

"Do you mind talking about him?" I ask as she pours us more tea.

"My father said that if you are silent about those you lose, they'll never be at peace, so I talk about Jim when I have a willing listener. So thank you for hearing my stories."

My mind flashes to Kees and Liese. I must ask him to tell me more.

My tea goes cold as Céline shares stories about the early years of her marriage, a shadow of sadness passing across her face when she says they never had children. "Friends used to ask how I could be content with just Jim. How can you live with only one person year after year? Tell us your secret."

"People ask me the same thing sometimes now that our two grown children have moved away. 'Don't you get tired of just being with each other?' they ask. I say no but also tell them that Joe and I have always managed to have some time apart."

"Perhaps like the time you're spending away from him right now."

"Perhaps . . . although I do wish I were still on the trail with him."

"I'm sure this separation makes you sad, but maybe it will be good for you. Jim and I both used to travel for our work and coming home to each other was always such a joy."

I nod and sip my cold tea. "We both traveled for work too, even when the kids were little, and homecomings were always special. And now that we're retired, I'm sure we'll be together a lot and will have to be careful to give each other alone time."

"It is important to realize that what makes a great marriage at one stage of your life may have to be revised for the next. Retirement and all that time together can be difficult." She laughs. "Even for very good marriages. Jim and I did have to adjust. . . ."

"I'm sure there will be ups and downs, as there always are. And a bump or two. We've already had a couple, I'm afraid."

"Like being on the Micheline train." Céline laughs, picks up her cup, and drains her tea.

"Very true. I always think the best way to describe a good marriage is what the fox says about his rose in *The Little Prince*. You have to make your relationship the most important thing in the world and then do everything you can to take care of each other. All those bonds you build between you are what make your love unique." I feel tears well.

Céline nods. "Seems we're both very lucky." She pauses and then asks, "Tell me more about your loved ones."

I talk about Joe and my large family. About falling in love with France. I tell her about our children and take out my good luck picture. Sudden longing for them stabs.

"They must be proud of their *formidable maman, non*?" she says with a French fist pump. "Jim and I hiked here, and I know you must be fit to climb these mountains."

It's now my turn to look away. "Well, I'm not sure they would be so proud. . . ." I pause to clear my throat. "If they knew I had to quit."

Céline asks for details about my injury, and I can't relate them without crying. How is it I can express myself so freely with this stranger—a new friend I'll likely never see again? Maybe it's because she, like Annie yesterday, is kind and open and doesn't judge.

"*Ma petite,* you have just done half the hike—the most difficult part, from what I hear. You just need *un peu d'encouragement.*" She goes into her purse and passes me a tissue. "Try not to be upset with yourself. You are injured. Knowing when to stop is not weakness."

"Right now, I just feel like I failed. And I think that maybe people—even those closest to me—won't respect me if I don't finish what I start." I swallow hard. "Ever since I was little, I've tried to accomplish things. Get good grades, make the honor society, win a scholarship. Even little things like rearranging my room, organizing the kitchen drawers, baking cookies for my siblings. And when I got older, it was the same. Nail the promotion, make the sale, run the marathon. Getting things done. It's what's always driven me."

"And if you *don't* get things done?"

I stop for a moment. "Well, maybe others might not care about me."

Before I ask, she hands me more tissues.

"But you must know that is not true." She gives me a minute and then continues. "Whether it's a hike or something else, give yourself credit for what you *can* do. You are a hiker, like I was, and you know that much of the reward is the walking itself. You must not hurry a hike because it is not about reaching the destination first. Worrying about doing a hike quickly is like not enjoying the croissant while it is warm because you are looking for the perfect plate."

I chuckle, closing my eyes. "I know, I know, but it's so hard for me."

The waiter stops, bends down to scratch Bernard behind the ears, and asks Céline if we'd like more tea.

"*Non, merci.*" She shakes her head. "It seems Americans always measure things to decide their value. How fast, how high, how much? Jim and I used to talk about it often."

I pause. "I never thought about it that way, but you're right."

"Just remember that you do not have to measure and you have nothing to prove. Think about what you would tell your children. Maybe, 'The *chemin* was difficult and you did your best.' Treat yourself with the kindness you would show those you love."

With a few simple sentences, she's made me feel I've just hung the moon and the stars. A sky full of Corsican stars. Like my mother did when I was little.

"What is it Jim always said? 'Lower the bar.' He said I set standards for myself that were too high. When I think of his words, they are like his arms around my shoulders."

I look up at her and smile.

"He also used to say, 'Bloom where you are planted.' This confused me at first, but he explained that it meant to be content with where you are. He always lived his life like that—happy with what he'd done, never dwelling on disappointment."

"He was a smart man, your Jim."

Céline nods and leans forward. "You are *l'ainée*, yes?"

"Yes, the eldest."

"You said you have many younger siblings. . . ."

The eve of my departure for college. I was eighteen, eager for escape. The Mariners Inn in Northport, on Long Island Sound, the rising moon shining a path across the water—my father, my grandparents, and I sharing a going-away meal. My mother had been in the hospital for a week. Her ulcerative colitis attacking again. Colon cancer threatened. My father sat first. I took the seat to his left to avoid facing him. Had we ever had a conversation of more than a few sentences? Chatting with his children, at least with me, was not his strong suit. He would have been uncomfortable having dinner with me alone, which is why I was pleased my mother's parents initiated the send-off. They chose the venue and would pick up the tab. Between appetizers and main dishes, my grandmother pulled me aside in the ladies' room. "We're counting on you, Marianne, to help your father with the younger ones, should the worst come to pass."

Why is she conferring this obligation just as I was about to leave? And why did she always have to speak in euphemisms? If my mother, her daughter, died is what she meant.

Back at our table, the sun set, the dining room in flickering candlelight. A plump scallop slipped from my fork into drawn butter pooling on my plate, spattering my new silk blouse. Try as I might, the stain would never come out.

". . . and your parents made you responsible for much, yes?" says Céline.

"They did."

"And you thought you had to do it all on your own without help."

How many times have I read it in self-help books? But this time, perhaps because I'm in France, perhaps because this lovely woman said it, or perhaps because defeat is so recent, I allow something wound tightly inside to unfurl.

"It takes a lot of energy to always control everything, doesn't it, Marianne?"

At that moment, an iridescent kaleidoscope of butterflies catches my attention as they flutter about the purple bush behind Céline. One separates from the others and lands on Bernard's head, still asleep on my boots. His ear flickers but nothing else stirs.

"You must practice letting go," she continues. "And asking for help when you need it. We need the assistance of others even though we convince ourselves we'll always be young and strong. It's hard to learn that's not true, especially if we're athletes."

I look at her and smile. "Did you just call me an athlete?"

The train station overflows with colorful coolers, backpacks, and other trappings of outdoor activity. The air is charged with anticipation, even before we hear the locomotive's distant whistle. The railway platform fills steadily with passengers anxious for their ride, most of them day-trippers returning to Ajaccio. The brakes screech, and the noisy three-car procession jolts to a stop, the engine hissing a sigh of arrival. A conductor steps from the middle car and announces the departure time. In ten minutes Céline and Bernard will be on their way. She carefully writes her address on a slip of paper she pulls from her purse. I read her perfectly rounded handwriting and tuck it deep in my shorts pocket. The lump in my throat makes it difficult to speak, but I promise to write. I carry her bag, help her into the car and get settled in her seat, Bernard at her feet. I clasp her warm hands in mine.

"*Au revoir, ma belle,*" she says, and then gives me two *bisous* and a hug, a gesture the French do not bestow lightly. I return her embrace and then step down, her lavender scent still with me. I wave as the horn sounds, the engine engages, and the train lurches to a start. It gathers speed and then disappears, echoing in the dark tunnel under the Vizzavona heights toward Ajaccio.

Those who accompanied the now departed travelers have scattered in the wake of the whistle. A forgotten scarf draped over the back of the lone bench and I are all that remain. I sit down, floppy, like the well-loved stuffed puppy of my childhood, paws limp, ears droopy and stitched back on, my heart visible, dangling by a thread. I finger the scarf, unable to pull my gaze from the now deserted rails. Silence rings in my ears.

Predictable tears drop, but my emotions shift from loss to joy. I am so happy to have met this woman who simply enjoyed my company. I dig my hand deep into my pocket for a tissue and find Céline's address. I'm overcome with the need to write her immediately. I jump to my feet, go into the ticket office, and buy a stamp and a postcard of Vizzavona. I carefully record Céline's Montpelier address, tuck it back in my pocket, and hesitate before writing my message in English. She'll appreciate the reminder of Jim.

"From one athlete to another, I will never forget you. Hugs for both you and Bernard." I affix the stamp and ask the clerk about the closest mailbox. He tells me it's two stops north in Vivario. "But I'll mail the card for you tonight if you'd like. I live there."

What a lovely man. A lovely Corsican man.

The note to Céline safely on its way, I settle back on my bench in the sun. My fingers move down to massage a string of age spots by my knee, just beneath my bruise. I think about the forces that have accompanied me though life: fierce independence buried beneath crippling shyness, or maybe it's the other way around. Whatever their position, both stop me from asking for help: too timid to ask, too stubborn to accept.

A shadow passes overhead. I look up as a large bird of prey—a falcon of sorts—soars over me, climbing and plummeting, each time closer. I feel it swoosh past my head only to again take flight. Maybe this mythical bird of victory is sending me a message. Forgive your inner critic for being so tough. No one I hold dear cares how quickly I climb over a mountain. After decades presuming "not thin enough, not fit enough, not perfect enough," I've been reminded that indeed I'm enough as I am.

Perhaps life's most important lessons need to be learned and then relearned over and over again. Receiving help and letting people see you're fragile is okay.

A late afternoon torpor falls over Vizzavona, thick shadows extending across the tracks where squat tufts of wildflowers poke between ties. A haze of Queen Anne's lace in pastel pinks on the far side of the rails gently waves at me as I linger under the murmur of leaves. If I hadn't been injured, I wouldn't have had these days on my own, wouldn't have met Annie and Céline, and wouldn't be sitting here feeling I'm where I belong.

The appearance of my ugly bruise continues to deteriorate, now purple with an ugly sallow tinge around the edges, but while the ache in my thigh still nags, it pulls just a little bit less. The swelling has gone way down, but have I healed enough to continue? What if I just stop driving myself so hard? Would that be enough to get me back on the trail? Or maybe I should just stop pushing altogether and say to hell with the rest of the hike? Take the train back to Bastia—the escape hatch I envisioned on night one—and wait for everyone there.

But what would that do to Sarah and Joe? She'd be stuck with a troop of testosterone and he'd feel guilty for going farther without me.

I breathe deeply, filling my lungs with optimistic oxygen, conscious of the comfort of convalescence. Who I am has come through this intact although my armor of rigor has softened. I exhale noisily, my breath warm, and get to my feet to find my way back through the forest to the *gîte*.

I look up the wide, bare path that divides the forest like the part in my hair, narrowing as it rises to infinity. There's a girl well ahead in a sunny yellow tee, a blink of color contrasting with the evergreens. I follow her golden swath until she disappears over the rise. Is it my imagination, or is there now a gentle glow at the point where the pines meet? The sloped straightaway leads through the wood, and I settle into the rhythm of putting one step in front of the other, my moving meditation toward the light.

I come to a sunny break in the forest canopy, slanted rays illuminating the Cascade des Anglais—the English waterfall—where the River Agnone splashes over the rocks. The falls are not huge—more entertaining than awe-inspiring—but have carved a succession of deep turquoise pools that sluice into water slides cut into the rock. This spot, towered over by beech and pine, was one of Céline and Jim's favorite places to picnic. I look around, half-expecting to see them sitting there, legs swinging over a ledge.

A plaque explains that once the railway was built, the falls became popular with aristocratic English visitors at the end of the nineteenth century, hence the name. I think about how the years make no difference in a place like this. Except for taller, leafier trees, it must look exactly as it did when Céline and Jim first visited sixty years ago. As I have so often since we began The Twenty, I consider the spirits of families that have gathered from across the island, spirits that will forever haunt these old stones. I think about the countless lovers who have visited this place over the years in turn-of-the-century Victorian lace-ups, loafers, sneakers, flip-flops, and hiking boots. Those we love will eventually leave us while the rivers and mountains remain.

I scramble to a rocky overhang at the top of the falls, stand, and breathe slowly, lifting my arms and eyes to the sky. I linger in the pose, my body and my emotions strong. I tell myself to let go. To just totally let go. Stop spending so much energy trying to control things, because in the end, they can all fall apart.

I take some time to contemplate my place in the world and my relationship with the Almighty—private journeys for me, best accomplished alone, inside my head, deep in my heart, often in the wild. I've always rebelled against the touchy-feely, community approach to my salvation, especially when forced. It always made me uncomfortable, and it often made me mad. These are my concerns, not yours, and no, I don't want to share.

Is it any wonder I ran screaming from the family prayer of my youth?

It was well into Saturday evening. As they did daily, my parents called us to their room and we dutifully filed up the stairs. In the early years, it was just two of us, my sister and me; in subsequent years it was three, four, and then five, six, seven, and so on. All of us knelt around our parents' bed, palms in prayer on the white chenille bedspread, the crucifix over the headboard peering down. "God bless Mommy and Daddy, Marianne," plus as many children as had been born so far. An Our Father, a Hail Mary, and a Glory Be were recited in quick order, followed by requisite offerings of gratitude. I fiddled with a cotton tuft on the bedspread when it came to my turn. Even in grammar school, I resented being told to bare my soul and share my innermost thoughts. I wanted to say, *I'm thankful for books and dreams and stories in foreign lands*, but instead I said, "my family," knowing it's what they expected.

In 1972, I was sixteen, my youngest brother had just been born, and the opening litany became, "God bless Daddy and Mommy" followed by the names of eleven children.

A year later, my mother invited my new seventeen-year-old boyfriend, Joe, to family prayers while he innocently hung out with me listening to the latest Allman Brothers album on our front porch. I can still conjure the image in sepia. My parents' room. On our knees. Around their bed. My face flamed with embarrassment, and I refused to be grateful. I knew he'd break up with me the minute the agony was over. And while I told myself I hated my parents with no compunction, I knew that when my father insisted we accompany him to Saturday confession, I'd be overcome by guilt and come clean.

I pick my way down to the base of the falls and sit on a rock still warm from the sun. I watch the watery reflection of a jet's contrail advance across the sky as it surges and swells in the day's waning light. I splash my legs in the cobalt pool and consider how my mood has changed since my morning in Albertacce's Golo River. I lose myself in the tumble of the current, marveling as it dances and splashes over rocks in its path. I study fresh freckles on my arms and legs, each a reminder of the summer's sun.

But I'm yanked from my reverie when, without warning, a toddler, his chubby cheeks pink with sunburn, splashes me as he accidentally slips into the deep pool. I plunge from my perch into the ice-cold water, grab him as he goes under, hold him high and return him to his terrified mother.

She grabs the boy, crying and shrieking in Corsican that morphs

into French. *"Merci, merci, Madame! Mon bébé! Mille fois merci."*
The child is laughing under his mother's kisses, thinking it was all
a game. The woman tells me she can't swim, thanks me again, and
wraps her son in a towel. All those around the falls applaud me.

I pull myself back up on my rock, soaked and shivering, and realize my thigh felt no pain. It just may be getting better. I'm happy to
be heroine-of-the-moment and to have saved the curly-haired boy
but suddenly remember: Oh no! Céline's address is in the pocket of
my now soaked shorts. My gut twists as I retrieve her address. It's
dripping and illegible, the blue ink running, and try as I might, I
cannot remember her last name. I gasp and then breathe in again
sharply, knowing I've lost my friend in the frigid pool.

I'm shaking and must get in some dry clothes before the sun disappears. I wave goodbye to mother and son, and she calls, "God bless
you" and blows me kisses. She has yet to release the toddler from her
embrace. Walking back to the *gîte* in the blue hues of dusk, the day's
final light casts soft shadows on the green leaves of summer. The sun
drops behind the mountain, its afterglow turning the sky into swirls
of mandarin and purple. The cool breeze nips at my neck. Physical and
emotional exhaustion pulse through my bones, but I'm not yet ready
to end the day. I exchange my wet clothes for my sundress hanging on
the bedpost and head out to claim a place on the Monte D'Oro terrace.

A breeze through the pines cools my arms, raising blond hairs
and releasing the sharp fragrance of oozing sap. While I continue
to miss Céline, I'm comforted knowing that in the days ahead, she'll
receive my postcard. I look toward a corner table under vines where
an elderly couple is having dinner. I close my eyes and imagine Céline
and "Geem" sharing a meal in Vizzavona and my chest aches thinking of Joe. I imagine him eating wild boar and mushroom casserole
and tally the hours until I see him.

The waiter puts a frosty glass of Corsican white in front of me. I take long, refreshing swallows, knowing that most anything would taste divine here in the shadows on this midsummer night. Relaxation flows to the tips of my fingers and my toes, and in the margins of my consciousness, like a throb I can't control, the unknown of the next five days dances just beyond my reach.

Monday, August 8
The Hike–Day Eight:
Réfuge d'Onda to Col de Vizzavona

↗ **Ascent:** 3,301 feet

↘ **Descent:** 5,538 feet

→ **Distance:** 11 miles

Guidebook Description: We pull up onto a high ridge, where there are some truly fantastic panoramic views before we descend into a glacial valley.

My Plan: Rest in Vizzavona for a third day and decide if I can rejoin the team.

The first sound of my predawn consciousness is a song. A child singing as she passes by.

Promenons-nous dans les bois,

Pendant que le loup n'y est pas.

Let's walk in the woods while the wolf isn't there.

Sleep gone and beyond recapture, I throw on my shorts and a T-shirt and head out to the blush of sunrise, waiting for the morning. I sit on the stoop, fill my lungs with cool air, and feel the warm approach of what will surely be another sweltering day. I await the full sun, watching dawn intensify from luminous green to pink until the sky is all rosy. I have twenty-four more hours in Vizzavona to continue stretching my leg, resting my body, and healing my heart.

I pass through the deserted hotel reception to order café au lait and a croissant from the bar. In the angled morning light, I actually find the foyer and its overly decorated *fin-de-siècle* detail charming. Even the faded wallpaper makes me smile. Must have been my miserable mood on arrival that wouldn't allow me to see past the dust. It's barely 7:00 a.m., and so I have the terrace to myself until a German family of day hikers arrives for breakfast before they hit the trail.

The remainder of the day is interminable but delicious purgatory while I wait for our group to return. My eagerness to be with Joe again is expected, but my anticipation to be back with the gang surprises me. I deeply miss them, each and every one. I pass the time lying in the sun munching granola bars, writing in my notebook, stretching my leg on a patch of lawn, and pacing on the pebbly path to keep my thigh limber. I wonder about the views I've missed, whether any heights have ignited Joe's vertigo, if Kees is feeling better, how Jim's knee is holding up, and if Sarah is managing as the only woman. She must feel like Wendy with Peter Pan and the Lost Boys. They should be here by about four o'clock. With just two hours to go, I make an attempt at beautification with my limited resources: freshly washed and sundried clothes, clean hair, and a touch of lip gloss will have to do.

In the molten light of late afternoon, it's almost five. They should already be here. My heart thumps—a flip-flopping fish on the floor of a boat. From the tiny open-air stone chapel, Notre Dame des Neiges, behind the *gîte*, a haunting hymn sung a cappella by a visiting choir carries through the trees, heightening my concern as I pace on the terrace.

The complaining hinges of the gate finally open, and Joe and Phil drag themselves in. I jump up saying, "Thank God, you made it!" My eyes meet Joe's and he holds them fast. I throw my arms around him as his pack thuds to the ground. "I was so worried because you're so late."

"The others are even farther behind," Phil says. "It was a long, tough day."

Joe returns my hug, buries his face in my hair, and then collapses in a chair. I give Phil a quick squeeze and he disappears into the bar for cold drinks. Joe has a hard time speaking, he's so spent, but he manages, "Babe. I am so happy to see you. To see you smiling. And upright. I felt so guilty for leaving you and was so afraid you'd be feeling worse. Kept picturing you unable to walk at all."

I sit next to him, fingers laced in his. "I'm better, I really am." I pull up my shorts to show him my thigh. "I know it's ugly, right? But it feels so much better than it looks and so much better than it did two days ago."

He caresses my thigh and closes his eyes. "Today was really, really hard, and I'm exhausted. I'm so sorry, but I just need a quick nap." He hands me his hat, his chin drops to his chest and he's out.

Phil returns guzzling a Coke and with an Orezza for Joe. "Looks like this'll have to wait." He hands me the bottle of water and then sits as he finishes his soda. "It wasn't the same without you, Marianne," he says and then burps, followed by an apology.

I laugh. "Definitely wasn't the same without you as well, Phil. Was actually pretty quiet." He burps again for emphasis and then goes on to fill me in on the terrain of the two days I missed. Lots of glacial lakes, some amazing views, and plenty of rocky climbs. He asks about my leg, I show him my bruise, tell him how I'm feeling, and share about my RA that may have complicated things. It feels good to have let him know about my uninvited guest.

"You should have told me before. I could have helped you out."

"I should have, Phil. You're right, as you always are. You're right about everything in the mountains."

He laughs. "Well, you're looking quite chipper, Marianne, so I hope you'll be coming with us tomorrow."

"We shall see. . . ."

After fifteen minutes, Kees and Chris arrive. They really were far behind.

"We missed you, Marianne," says Kees. I'm touched by his gentle offering and get up to give him Joe's water and a hug. Chris wastes no time heading straight inside with a quick salute. "Good to see you, Marianne." I follow him into the bar to buy a round of Orezzas. Twenty minutes later, Julien leads Sarah and Jim through the gate. Seeing Sarah's now familiar Life is Good T-shirt makes me smile. But Jim can barely walk. I hand each of them a bottle of water.

Sarah drops her things and gives me a huge hug. "I need a serious dose of estrogen, Marianne. Enough with just the boys."

"I missed you, Sarah. Can't tell you how happy I am to see you." She goes in to use the facilities while Jim and Julien go for drinks. Sarah returns and Jim soon follows. He says to now awake Joe, yawning Sarah, Kees, Phil, and me, "Just told the guys inside. I'm done. My knees have had it, and this just isn't fun anymore."

"Oh no," says Sarah. "I'm so sorry, Jim."

"Told myself I'd keep going as long as I was having a good time. But that ended at lunchtime yesterday. I'll take the train back to Bastia tomorrow, spend a couple days in town, and fly home from there."

Once I realize Jim is genuinely happy to be done, a childish thought flashes: at least I won't be the only one who didn't make it through all thirteen days.

"Am I crazy to feel that way?" I whisper to Joe.

"Absolutely not. I'm sure I'd feel the same if I'd quit like you."

I whack him with my notebook.

Julien and Chris join us on the terrace, and Julien proposes a toast, raising his beer. "*Santé* for all eight of us who are together tonight. We will lose James tomorrow, I am sad to have to say, and I do not know about Marianne, but for now, we are together." We clink our glasses, down our drinks.

I follow Julien back into the bar to have a word and then return to the terrace to collect my roommates. Joe and Sarah follow me to the *gîte* and I help them settle into our cozy room-for-three. Joe and I will be next to each other on the twins and Sarah takes the bottom bunk. While Joe showers, Sarah tells me about the past three days. "The terrain was tough, but I assure you, it was nothing like the first five days. And the food was crap. Overcooked pasta mostly, but Julien says tonight's meal will be good." She doesn't ask if I'll rejoin them as I'm sure she assumes I'll tell her when I'm ready. "Julien assured me that the stages we have left will be extra-long with brilliant views, but there won't be many scrambles and only a couple cables."

"Do you trust what Julien says?" I say laughing. "He does tend to soften things in his descriptions. . . ."

"It's true. He does. But what he said is actually what I heard from some other hikers yesterday. These next five days will be longer but have 'gentler edges,' is how they put it."

It's Sarah's turn for the shower, and while she's singing, Joe sits across from me on his bed, elbows on his knees. "So. Tell me about your days on your own."

I fill him in on Albertacce and my lunch at Chez Jojo's, on my terrifying taxi ride and my arrival at the *gîte*. But when it comes to telling him about Céline, I hold back. I lie down on my bed, toying with the curtain fringe. "I met a really nice French woman at the café by the train station," I tell him, but can't get much more out. I think about recounting our conversation, but the words sound trite. *We had tea and she told me to go easy on myself.* The clarity of emotion that surfaced while I was with her will dissolve like spun sugar if I try to explain. Joe is spent, and despite his best attempt, I know he can't focus on any serious conversation. I promise I'll tell him the rest of my story in the morning—but doubt I ever will. My afternoon with Céline will remain mine and mine alone.

"See you at dinner," Sarah says, showered and dressed, leaving for the canteen down the hall. I sit up, and Joe shifts over next to me on my bed. He lifts my chin with his finger. "So, Marianne," he says. "How *are* you?" And I know that what he means is, "Are you feeling good enough to come with us tomorrow?"

I straighten my spine and smile. "Vizzavona's not the end for me. I told Julien just now. I'm not going back to Bastia with Jim—I'll be back on The Twenty with you."

Of all the paths you take in life, make sure a few of them are dirt.

–John Muir

PART IV: CORSICA
DAYS NINE THROUGH THIRTEEN

Tuesday, August 9
The Hike–Day Nine: Col de Vizzavona to Col de Verde

↗ **Ascent:** 4,478 feet

↘ **Descent:** 4,062 feet

→ **Distance:** 13 miles

Guidebook Description: We have one of our longest treks today at thirteen miles.

In the crystalline air before dawn, Joe and I park ourselves on a picnic table and watch the new day come alive. What begins as a glimmer becomes a glow and then a tidal wave of light as we turn our faces toward the sun like flowers, soaking in its warmth. Joe pulls me close.

"I'm not very good at letting you help me, am I?" I say, putting my hand on his knee. "It's almost like I've trained you to let me fight battles—and Corsican trails—on my own." I take a sip of tea. "I thought about it a lot while you were away, and it's starting to become clear. Why I feel I have to be so independent and do things on my own. I know that I push away your help sometimes."

Joe raises his mug of coffee, takes a long gulp, and then looks straight ahead. "Definitely true. With whatever it is you're doing, you never want me hovering." He bends down to relace his boots and then sits back up. "You may not realize it, Marianne, but I can see it in your jaw. Right away. Whenever you think I haven't given you enough space or, even worse, that I'm babying you."

I nod, thinking hard, knowing he's right. "Except that sometimes I really do want you to help me. But I don't tell you and then I get mad that you haven't." I move my hand from his knee to under my chin, my elbow on my knee. "I guess I just always thought you would know. . . ."

"Do you see why I'm confused?" He picks up a chestnut and launches it into the trees. "How am I supposed to know about those few times when you want me to step in?"

I jump off the table, wince as my thigh pinches, and brush off my shorts. I turn to face him. "I'm really sorry, Joe. I am. I'm still a little baffled by it too, but I do think it's all starting to make sense to me. . . ."

"Breakfast," calls Julien from the canteen door. "Chestnut pancakes today. We will leave in one half hour."

"Ready to get back to The Twenty?" asks Sarah as we fill our water bladders at the canteen sink after saying goodbye to Jim.

"You have no idea. But I can tell you've been talking to Joe."

"We were talking the other day over dinner about the training you did, and he told us about that being your battle cry."

"I can't tell you how sick I was of hearing it by the time we got to Corsica."

"I would imagine! Well, so happy to have you back, Marianne. Didn't much like being the only woman, and I missed talking to you."

"Me too, Sarah. But I'm definitely back and ready for lots more chatting."

"Hey, what did Julien say when you told him you were coming with us?"

"He was terrific. Told me to take it easy and not to worry if I'm slow on the ascents. I'm going to carry my pack, but it'll be lighter. He'll take my share of the food and my sleeping bag. And Joe is taking a few things too."

"Brilliant! I think Julien missed you and your French, and I know for sure that Joe was pretty miserable without you. He kept saying things like, 'If Marianne were here. . . .' and 'I know Marianne would have loved this cheese. . . .'"

"Yup. Sounds just like him. And I have to say I was pretty miserable without him too. But as you told me, this leg needed some TLC." I pull up my shorts to show her my three-day old contusion—still red and purple in the middle but now less distinct around the edges—green and blue, yellow and brown. "It's still really ugly, but it hurts a whole lot less than it did."

"Well, I would keep that thing hidden for now," says Sarah. "Don't want you scaring anyone away."

I hold both trekking poles in one hand and pump my arms like pistons as we go up the road to the trailhead, my steps light, with only the hint of a hobble.

"Full of piss and vinegar, aren't you," Chris says from behind me.

"I am. Wind's in my sails. Got pep in my step. I'm like a dog with two tails. All those things."

I turn and see Joe roll his eyes, but he's smiling. "Good to see you being silly again."

"Feels good to be silly." I flash a cheesy smile, spread my fingers, and make jazz hands holding my sticks. "Can't even explain how much better I feel than that night at Castel di Verghio. But please don't worry about me today. I'm going to hang with Sarah, and I *promise* I'll let you know if I need help." My new resolution.

"You absolutely will?"

I nod. When you go ahead, as I want you to, just turn and check now and then."

"Done."

The skin on my shoulders has become tender after three days of leisure. But working in my favor is the fact that today's terrain will be less demanding and hard-edged than that of the first half. We have a thirteen-mile day ahead, the longest yet distance-wise. But from Vizzavona, the lowest point on The Twenty, the route is relatively clear-cut, and the gradient won't be as grueling, except for some initial steep zigzags, a chain or two, and a couple scrambles to reach the ridge.

"Ha!" says Sarah. "That's Julien's idea of straightforward?"

I shrug. "Not much we can do about it, right?"

So, up we go, geometry in our favor—a lot of ascent but over many more miles. While I'm still stuck in the sixty-year-old body I started this journey with, I've left my rebukes under the gîte's twin bed. I tell myself, *You* get *to do the ninth day of this hike instead of you* have *to do it.* I'm filled with new energy, my mind clear, muscles loose.

I'm breathing hard as we go up an old mule track, my footfalls matching Sarah's, or maybe she's slowing hers to match mine. I just continue stepping gently through the soreness in my right leg, favoring my left. *Be happy with how you hike*, I tell myself. *You're like a tortoise, slow and steady but always reaching the finish line.*

Joe is just ahead, and he often turns to check on me. I give him the okay sign. Before long, Sarah and I are beyond earshot, and she belts out Sly and the Family Stone's "I Want to Take You Higher." This time I join her in song, my soprano to her alto, reveling in the unbridled joy of this and other climbing tunes. We stop and improvise with our hiking poles as microphones. Even the guys, if they could hear us, would have to admit we're pretty good.

We catch up with our crew and a dozen other hikers late in the morning when everything has slowed to a crawl. Literally.

"Joe, do you mind taking my poles?" I ask. "It's just. . . ."

"Say no more. I got them." He takes my poles and attaches them to his pack with his. "Asking me to help wasn't that hard now, was it?"

We go down on all fours since using our hands is the only way to advance on this long stretch of scrambling. Finally back on our feet, we take turns squeezing through claustrophobic rock columns with the help of long cables. I let my arms do most of the work. Once up top, we're on a broad, bare saddle with sweeping vistas over fertile plains on Corsica's eastern coast. Time to use our poles again.

"What'd you think of the morning?" Joe asks over lunch. "Pretty tough, right?"

"It was, but I actually like the scrambles and the cables. The views were so gorgeous, and I just focused on that. Plus, Sarah and I sang most of the way and she had me laughing with silly stories about her family. And by the way, Joe—I saw you turning to check on me pretty often. Appreciate it."

"After what happened a few days ago, of course I checked on you.

But I knew you were with Sarah, so I wasn't too worried. Leg holding up so far? And your RA?"

"My quad's still sore, but my painkillers are taking the edge off. I just keep relying on my left leg more than my right. And my joints, well, they're achy too, but nothing I can't deal with."

Joe shakes his head. "Listen, I didn't say it before—didn't want to jinx things this morning." He stops, his eyes misty. "But I can't believe you're actually back on the trail with me." He stops again. "When I saw what your leg looked like a few days ago, I thought for sure you'd have to drop out. For good. And it terrified me, thinking you might be hurt so badly. I'm just so, so proud of you."

"Thanks. Means the world to me. I'm just going to take one step and one day at a time. That, and to let you know when I need help."

"I think you're on your way, Miss Independent."

"And I think I've learned my lesson. If I need help, I have to ask."

He squeezes my thigh without thinking. "Sorry," he says as I cry out. "I swear I'll save any more leg touching for after we're done."

"Promise?"

He nods.

"Well then, I definitely have that to look forward to." I lean over to kiss him.

Post-lunch, we pick our way down a steep, rocky slope. Sarah and her knees struggle with each step, so it's now my turn to adjust my pace to stay back with her. We reach a secluded mountain pool, its perimeter dotted with yellow and red wildflowers. Before Julien has the chance to suggest a stop, Sarah ducks behind a bush to slip on her bathing suit and Phil strips to his briefs. They splash into the deep, dark water and are doing the backstroke before I can unlace my boots.

The rest of us wade to our thighs, all except Chris. Boots, socks, and shirt off, he stands tall on a rock, hands on his hips, head and chest high, staring up the rise. I follow his sightline to where two German girls in their twenties, sisters we met at breakfast this morning, approach. Chris is transfixed and I know what he's thinking: *Might they accept an invitation to a GR20 pool party?* After hours of hiking, our group is bedraggled, but the *fräuleins* appear fresh and rosy-cheeked, their long, tight braids wound round their heads. Hiking briefs cut across their firm thighs and hug the rounds of their bottoms. Their toned arms—youthful limbs capable of anything— give a wave as Chris calls, "Cheers!" But they veer away, maintaining their pace, avoiding the possibility of an invitation.

Sarah says in her oh-so-sophisticated British way, "A youth-worshipper I'm not, and I don't expect to look like I did when I was twenty, but don't you miss, just a little bit, being as lean as they are?"

"I'm sure I was never as lean as they are." I laugh. "But would you really say goodbye to all our wisdom and experience to have bodies like theirs? Give up our crow's feet, less-than-perky breasts, and sagging butts?"

"Sarah?" I ask when there's no reply.

"Give me a minute—I'm thinking."

Cresting the stony mountain behind the lake, we gaze over the vast valley below. A lush green grassland oasis dotted with mini lakes defies its mountainous rocky rim. It gives the impression that pieces of lawn are floating on an expanse of water. Is this gentle interlude real, or are we hallucinating?

Julien assures us we are not. "The lakes are called *pozzines*. It's from the Corsican word *pozzi*. It means water wells."

We step lightly after the difficult broken rock descent to the marshy basin. It's like a golf course green scattered with herds of cows, sheep, pigs, and wild horses grazing—welcome spongy turf for battered feet. To the clank of cowbells, the cushioned pasture takes us to the final descent and the Col de Verde, a scattering of cabins, campsites, and a café in the middle of dense coniferous forest.

We drop our loads, and Joe buys Julien a glass of *myrte*, a beloved Corsican eau-de-vie, made from myrtle leaves and deep blue berries. Julien gives me a taste of the fruity liqueur, redolent of rosemary and which Corsicans hold as a sacred symbol of fertility. I buy myself a glass and a beer for Joe.

"This *myrte* is *délicieuse*," says Julien, "but my girlfriend—my Corsican girlfriend—makes the best one. It is a secret recipe of her *grand-mère*. She will not even tell me how to make it."

Over drinks on the shady umbrellaed deck, Julien breaks the news that tonight we'll be sleeping under one roof in bunk beds—six of us in one cabin. He, of course, will be atop an alfresco picnic table. None of the men reacts to the announcement, but I look over and see Sarah roll her eyes and shrug. All I can think is, I don't much care where I sleep as long as I'm back with my team.

We shower in soothing solar-warmed water as daylight dissolves to darkness and swifts initiate their noisy, screeching calls, swooping above and then dipping into the trees. Bellies sated with crispy pork grilled over an open wood fire, we retire to our bunks, all save Chris and Julien who stay in the tavern for the trail version of karaoke night. Although not planning to sing, Chris is on the prowl. "Who knows?" he says. "The Deutschland sisters may make an appearance." Julien announces that he'll actually be part of the show. "You might be surprised. I play the guitar, and my singing, especially Corsican songs, is actually very good."

My legs are heavy as they push me up the ladder to an upper

berth. I slip into my sleeping bag and lie back on the mattress—a bit of welcome softness after thirteen miles of sharp edges. My thigh muscle pulses gently, but I actually enjoy the throb. It distracts me from my sore wrists and inflamed knuckles and reminds me of what I managed to do today.

From the fireside in the bar just steps away come ambient sounds: hushed conversation, spirited laughter, the strum of a guitar, and Julien's tender crooning. Melancholy strains of *lamentu*, Corsica's beloved folk music that tells stories about death, departure, and shadow realms, drift through the pines, oozing the longing and ache of shepherds and their kinsmen whose lives of unrealized dreams of liberation have disappointed. I recall what I read about the island's polyphonic choral tradition, central to Corsican identity and evoking the music of so many of the island's serial inhabitants: pagan mantras, Islamic prayer, Christian hymns, and sacred madrigals. For a time in the 1970s, *lamentu* was declared illegal, authorities fearing the keening laments and incendiary lyrics stoked the longing for independence into fiery rage.

"Whenever Corsicans, especially men, get together," Julien told us over dinner, "there is *lamentu* music. It is very important to all the people of this island." I finally drift off to the all-male a cappella harmonies, layered, vibrating voices reminiscent of the medieval music of the Latin masses of my childhood.

I awaken with a jolt. What was that? Has a woodland critter found its way into our little cabin? I listen carefully. Silence. Must have imagined it. But then, just as I relax, the stillness is shattered by the splutters and grunts of late-night snoring. Apparently, it's time to make some noise. Is snoring, like flatulence, worse at higher elevations? And just when I think the racket can't get any worse, a series of God-awful eruptions explodes from Phil's berth across the room.

"Oh, God," I say out loud. The rumble of long complaining farts now punctuates the snoring tsunami. It's a full-on HAFE cacophony.

"'Oh God' is right," says Joe from the bunk below. My stomach soon aches from laughing so hard.

Wednesday, August 10
The Hike–Day Ten:
Col de Verde to Cozzano

↗ **Ascent:** 2,927 feet

↘ **Descent:** 4,724 feet

→ **Distance:** 13 miles

Guidebook Description: Today a forest trail ascends steeply up through the woods onto a high ridge and then descends into a Corsican village.

M orning dawns on a foul note. The place needs serious airing. I slide down from my bunk to prop open the cabin door with my backpack. My companions are stirring and I see that Phil is sitting up in his bunk, rolling his massager over his thighs.

"Morning Phil," I say, climbing back up to my bed. "Sleep well?"

"I did, and if I were feeling any better today, Marianne, it'd be a little scary." He chuckles, as usual, amusing himself. I do envy Phil's eternal sunshine.

"Too bad the rest of us can't say the same," says Joe. "From now on I'm calling you 'Phil-harmonic.' You were making some serious music last night."

"You call that music?" Sarah asks, ruffling her bedhead.

"I think all the beans we've been eating has supercharged my digestive system," says Phil.

"I'm surprised your sleeping bag didn't levitate with all that hot air," says Joe.

Dawn becomes day as we set off for Cozzano, a granite village in a green valley, for a taste of rural Corsican life. Julien explains that the island's real estate laws are written to keep family property together. "It is very *difficile* to sell your house or your land to someone outside the family. But because so many people move to mainland France with no family left on Corsica, they cannot sell their property. That is why you will see many houses and farms with no one living there. We will see some in Cozzano."

"So they're basically abandoned?" I ask.

"Yes, I am afraid it is so." Julien shakes his head as he heads up the trail.

"Sounds to me," I say to Joe, "that so much on Corsica is about keeping the family together, but sometimes there are unintended consequences. Like lots of deserted villages with homes in bad shape."

"Maybe it'll get so bad that they'll change the laws at some point."

But it seems to me that the laws, like so much of the Corsican character, will be nearly impossible to change.

Joe hikes ahead of me, hanging behind the others so he can keep me in his sights. His vigilance and thumbs-ups make me smile. The morning is cool, but when we switchback up the valley of a narrow torrent and cut straight up past the tree line, we're in the teeth of another scorching day. By the time the two of us reach the spot for our lunch picnic next to dozens of grazing cows, the others are halfway through their meal, and Kees and Chris are already napping. But I'm perfectly content to have arrived late. Joe fixes and hands me a plate that includes generous hunks of bread and sheep cheese.

"How's the eggplant?" he asks.

"Hanging in there. But it definitely needs this break. Thank God the rest of today is downhill so my poles can rescue me."

"Definitely a good thing," he says, taking a bite of wild boar sausage. "You know, until I asked, you haven't mentioned your leg even once today. Those three days off must have been what you needed."

"They were *exactly* what I needed."

We cross a high plateau, grassy and stream-laced, to the Arête a Monda, a long craggy north–south rim. The eastern views are to the sea and Italy's Tuscany on the horizon. To the west is the expanse of a broad tree-filled valley dotted with jumbles of orange-roofed villages, including Cozzano, our destination. We stop and look back north across what we've hiked and see Monte Cinto and Paglia Orba, well behind us in the distance.

"Would you look at that," says Sarah. "Look how far we've come."

"I love Monte Cinto," says Julien. "But like I told you, Paglia Orba is so special. Look at that shark fin."

I glance at the distinctive peaks on the horizon, but then my sight rests on the verdant area of Vizzavona. I remember Céline and think, yes, indeed. We've come so far.

Ahead, the trail crosses convolutedly from one side of the ridge to the other, as dictated by the openings in the rocks. "I know you are all very tired, so you must be careful," says Julien. "This next part is *difficile*. I think you say "tricky" in English, so you must watch every step so you do not twist the ankles. Go over the rocks right where I go because I will pick the most safe way." So, back and forth we go until our descent to Cozzano.

He sits below us on a rock, leaning over, hands on his knees. His sleeveless tee is spattered with fresh red blood creeping through the cotton, as is his face from a deep gash on his forehead. A female companion stands with her arms above her in a "Y," the international Alpine distress signal. *Yes, I need help.* Sarah drops her pack to rush down. Julien follows.

"*Qu'est-ce qui s'est passé?*" she asks the man's two younger companions. What happened? We all stand back, allowing the doctor and our guide to tend to him. He's about our age and, evidently, this is not his first injury. His leg is banged up with red-blue bruises and he has scabbed-over cuts on his arms and hands. The man is quiet, dazed, letting his friends do the talking.

"He lost his balance, hit his head, and then fell down several feet," says the woman in Eastern European-accented English.

Sarah cleans his face with supplies from Julien's first aid kit and then covers his wound with a bandage to stanch the bleeding. She asks him to follow her finger with his eyes, helps him stand, and then says to Julien, "Let's stay just a few more minutes." She turns to the injured hiker. "Want to be sure you're stable." She looks down at his legs. "It looks like you can carry on if you take it easy, but you need medical attention as soon as possible."

He nods. "Thank you," he says, finally speaking, pausing between words. "I am so grateful."

Julien says to the hiker's companions, "Take the trail below to the right and you will get to a village more quickly. Cozzano, where we are going, is too far away." We wish the hikers well—*bonne chance et bon courage*—and continue down the trail to the left. It reminds me that a false sense of security is never good.

"It is that grabby granite," says Julien. "It will slice the leg or the face if you fall. I am sorry the man is hurt, but think it is good to see this. We must remember how dangerous the mountains are and that there are accidents. They are very beautiful, yes, but they can be, how do you say it, Marianne? *Mortel.*"

"Deadly. They can be deadly."

"Hey, Babe. Turn and look at me. This shot is perfect with the sun coming through the trees." I swing my head to look back.

"Aren't you going to turn all the way around? You know, no pictures from behind?"

"Nah. Go ahead. Shoot away." I'm done being bothered by the breadth of my bum. Thank you, Sarah. Merci, Céline.

After seven hours on the trail, more than half of them in descent, we arrive at the Bella Vista gîte just outside Cozzano village. Straightaway, Julien, Sarah, Kees, Phil, and Chris head out to explore. Today happens to be Cozzano's summer festival that celebrates the village's patron saints, and parties will go on well into the night. It's only a quarter mile into town, but it might as well be ten. As much as I'd love to join them, my body screams, and I listen. My leg needs to be iced, and I'm not walking another foot. Joe gets a bag of cubes from the owner, and we sit on the terrace with a Pietra and an Orezza, trying to figure out which buildings on the street are abandoned, until my thigh is numb.

The *gîte*'s common room has huge sinks for washing clothes and plenty of hot water. We take long luxurious showers and then do laundry, hanging it on the branches of a fruit-laden pear tree. For the second night in a row, we'll share bunks in one room. This time, however, there's a wide glass door through which afternoon sun bathes the bedroom. Tonight we'll leave that door open to prepare for Phil-harmonic.

Thursday, August 11
The Hike–Day Eleven:
Cozzano to Crocce

↗ **Ascent:** 4,580 feet

↘ **Descent:** 1,946 feet

→ **Distance:** 13 miles

Guidebook Description: We start by ascending through maquis scrubland and then a thick chestnut forest to reach the highest plateau on Corsica.

Julien says over breakfast, "We must leave very soon because today the weather will change. There will first be sun and then rain, and I think we will have a storm. But we will try to get to the refuge at Crocce before everything starts."

"What does *everything* mean?" asks Joe.

"Everything means everything. Rain, wind, thunder, and lightning. And maybe some hail and snow."

Joe leans back, lifts his hand, and rubs his neck. The mention of an electrical storm puts his engineer brain on high alert, conjuring danger, while all I can think is, *Please don't let it get too cold.*

"Be sure you can take out your bad weather gear quickly," says Julien. "Mountain weather changes fast."

Chris arrives just as we're packing up to leave.

"And when did you leave the village *fête*, Christopher?" asks Julien. "It was already very late when I said *bonne nuit* to you."

"Actually, just got back. Had enough time for a shower, though." He takes a bite of his energy bar and says not another word.

The inevitable ascent out of Cozzano's valley is a brutal effort. We have to regain over three thousand feet just to get back on the GR20. I give myself a pep talk: *I'll get there when I get there. Don't try to keep up and don't you dare scold.* I focus on the wind in my hair and the satisfaction of being able to walk on my own, no matter how slowly.

The climb takes hours through thick brush and then chestnut wood, back and forth across a steep fire road. The sun soon blazes despite a rippling, mackerel sky, and I remove my layers until I'm down to just a tee. Now and then big-eared pigs tag along, their presence and their snorts as they search for fallen chestnuts distracting me from my thigh. When we started this hike, I can't say I thought much about chestnut trees at all, but I'm now keenly aware of them, Corsican companions for a lifetime.

I stop and look back over the orange tile roofs of the village, now in miniature. I smile and shake my head, having seen Chris, not far ahead, stop frequently to bend over and breathe. He's having some difficulty coping with this climb after his festival all-nighter toasting Cozzano's saints. Despite his exhaustion, however, I suspect that seeing the sunrise with the Cozzano carousers will be a highlight of his vacation.

I'm just behind the group when we reach the Bocca de l'Agnone, gateway to the Plateau de Coscione, where the rocks give way mercifully to undulating grassland, the highest on Corsica. As Julien predicted, a front is on the way, sudden, fierce gusts driving ominous convection clouds across the sky. By lunchtime, the clouds have dissolved into a fine mist and the sky has turned pewter. Our midday meal is a quick affair, as we need to beat the storm to Crocce.

"I think we will arrive by three if we are fast," says Julien, checking his watch.

The reek of wet grass and earth greets us as we cross the lush stream- and gully-riddled moorland. On terrain that allows easy conversation but under an increasingly troubled sky, I talk to Kees. His few sweet words of two days ago—when he told me he missed me in Vizzavona—have me wanting to know more about him. "You know, the first half of The Twenty was definitely harder but the second half seems more remote." I see him nod. Always the reticent man.

We pass a herd of cows, huddled with their heads down, and I try another tack. "Was hiking the only sport you and your wife shared?"

"One of the things Liese used to say was, 'Children always look for adventure, so why not big children too?' She always wanted us to do exciting things."

"I totally agree with her. So what else did you and Liese do together?"

"We did many things, even when our children were little."

"How many children do you have, Kees?" I ask.

"Two sons. We did many family hikes and biked. We also skied, mostly in the Alps."

"Did you travel much?"

"Yes, in Europe. Whenever we could. But once the boys were grown, they were busy with jobs and their own travel, so Liese and I just went on our own."

I hesitate before sharing what I say next, but decide to forge ahead. "Thanks for talking to me about Liese, Kees. You know, when I was in Vizzavona for those three days, I met a widow who told me that if we don't talk about those we've lost, they'll never be at peace." And I think, *perhaps neither will you, Kees.* "So I think it's really good that you talk about your wife." Kees is silent for a few moments, and I fear I've upset him.

"Thank you for asking about her," he says as he dabs at his eyes. "I should talk more about her. I think it will help me."

I give him a few minutes before I switch subjects, remembering that when we first met, he told us he was an attorney. "What kind of lawyer are you, Kees?"

"I work with refugees. So many come to my country, and they all have very sad stories. I do what I can to help them, but it can take years to get them papers."

An enigmatic man with such a soft heart. *Still waters,* I think. *They do run deep.*

We're now under stifling humidity pressing from above and shrouded in thick fog. The visibility is near zero, beyond us only gray. Kees and I are in the rear with Sarah and Chris, moisture glistening on our hair. As expected, Chris is significantly slower than usual. I've insisted Joe go ahead as I'm in good company. Clumpy, soft hummocks squelch under our boots, and I shriek when I accidentally sink into a spongy spot to my ankles, icy snowmelt seeping into my boots. My socks are now soaked and crumpled under my heels. Kees plods ahead while Chris and Sarah, who have also fallen prey to the sodden moss, stop with me to wring out our socks and add extra layers.

"This weather is evil," says Chris as we don woolen hats, pulling them over our ears. "Looks like it's going to be a rowdy afternoon."

"Wasn't it just a few hours ago we were moaning about the heat?" asks Sarah.

"I think it's dropped twenty degrees in ten minutes," I say, seeing my breath.

The three of us now lag well behind as we leave the treeless plateau and enter the misty gloom of a primeval chestnut forest. Mountain gullies thick with ferns, layers of white tree mushrooms, and mossy vines crisscross the wood. The perfect place for Corsican sprites.

"Look," says Chris, "a fire salamander. There, on the right."

And sure enough, a slimy six-inch salamander, black and splotched with vivid yellow markings all the way down its long tail, is crossing a shallow stream. Chris bends down, and Sarah drops to her knees to get a closer look at the amphibian, now frozen in its path. I squeal with schoolgirl delight as I crouch next to Sarah. "I have never, ever seen one before. Had to come all the way to Corsica!" I can't take my eyes off this slim blunt-snouted creature—much better than a sprite.

"Let's consider ourselves lucky," says Chris. "Salamanders only come out in wet weather. Our timing is perfect."

We study its splayed digits at the end of short limbs that project at right angles to its body. It finally advances its legs slowly, deliberately, like a baby crawling, one limb after another. How appropriate that we've come across this mythical creature in a magical wood.

"You guys know salamanders were the symbol of the French king Francis I? And that people believed they were born from fire?" I ask.

"I knew about the first thing but not the second," says Sarah. "Interesting."

"Well, there's definitely no fire here, and we really should go," says Chris, looking up into the trees and then down the trail. "I can't see anyone ahead, and it's getting bloody cold." He pulls his gloves from his pocket. Sarah and I do the same.

Determined drizzle intensifies, and then the first fat raindrops fall, splatting on the ground like so many ripe berries, creating wide saucer ripples in the stream. I hear heavy drops drip from drooping branches. The heavens crack open abruptly, shaking the ground with elemental thunder. The air is suddenly electric, and a dead branch whips across my cheek. Beneath detonations, we hustle from the hollow to open, treeless highland where the others await us on the rise.

"*On y va!*" shouts Julien, the minute we're back together. It's clear he means business. Let's go!

I gush about the salamander as Joe increases his pace. "It was just the coolest thing, and you missed it. Never thought I would see one of them in the wild. They're actually kind of cute."

Joe swings around and crushes my chirpiness, his expression pinched. "Tell me later, okay? Or someone's going to get hurt." He speeds up and turns to be sure I can keep up.

I do feel a bit ridiculous because Joe's right to be dramatic, of course. There are more important things to think about than remarkable forest creatures. His fear of lightning for one, and the fact that shelter is still miles away. While I'm determined to go easy on myself, driving hard now could literally mean the difference between life and death.

"We've got to get ahead of this or none of us will make it safely. Especially at this altitude. The storm is close." His words are strained and tight.

I quicken my step but can only go so fast, fear and quad strain creeping in as the temperature continues to plummet. I take a deep breath and force myself to ask, "Joe, can you take my pack? Please?"

"Of course! Let me have it. Should have taken it sooner."

I hand it over and unburdened am able to accelerate my steps.

We witness a fit of fundamental fury under an angry purple and yellow sky. Against the bruise-colored backdrop reminiscent of my thigh, flickers of lightning illuminate the landscape. The heavens open and we morph from determined hikers to drowned rats on a long march. Sharp bursts of hail rattle around us, and ice pellets bite my cheek and forehead before I can pull my hat down further and my bandanna up. My fingers have lost all feeling despite my gloves, and my joints stiffen in the cold. I shiver uncontrollably and am careful not to bite my tongue. Forget about exciting—this is now perilous.

Bad-tempered thunder rumbles closer, like wooden casks tumbling from on high. A sudden crack I feel in my chest is so sharp it seems a celestial boulder has been rent asunder. What were distant skewers past the mountains are now proximate zigzags of electricity, several hitting the ground. I follow on Joe's heels, hoping he's okay. I count the time between flashes and claps—*one Mississippi, two Mississippi*—never making it to three. I wish we could stop to watch the meteorological show, but being caught in an electrical storm in the mountains is not the time to observe. My shoulders tense and I lengthen my stride, recalling Julien's warning about hikers killed by lightning. It's now dangerously close. Thick fog has rolled in, and we're submarines in pea soup, barely able to make out each other's silhouettes. I allow my drowning thoughts to race over the peaks, across the sea, and back to the golden fields of Provence. Perhaps if I imagine myself in Luberon heat, I'll stop shaking.

As if my Provençal summons has taken charge, the fog thins and lightning sprays weaken, leaving only faraway flickers and receding rumbles. The downpour has turned to a foggy rain. Through the mist, we can now see a gentle rise topped by our day's destination: the stone Bergerie de Crocce surrounded by tents, like mounds on the moon.

We arrive, faces chapped red from our August encounter with

winter. Our cold soaked clothes give off clouds of steam when we warm by the fireplace in the mess hall.

"They delivered our duffels here, right Julien?" asks Sarah, anxious to change clothes.

"*Oui*. They are in the barn, a little up the hill. We will go outside, and I will show you." Must we leave this cozy hearth so soon?

"Over there." He points to a low gulag-like, cement-block structure two hundred yards up the hill.

"You mean where those pigs are jumping out?" asks Phil.

"*Merde!*" says Julien, who takes off running.

"They'd better not have my dry clothes," says Chris.

"And they damned well better not have taken my hair wash," says Sarah.

Everyone manages to sprint after Julien. I do my best with a race-walk.

A half-dozen hogs the size of hippos escape the concrete cube, scrambling over each other and wooden barriers meant to keep them out. They do look happy, and why not? Their mouths are full of granola bars and crackers, apples and apricots . . . wrappers, cores, and all.

"*Fiche-moi le camp!*" says Julien, wildly gesticulating to chase away the thieves. Get lost!

"Go eat your own slop," I call.

"Leave ours alone!" Sarah shouts.

I look over at her and we dissolve into laughter. Contagious hilarity overtakes us all as we climb over the barricade to survey the damage. Inside, it smells of wet hay, farm animals, and sugar.

"*Zut,*" says Julien. Damn. "They ate all our cookies."

I wait my turn outside Crocce's primitive dirt-floored toilet barely shielded behind vertical wooden planks, two inches between each slat. A sound like balloons bursting in a barrel of yogurt emanates from the stall. Trail food isn't agreeing with someone's system. Could be awhile. I duck behind a nearby rock.

The shower stall is constructed like the toilets, but without a door, the earth dank and slimy underfoot. How audacious we've become in our nakedness, I think, because there's no place for privacy on The Twenty. I strip frantically, peeling off still-soaked layers, chilly air touching my pale breasts and buttocks. From head to toe I'm cold and pruney, as if I'd been in the ocean all day. I yearn for unlimited steaming water but have to make do with two minutes in the luke-warm flow. I then struggle to pull on my dry clothes over damp skin. There's no line waiting outside, so I stay in the cool stall for longer than needed, reluctant to go back into the biting wind.

And it dawns on me as I stand there shivering, lifting my leg to go into my pants: *Memorize this moment in a makeshift shower on a Corsican hill. Life isn't always about running from the rain and avoiding what hurts. Take it in. Embrace it all.*

The canteen is humid, its windows fogged. We sit on long benches at heavy tables, a fire raging, logs crackling. I add my dank, smelly boots to the line of others drying on the hearth and hang my wet clothes from hooks along the side. The thunder is back and, while remote, it rattles the roof, the lamps on the wall quiver, lights flickering.

"Cocktail time," says Joe when I slip in across from him, despite the earlier than usual hour. Our still-glacial cores need some red wine at once. It's Sarah's turn to buy, so she delivers a tall carafe and overpours my glass, crimson pooling around the base.

"Oh no, Sarah!" I pretend to cry. "I need every single drop to thaw me out because that shower sure didn't do the job."

"Plenty more where that came from," she says. "After surviving that storm, I'll buy two rounds! Cheers for getting us here safely, Julien."

We clink our glasses and are quiet as we lap up liquid relief, Chris with a Pietra, Phil with a Coke, and the rest of us with hearty Corsican red.

"Definitely helping my chilblains," says Sarah, rubbing her hands and then emptying her glass. "Think we need to worry that they're filling the carafes from gigantic bottles with no labels?"

"But that is the best kind of wine," says Julien. "Family recipes."

Sarah buys a second round ("Cheers to being warm and dry!") and Joe buys the third ("Here's to our final two days on the trail!"). And so it goes for the next several hours, right through our dinner of *figatellu*—a pork and liver sausage, pasta with ham and vegetables, and fig cake for dessert.

We've barely moved since we sat down hours ago, except to buy and deliver drinks. And we've all resorted to speaking in short sentences. Complicated expressions are beyond our abilities. But it's finally time to retire when I see Joe get up slowly, motioning toward the door.

Sarah gets up too, holding onto the table to steady herself. "Well, I'm afraid I'm a bit squiffed tonight. This wine fest's done me in."

I stand, feeling the same—a woozy blur of alcohol and exhaustion. It's pitch-black outside and the air is thick with moisture. Between the wine and slapping wind, we barely manage a straight line. I expect a carpet of brilliance above, but the resurgent fog won't allow a single star to shine through.

I awaken in the middle of the night to the heavy drum of rain on the tent. I cuddle close to Joe, burying my face in his salty neck, breathing in his spicy smell. He doesn't move, not even a stir. Sarah and I definitely weren't the only ones overserved.

Friday, August 12
The Hike–Day Twelve:
Crocce to Col de Bavella

↗ **Ascent:** 3,130 feet

↘ **Descent:** 4,173 feet

→ **Distance:** 11 miles

Guidebook Description: An alpine path leads up and over a tricky rocky section and the famous granite peaks of Bavella.

I awaken to the wind's rattle. We've slept for ten full hours, and it looks like Joe may make it to eleven. I watch a bug inch its way across the outside of the tent until a strong gust blows it away. I dress quickly and peek out to smell sweet morning air on the open plain under a low enveloping sky. The clouds are thick, but sparkling slivers of post-storm light manage to slice though. Shadows of hikers inside translucent tents dress for another day on the trail, and a string of swine sashays up past us to the outbuildings for breakfast.

A headache bites at my hairline, and my stomach rumbles. I desperately need bread to soak up last night's liquid. I wonder if Sarah feels the same. No loud noises are allowed this morning, so I whisper

to Joe, gently rousing him, "See you up at breakfast." I've no indica-
tion he's heard me.

"A little wobbly?" asks Sarah, alone at the breakfast table. "I'm on
my second cup of tea and my second baguette." She hands me the
basket of bread. "But what I really need is a proper breakfast. Where
are the buttered eggs and bacon?"

"No such luck, but I think I'm going to be like you and need three
cups of tea to make it through the morning."

"That and a gallon of ice water."

"I swear I'm not complaining—this bread and butter is delicious—
but you know what I'd really like right now?"

"Chocolate ice cream?"

"A big bowl of cold creamy vichyssoise sprinkled with fresh chives
and, of course, lots and lots of salt. My stomach and my head are
crying for sodium, and I'm not sure I can get enough briny food."

"You really are a salt fiend, aren't you? I would take a bowl of ice
cream over a bowl of soup any day, even after a night of too much
wine."

"I'm just going to close my eyes and dream about cold potato soup.
Either that or a salt lick." I rest my forehead on my arms folded on the
table, willing the pounding to go away.

In the summertime damp, we head up a denuded sandy slope to
the col, a dull plod compared to what we've become used to. Julien
and Phil well ahead and upright, despite steady gusts. The rest of
us lean into the wind like scrub pines slumping to Mother Nature's
will. The morning tramps by in a blur, my throbbing temples distracting from muscle pain. From the pass, we catch our first glimpse
of the famous Aiguilles de Bavella (the Needles of Bavella)—sharp,

towering granite spikes, dominating the horizon and rising like so many church spires—through which we'll climb this afternoon.

"How's your head?" asks Joe as we take a break before a remarkably sudden descent.

"Finally stopped hammering, but now my stomach is screaming for protein. Yours?"

"Just realizing I need some aspirin."

I drop my pack and pull out my pouch of pills. Four please," he says. I swallow two on top of the two I took at breakfast. Neither of us is in the mood for conversation.

We lose two thousand feet over a short distance with knee-shattering steps straight down the rocky face. Phil hops his way ahead of us. I could never do it without my poles. Julien stops and points to the head of the valley.

"That is where the Réfuge d'Asinau was," he says, "before the fire. You see the black place way down there and the tent?" We look down on a doublewide yurt of white canvas by the side of a charcoal wasteland.

"On March twenty-fifth this year, Asinau burned to the ground."

"What a shame," says Sarah. "Lightning?"

"I speak no words about it," says Julien, looking down at the charred brush and white-gray dust. "It is a Corsican affair."

I look at Sarah, both of us wide-eyed.

Chris jumps in. "You mean like a Sicilian affair—omertà and all that?"

"I say no more."

Sarah and I remain astonished. Sounds like Julien doesn't want to be on the wrong end of a gun barrel.

Wobbly legged, we reach the yurt, the air tinged with five-month-old smoke. At the edge of a ring of dust is a forest boneyard, black and burned like knobby fingers.

"Spooky," I say to Phil. "You have any idea what happened?"

"Actually, I heard it was a 'business decision.'" He makes air quotes with his fingers. "The owner of another refuge set the fire so hikers would change their route and go to his place instead. They say he even adjusted the blazes for the trail, but who knows? Corsicans just don't like competition."

Julien approaches. Speculation ends.

A wizened old man with hands that shake sells cold drinks and snacks inside the tent. I feel I've hit the jackpot when I see his offerings include a tray of hard-boiled eggs.

"Sarah," I call. "Quick!" We each buy two. We sit on a rock and I take out my salt shaker.

Sarah says, "I have to admit, I thought Joe was daft giving you salt as a gift, but now I think it's brilliant. Willing to share?" We dust our eggs in sodium and devour them. I go back for two more.

The trail heads into the valley beneath the imposing Aiguilles de Bavella. It becomes a gentle path padded with pine needles as it follows a stream on the valley floor.

"It will take much climbing to get up to the *fabuleuses* views from les Aiguilles," says Julien. "They are some of the best *vues panoramiques* on Corsica. Do not hurry because we have a lot of time. But your legs will pay the price for what we see from the top." His propensity for sugarcoating is well behind us.

I hope his comments are directed at me because I do plan to take my time. This is our second to last day on the trail, and I am going to enjoy it.

"Just how hard *will* it be, Julien?" asks Sarah.

"There is nothing more hard than our first three days. It is *difficile*, but you will not have a problem, Sarah."

I have four hard-boiled eggs in my belly to sustain me, I think. Four eggs and a teaspoon of salt.

The trail cuts sharply to the left and pulls up immediately. The ascent is steep and gets steeper still when we leave a thick, ragged stretch of maquis to look up at the wall of red rock towers. I'm already the caboose, but I pay it no mind as Joe waits for me on a rare flat rock. I drop my pack, still lightened by Julien and Joe, to get us some energy chews. We see a ferry on the sea far in the distance and anticipate sailing back to the mainland—only a couple weeks away.

"Can't get nostalgic about this effort just yet," Joe says.

"I know. Still a day and a half to go, Mr. Positivity."

As we enjoy our breather, just below us two adult sheep appear. "Look, Joe. Mouflons! And they're so close."

"I think we're the only two to see them—everyone else is too far ahead."

"Aren't you glad you hung back with me?" I hit his shoulder with my fist. "Being first and going fast isn't always the best way to go."

"True. Being a slowpoke does have its advantages." He hands me the wrapper from his chew.

Back on the trail at the base of the famous jagged pinnacles, we scramble over loose stones and rough boulders on the final haul to the top. Everyone waits for us before a very steep chain-assisted section, where Julien coaches us up, one by one. "Thank God we're doing this now and not this morning," says Sarah. "Not sure my head could have handled it."

"I know my stomach couldn't have." I hold my arms across my abs.

We pick our way around the bottom of the Aiguilles and have a long lunch break to take advantage of the panorama toward the west, including a sparkling slice of the Gulf of Ajaccio.

"Can you believe tonight is our last on the trail?" Joe says, sitting next to me, sharing a wedge of cheese.

"I can't, but it's even harder to believe that I'm still here on day twelve. I just don't know whether to be happy or sad, though. I'll be ecstatic to be back to hot showers and real beds, but sad too. About going back to civilization."

"Guess I'm feeling the same, but my body is fried. Psychologically, I prepped myself for thirteen days, and I don't think I could do even an hour more."

"You *must* be fried. At least I had a three-day breather."

"But you were injured—and that must have taken a lot out of you." He puts his arm around my shoulders. "And now you're going to *finish* The Twenty. You're going all the way to Conca."

We spill from the woods onto the road at the Col de Bavella. There's a towering white statue atop a pile of rocks—Notre Dame des Neiges—dotted with candles, tiny plastic statues, and other offerings overlooking the touristy jumble of accommodations, cafés, and souvenir shops down the road. Lines of cars, coach buses, the smell of exhaust, and hordes of day-trippers who came up from the coasts besiege us under scattered laricio pines.

"Culture shock, isn't it?" I turn to Joe. "Exactly what we were talking about. Vizzavona is so sleepy compared to this."

"Forget what I said at lunch," says Joe. "Maybe extending our walk by a few more days on the trail wouldn't be so bad."

Saturday, August 13
The Hike–Day Thirteen:
Col de Bavella to Conca

↗ **Ascent:** 2,320 feet

↘ **Descent:** 5 5617 feet

→ **Distance:** 13 miles

Guidebook Description: The granite spires and pine tree forests make for a memorable last day's walk.

The sun has yet to rise on our final day on the trail. I sit on the top bunk in our room at the *gîte*, careful not to bang my head on the ceiling. *You're going to have to handle one more day,* I tell my beaten body, but then quickly change it to: *I get to have one more day.* I tuck my legs beneath me and do a silent happy dance on my knees, already looking forward to sleeping in tomorrow morning.

Breakfast is a giddy gathering with smiles and laughter all around. To the very end, Chris is last to arrive. "Cheers, my friends," he says, toasting with a Pietra. "Almost there."

"We will walk two miles more than yesterday," says Julien, "but it will take not so much time. We have no Bavella needles to climb, and most of the way will be down." And so, on this final morning, he tells us not to rush, giving us the luxury of waiting for the sun to bless our exodus.

Joe and I huddle outside the *gîte* to witness our last GR20 sunrise, its prismatic pink light creeping up to and then bursting over the valley that stretches toward the sea. The sun turns the lowland gold and casts a dazzling morning glow across the gray cliffs to the north. A beautiful start to day thirteen.

"Look," says Sarah as we head for the trailhead. "The first sign for Conca." And there it is: a wooden plank heralding our final destination in all caps, the red-and-white blaze beside it. "*On y va*," she says. "Let's get to it."

By midmorning, after descending stream-carved trails, some up and some down, we reach Paliri, the farthest south and final refuge, for cold drinks and to top off our water supply. I wander up to the high point of the belvedere with my Orezza. West and north, from where we've come, is an endless mountain spine. To the east, the sea is closer than at any point on the trail, its sapphire water shimmering like splintered glass, the indigo of the open Mediterranean in the distance. Just over the horizon is Italy, and I imagine our visit there in two weeks. I smile about the promise of additional adventure on the mainland. I turn south and look past the diminishing line of mountains toward Bonifacio, Corsica's southernmost town. I picture its celebrated coves and shell beaches tucked at the bottom of cliffs—those we'll explore in a few short days. Across the windswept straits lies the Italian island of Sardinia, nearly three times the size of Corsica and the next stop on our journey.

I rejoin the group at a picnic table and ask, "So where's everyone traveling next?"

"More mountains, of course," says Phil without hesitation. "Maybe Slovenia's Julian Alps or the Balkans in Bulgaria."

We continue round the table.

"I am taking a family to hike la Vallée du Fango here on Corsica, near Calvi. It is not too long but it is a very steep canyon that goes down to the sea," says Julien.

"Next summer, I will bike through Switzerland," says Kees, "for three weeks. Maybe with my sons."

It's Joe's turn. "We did the Grand Canyon rim-to-rim hike a few years ago but want to go down the Colorado River itself." A voyage with no climbing sounds just about perfect right now. I know we'll have to battle rapids, but at least we won't be scaling any peaks. Floating downstream on a raft, hands behind my head, legs stretched with ankles crossed may be a romantic notion, but I'm going with it. I give Joe a thumbs-up.

"How 'bout you, Chris?" I ask.

"Somewhere in Central America, just not sure where yet."

"Well," says Sarah, "you all know I'm heading to the Congo with Doctors Without Borders next month, so I'm sure my next trek will be in Africa. Maybe something like going down the Congo River."

"*Et toi*, Marianne?" asks Julien.

"I'm with Joe. But I've always wanted to hike the Milford Track in New Zealand. Anyone done it before?"

All shake their heads.

"Well, it's hardly the GR20, and it takes only four days, but it's supposed to be beautiful. I think I'm going to take some time to appreciate this one and stay away from any serious trekking for a while."

Joe smiles and nods from across the table.

Gargantuan rocks eroded into spires line a high ridge. We eat an abbreviated lunch in their shadow, our enthusiasm for reaching

Conca obvious as we gobble down our midday goodies. We make
the final strenuous, snaking climb of our 124-mile trek to reach the
Bocca di u Sordu followed by a series of tight switchbacks to the final
brèche—our last mountain gap, the Bocca d'Usciolu. We squeeze
through a V-shaped red rock niche, the traditional gateway to Conca,
imagining we've stepped through a magic portal to the other side.

"It is all down from here," says Julien. "Our next stop will be the
finish."

As he proclaims it, "the finish" feels like a benediction. My body
does internal cartwheels; my weary soul rejoices. I try to find something meaningful to say as we start the final descent, but all I manage
is, "Let's do it!"

"We're bringing her home," adds Phil with a broad laugh, lifting
his arms in celebration. His words and boyish delight are liquid gold
in my veins.

The exposed rocky terrain transforms as we lose altitude, and the
temperatures soar. The boulders disappear, and the trail becomes
gravelly and then sandy. We wind under spindly pines rising from a
two-foot-high blanket of ferns, exchanging the high desert for forest.
Soon we're treated to our first views of the orange roofs of Conca, the
fabled terminus village, far below. Julien jumps and does a perfect
heel-click. "We will be there in less than an hour."

I'm elated, but my stomach tightens, and a lump rises in my
throat. Conca is our holy grail, but do I really want The Twenty to
end? Our sense of accomplishment awaits, but images and memories
cartwheel, as I'm keenly aware of a reluctance for the journey to be
over. We'll soon have to leave these people whose company we've so
come to enjoy.

I see that Sarah is limping, so I hang back to keep her company.
I want to spend as much time with my British mate as I can. While

adrenaline can overpower exhaustion, camaraderie can keep hurt at bay and stave off the sadness of an impending farewell.

"Knee bothering you?" I ask.

"Is it that obvious? Bloody vicious throbbing, actually."

At that moment, a big-bellied seventy-something gent materializes ahead. We're on a rare straightaway, so we step aside to take him in as he approaches. He's tall and bony with the legs of a cicada sticking from a jockstrap that, along with a small backpack and a pair of black army boots, is the extent of his attire. The freckled skin stretched over his skull is bordered by lank locks of gray hair hanging from just above his ears— a French mullet of sorts. One hand holds a water bottle sloshing red wine, the other a wooden walking stick, and he's chatting to himself. He raises his bottle and the chin of his rosy face and says, *"Bonjour, mes jeunes filles"*—good afternoon, young ladies—and passes us by. Our mouths agape, we turn so our eyes can follow him up the trail to confirm what we saw. And sure enough, he is there, Monsieur Commando, vanishing 'round a bend, sunburned, dimpled cheeks behind him.

"Did you *see* that?" Sarah says, poker-faced.

"I sure did."

"Curious sight, that." We look at each other and collapse into giggles.

"Think that guy's going to walk the whole thing in that getup? I need a pee break, or I'm going to wet my pants."

"I'm afraid I already have," says Sarah.

Sarah and I become Tony in *West Side Story*, but the object of our affection is Conca and not Maria. *The most beautiful sound I ever heard* . . . We provide the soundtrack for our unruly rabble's final miles as we scramble down the final stretch.

At long last, Julien announces, "For fuck's sake, we did it! *Ça y est!*

On est à Conca!" We're in Conca! I hear his declaration and sense it like a song.

"*Ça y est* is right," Chris says. "Whatever that means, it sure sounds good."

Joe gives me a high five, a long kiss, and an even longer hug. I circle his waist with both arms and look up to catch his eye and share the moment. Heady with the prospect of ending this trek, jelly-legged and slack-kneed, I release him to lean against a tree and slide to the ground. I let out a long gratified sigh, tilt back my head, and spread my arms wide. How I wish I could have told myself when we started this journey that I would in fact make it to the end. Go easy on yourself, Marianne, and enjoy the walk. Joe will love you forever, no matter your speed on a trail.

Phil says, pointing in front of me, "Look, Marianne. A nuthatch feather—a *sittelle corse*. Catch it before it drops all the way. For good luck!" I see it and grab it between my hands. "Do I really need *more* luck, Phil? I just reached the end of The Twenty!" But then a shadow slips over me gently—the bittersweetness of graduation, a walk on the beach in the dwindling days of summer, the final day of vacation.

We take celebratory pictures by the final red-and-white blaze and the sign welcoming us to Conca, but dare not stop for long since our legs may refuse to continue. We have another half mile to go through the quiet streets of the village before we reach the café, La Tonnelle, for drinks.

"Your boots are a wreck," says Joe, looking at my feet as we walk the final hundred yards.

"And how do I look?"

"Not much better than they do." He pats my bottom with a wink, and I smack his back.

"Yeah, I know. My Garmonts really are a disaster. Look at them.

The toes are sliced, the laces are spliced together, and most of the treads are gone. Come on, boots—just get me to the bar—just a few more yards."

"Happy?" Joe asks. "To have it behind us?"

I laugh. "I'm not sure I even realize just how happy I am yet!"

And then we're there. I plunk down on a white plastic chair and can't strip to bare feet and slip-on sandals fast enough. I tie my boot laces together in a pretty knot, hold them up, touch them to my lips, and kiss them goodbye. I give a brief eulogy. "My dear, loyal, trusted Garmonts—you've done more than nine hundred miles across seven years, and I'll miss you!" Joe snaps a picture. I drop them without further ceremony in the trash bin.

To all appearances, my body is as battered as my boots, but inside my heart is the sun, beaming with rays of relief. I did what I set out to do: I started The Twenty, and I finished The Twenty. Damn, it feels good.

We head north to Bastia in our van, tracing Corsica's eastern shore back to where our journey began. Was it only two weeks ago? I feel I've lived a year since then. The sun warms the window next to me, the electro beat of Serge Gainsbourg's "Sea, Sex and Sun" and its risqué lyrics . . . *tes p'tits seins* . . . pulsing from the radio. Sarah and I share a smile. "Crikey," she says, her eyes wide.

As the dry landscape races by, my mind's eye plays a reel of the past seven months. Training for Corsica; excruciating joint pain; my RA diagnosis; dependence on my pink pillbox; anxiety about what my body can and can't do; meeting Céline; acceptance and relief; Conca. Though we all hiked the same path, we each had to walk it in our own time, with our own thoughts, in our own way. And with any luck, we each learned some lessons along the way.

I turn to look at Joe's tan, muscled arms, his hand resting carefully on my thigh, his toned legs, blond eyebrows, sunburned nose. How lucky I am to still feel a pulse in my throat every time I see him or take in the smell of his clothing. I stroke the soft, pale hairs on his arm and think of how well I know every inch of him: deepening creases at the corners of his eyes, sun-bleached sandy hair, strong hands. I still see the face I saw when we were seventeen, despite the addition of laugh lines and long eyebrows. But I love each and every mark of age because I was there for them all. We grew up, got married, raised children, built careers, retired, and grew older still. Together. All of it, together.

An outdoor restaurant under an umbrella in Bastia on the Place Saint-Nicolas. Our group's final meal. And for the first time in almost two weeks, we all get to order off a menu.

"Brilliant," says Sarah, looking across the table littered with shrimp tails, fish bones, and pizza crusts. "This was all just perfect." We commiserate about blisters and bumps, muscle pulls and thigh bruises, lost toenails and broken boots. Joe sits, his gaze to the sea, watching ferries come and go. I can tell he's already moving on, our GR20 adventure behind him. But I'm not quite ready to let it go.

"Here's to Jim," says Chris. "We were happy to have you with us."

"Cheers to Jim," we all toast.

Sarah leans behind Joe to tap me on the shoulder and raise a glass. "Cheers to old broads who get black, blue, and battered," she says, misty-eyed.

"And here's to tough broads who tackle The Twenty," I add. "*Tchin, tchin,* Sarah."

"Cheers, Marianne."

Our toast summons a Hunter Thompson quote, one of my favorites: "Life should not be a journey to the grave with the intention of arriving safely in a pretty and well-preserved body, but rather to skid in broadside in a cloud of smoke, thoroughly used up, totally worn out, and loudly proclaiming 'Wow! What a Ride!'"

I may not have believed it at times on the trail, but here I am, celebrating what we've done, Thompson's words ringing.

In liquor-loosened French, Sarah and I speak with Julien over final drinks about our time together, recounting our favorite parts. Julien adds one last tribute to us all, with a special wink for Sarah. "It's been *brilliant* being your guide and getting to know you all. You must know that I will miss you. All of you."

I sit back, look up, and watch a flock of birds—starlings perhaps—arc sharply and then billow like smoke against the lavender sky. An ineffable calm surrounds me as they broadcast their piercing twitters.

Our leg muscles rebel against the agony of rising from the table and walking to our hotel, but the time has come to disband our team. We share hugs and kisses and though we promise to keep in touch—and perhaps even visit—sadness lurks beneath the farewells. The responsibilities and realities of our lives make reunions highly unlikely. It takes seconds to say our final goodbyes and then—poof! Our companions are gone.

Those who contemplate the beauty of the earth find reserves of strength that will endure as long as life lasts. There is something infinitely healing in the repeated refrains of nature—the assurance that dawn comes after night, and spring after winter.

—Rachel Carson

PART V
POST-HIKE

Sunday, August 14
Calvi, Corsica

Nature runs on cycles. The earth and moon rotate. Seasons change. Flowers bloom and then fade. Tides ebb and flow. Loved ones are born, and we celebrate, but then we lose them to our memories. People come into our lives and then disappear, never to be heard from again.

The day after we complete The Twenty, we're not fully prepared, as we never are, for the cleaving, the post-journey letdown—a mixture of sadness and satisfaction—that takes hold while we recover. The world feels off-kilter, we have no energy to move, and we struggle with a lack of focus. We video-chat with Chris and then Caroline halfway across the world to help ground ourselves back in reality and fill them in on the highs and lows of our trip.

I phone my eighty-eight-year-old father to let him know we've finished our hike safely. "God bless you both," he says, and asks me to remind him where Corsica is. "And since when did you become such an athlete?" he adds.

My eyes brim with tears. He has no idea I'm crying.

We rent a car and drive ninety minutes west of Bastia to check into the Villa Calvi hotel, as refined as the trail is rugged. An enormous bed piled with goose down pillows and crisp white bedding dominates our bright, sunny room. I slip off my sandals to feel the cool of the floor tiles and then pull back the breezy curtains to step onto the balcony that looks out over the bay in the distance.

We're in an oasis of lavender and roses where the lawns are green carpets and tropical gardens flourish under skies the color of cornflowers. A perfect visual cocktail for our convalescing selves. We do our best to prolong the restorative effects of nature's remoteness on our spirits as we nurse sore muscles, bruises, scabs, and scrapes and attend to transitioning back to civilization.

The white-tiled bath is fully stocked with beauty products and elixirs. I slather my face in an algae cream mask, feel my skin tighten, and sense the toxins release. "Want to try?" I ask Joe, expecting a chuckle and a no.

But he surprises me. "You know what? Right now I'll do anything to make my body feel better, so sure. Pamper away."

I smooth the green mousse over his face and can't stop smiling as my typically buttoned-up husband not only sports a facial treatment but also actually enjoys it.

Mask applied, I soak my sore muscles in a bath milky with lavender salts, steam rising from the 105-degree water, my joints releasing. Be gone RA trespasser. I beat you. I continue to steep for an hour.

Setting aside penchants for long walks and Joe's aversion to bronzing on a lounge, we're happy to confine exploration to the path from our porch to the pool where icy Orezzas are on tap. We eat multicourse, candlelit meals under the stars slowly, deliberately, lulled by the soft murmurs of French at neighboring tables, savoring every bite of gourmet cuisine with fine French wine.

"Look!" I turn to Joe on our first evening on our own, unable to sit still in my seat. "Vichyssoise is on the menu!"

"I know it's a favorite, but are you really passing up the shrimp for cold potato soup?"

"I am." I reach across the table to grab the salt and have it ready. "Long story." I add, "involving Sarah."

"Marianne," Joe says, suddenly serious as he lifts his wine glass. "I will never forget the GR20, and I will never, ever forget that I did it with you." Even after forty years of hearing Joe say sweet things, this one's extra special. He reaches for my hand without a word.

Joe steps fully clothed on the scale in the bathroom. "Ten pounds," he says. "I lost ten pounds on The Twenty." He tightens his belt a notch. I recall Sarah announcing as she ordered dinner on our final night, holding the menu in front of her, "I'm eating whatever I want because I'd better have lost a stone on this trek." Fourteen pounds, I think. Could she possibly have lost fourteen pounds?

I step on the scale, naked, of course. Can't let the weight of underwear mask any loss. Try as I might, some things will never change. "Two pounds. Two whole pounds. Muscle weighs more than fat, right?" Before Joe can answer, I turn and do my best body builder imitation, striking a pose, flexing my arms, making my tummy taut. "What do you think?"

Joe laughs. "You look great, Babe."

I stifle the urge to add, "For a woman of sixty." My days of disparaging digs are behind me.

"You looked great when we started and you look great now," Joe continues, squeezing my arms. "Your biceps are impressive," he says, stepping back. "But I'm much more taken with your chest."

A week after downing celebratory drinks in Conca, our hiking companions are long gone, our muscles have stopped cramping in the middle of the night, and we've had the luxury of washing and drying our clothes in machines. We drive south along the west coast of the island, stopping to board a boat to see the abundant birdlife, red coral, craggy cliffs, grottoes, and secluded beaches with iridescent seabeds of the Scandola Nature Reserve. After many hours back in the car, we reach the narrow cobblestone streets of the medieval fortified town of Bonifacio, our final destination. Having spent two weeks on the island's dark granite peaks, the secluded seaside town's layered white limestone cliffs are a bright surprise.

As in Bastia before we began The Twenty, we find ourselves at a seaside café, this time perched high on the promontory of the *haute ville* (upper town) as if on a ship's bow looking over the cobalt waters below. "Did you know legend has it that Bonifacio was one of the stops on Homer's *Odyssey*?" Joe asks.

"Had no idea, but it makes sense because this seems like a place for ancient stories." Joe always manages to surprise me with the things he knows. My very own Renaissance man.

We look just over seven miles across the straits to Sardinia, tomorrow's destination. I'd convinced Joe to make the island pivot from French to Italian because the marine engineer in him will never say no to boarding a boat. But for now, with the trail behind us, I'm content to relax and savor these unhurried moments at the bottom of this storied island.

My fingers lightly brush the gray shadow of the bruise still apparent on my thigh, my physical souvenir. We relish the reward of honey-hued hair and caramel calves, but our biggest takeaway is having experienced the island from the inside out, from its punishing mountain middle to its rugged, chalky shores. We sit and sip the local wine as the sun slowly slips beyond the blazing horizon to the west.

When we first arrived in Europe in the silvery light of early summer, the weeks stretched ahead—indistinct encounters yet to come. But here we are—our final night on Corsica. It blesses us with the sweet gift of regret as we prepare to leave. *We'll be back*, we say, promising to return. Home is nearly in sight—the red, white, and blue of the States beckoning from across the ocean and where, at least for a while, we'll set our wanderlust on a shelf. But for now, six more weeks of travel await: to Italy's Sardinia and the Cinque Terre and then back to France—Provence and the Luberon.

Flags snap sharply in the legendary winds beneath Bonifacio as we watch yachts carve through the choppy whitecaps. I imagine the sea floor well below, littered with the wreckage of pirate ships unable to successfully navigate the straits. The distinction between sea and island blur as we look back, Corsica's jagged outline of rugged inlets losing its shape in the blazing midday light. From where we lean over the ferry's stern, the island's great shadow shrinks, soon to sink into the sea. We're leaving her behind, having written our story in her stones—the story of two sixty-year-olds reluctantly skidding into senior status.

Our journey has an enduring lesson, however. Age cannot be denied, even as we renew our appetite for adventure and despite how youthful we feel. Years accumulate and bodies break down as they must, yielding to time traveling in just one direction. But we're not simply victims surrendering to limitations without a struggle. We'll adjust our expectations and try to live as young as we fool ourselves into thinking we are, for as long as our bodies allow. I'll rejoice in what I *can* do and find peace with and be proud of exactly who I am, curbing my forever insistence that I do things on my own.

The Twenty has reminded us of our place on this earth, our place in a greater whole. We're simply part and not rulers of nature and must adapt to her rigors and rituals. It reminds us to not only get down on our hands and our knees to touch and appreciate the earth, but to fear her when we must. Our two-week adventure was a mere flash of the island's existence and showed us that nature does not round her sharp edges for pampered human rhythms. And so we leave Corsica, my stubborn self-reliance softened but in need of tempering still. My sentimental education will indeed continue.

"Joe, did I tell you Phil told me he thinks everything starts to shrivel once you retire? It's why he swears he'll never stop working."

"I think he'd be better off if he vowed to never stop climbing mountains."

"True." I look off to the still visible tips of Corsica's peaks. "That's exactly what I told him, and it's good advice for us too."

Joe steps back and says, "Hey hiker girl, look back—one last picture of you and Corsica." I let him snap several photos from behind me and then I turn, lean on the railing, and smile for the camera, Corsica fading into memory at my back.

Some experiences are like dreams, tenuous to hold—like snowflakes that melt upon landing. Will it be that way with The Twenty? What will I forget and what will I remember? That every day started with a thigh-numbing climb and ended with a knee-destroying descent? That from the very first stride, we advanced at a dizzying pace through fragrant maquis, soaring forests, and then delicate mountain mist? That farmhouses clung to cliffs on which we trod in the hoof prints of *sangliers*, mouflons, and other Corsican creatures? That there were nights when I woke, gritting my teeth in pain from charley horses I was sure would tear my calf in two? That we were seared by sun and frozen by hail? That views to the Mediterranean under black velvet skies glittering with nature's cosmic chandelier were around the corner from crumbling shepherds' huts, shriekingly cold showers, and campgrounds dotted with cow pies? That I was disappointed not to meet more Corsican people and that my cab driver wouldn't speak to me?

Or will what stays with me above all be what I learned on the journey? That Kees and Céline reminded me how fleeting life can be; that what I have isn't permanent; that what I've been blessed with can be taken away at any moment? That making a connection with two special Corsicans, Annie and Jojo, made up for others I missed? That The Twenty is about nature and discovery and not the speed at which I cover a thousand vertical feet. And that while putting 124 miles behind us, I learned to be gentler with myself. That I need not control everything. That sometimes I must let go, be kind to myself, go easy with judgment. Doing my best is good enough. And while I may remain frustrated when I need others' help, letting them do so does not make me weak.

I look up at Joe standing next to me in the breeze, face to the sun, eyes closed, blond curls peeking from beneath his baseball cap. There's stillness between us, a trusted stillness that's familiar and makes me feel safe because I know that as long as we're on this earth, he'll always be at my side. How did we know, when we were teens and then twenty-five when we married, what we would want and need at sixty? How did Jim and Céline, Kees and Liese, or any other couple know? Did the thought even cross our minds?

My sight blurs as I reach over. Joe takes my hand and tucks it in his jacket pocket, the silky material cool inside. I look up at him and think, while I may forget your hiking shorts and faded tee, your sandy stubble, the precision with which you lace your boots, or the way you so badly need a haircut, I will always remember that you were there when I learned lessons that were mine to discover and to learn in my own time. We have both come to understand, as we really already knew, that adventure is still possible for two aging travelers who seek it. That it's possible to walk the wilds of Corsica, and at the end of two weeks, restore our battered bodies in the sea.

EPILOGUE

Seventeen days after leaving The Twenty, we're on Italy's northwestern coast in the Cinque Terre. Joe and I are relaxing to the sounds of the surf out our guesthouse window when my brother calls. "What did you say?" I ask, jumping up. I press my fingers over my other ear.

"Dad died, Mar. A few hours ago."

The air drains from my lungs, my legs weaken, and I sit back down hard on the bed. I listen as my brother recounts the details but they barely register. He says he'll let me know as soon as arrangements for the wake and funeral are made.

I hang up, share the news with Joe, and fall back, recalling my final phone call with my father. I smile, certain he wouldn't have been able to locate the Cinque Terre on a map. And then I calm, convinced that having lost my mother nine years earlier, he never stopped missing her and had had enough of being alone. He just gave up, no longer wanting to go it without her. And despite his children's determination to include him, as his hearing and stamina went, he must have felt a bystander in the margins of our hectic lives. It was simply time to let go. May you rest in peace together, Mom and Dad. I know you always did what you thought was right.

"I'm so sorry, Marianne," Joe says, coming over to sit next to me.

I always feared that my father's death would stir up the unhappy muck of memory. But my core loosens and the cold stone in my heart starts to soften as Joe pulls me into a hug. Forgiveness is a process. It will take me some time and some space to unpack it all.

What happened in my childhood—all the good and yes, the bad—led me to where I am today, and I wouldn't want to be anywhere else. And I wonder if maybe the grief I feel is more about regret for a relationship that never was rather than for the one I've actually lost.

When friends and family back home say, "Tell us about your trip," I briefly recount our Corsican journey. But while they pay polite attention, their interest wanes after just a sentence or two. They ask a couple questions including where we'll go next, but quickly get fidgety, and so I cut the chronicle short. Our island exploits will remain, as so many others have, our story—just Joe's and mine.

Two months after we leave The Twenty, our passports packed away, we start our way west toward our children in California to start the next chapter of our lives. We make an extended stop in Park City, Utah, to be ski bums for a season and return to living gentle days of real-world practicality—cooking, spending time with the children, and hiking in the Wasatch Mountains. And when winter arrives and brings the snow, Joe becomes a ski instructor and I teach English to non-English speakers. We remain in touch with Sarah and Phil and think often of our companions from The Twenty, imagining them climbing mountains on journeys around the world.

One night, in front of the fireplace, cozy in the middle of a snowstorm, we discuss where in the world we'll go next.

"Remember on the last day of the hike when we all talked about where everyone would travel next?" I ask.

"Of course," says Joe. "I said doing the Colorado River and you said New Zealand's Milford Track. Don't tell me—we need to decide because you want to start planning. You always need a trip on the horizon and all that. . . ." He winks.

"Well, we don't have to decide right away, but maybe we should think about the Far East—Vietnam or Thailand—now that we're so far west."

"Either of those sounds great. Just start the research and you know I'll be on board."

I realize, though, as I know Joe does too, that it doesn't really matter where we go next. As long as we can plan and be there together, as long as we both keep putting one foot in front of the other, all will be right in our world.

ACKNOWLEDGMENTS

I am so grateful to see my second book, *The Twenty*, in print. Writing and publishing my first book, *Gap Year Girl*, was such a pleasure, and to now have my second book between two covers is truly extraordinary.

Every book that makes its way to publication is a shared effort, and I have many to thank for their assistance. *The Twenty* is dedicated to Joe, my husband and partner in everything, who always supports me in whatever I do. I couldn't have made it to the end of the hike or the manuscript without your sense of humor and encouragement. A loving thank-you to our children, Chris and Caroline, who were at home cheering us on stateside as we hiked across an island in the Mediterranean, and then continued their support through the long process of writing about the journey. My deep gratitude to our fearless fellow GR20 hikers—steadfast companions and solid athletes who always made me laugh: Julien, Phil, Chris, Kees, Jim, and especially Sarah, who made our journey the hike of a lifetime.

I want to thank Brooke Warner at She Writes Press for once again believing in me and my writing, and to the entire She Writes Press team, especially Lauren Wise, Julie Metz, Anne Durette, and Jennifer Caven. A profound thank-you to my Park City Writing Circle for always being such generous, wise counselors, not to mention great company: Anne, Ariela, Elizabeth, Joan, and Rina. I am beyond thankful to April Bosshard who invited me to her writing retreat in Champagne, France and was always there for constant counsel. You really are the story whisperer and made me a better writer. I am so grateful to Annie Tucker, for her always good humor, gentle editing expertise, and invaluable suggestions. I trust you implicitly and was always secure knowing my writing was in your capable hands. I also want to thank Noreen for unconditional love, Davida, who is always there for me, and Didi who more than once pulled me back from the edge. All three are kindred spirits. I have great fondness and appreciation for two terrific independent booksellers who helped when I asked: Dolly's Bookstore in Park City, and The King's English in Salt Lake City. And a final thank-you to my readers. You have always been so kind by posting reviews of my books and I am forever indebted to you.

The journey I recount in *The Twenty* is based on my imperfect memory of what took place on and off 124 miles of trail. There are pieces I omitted because so much happened over the course of our hike and the months spent training for it. I simplified and condensed some of the experience for the sake of the story and did my best to accurately recreate conversations and events.

I hope you enjoyed *The Twenty: One Woman's Trek Across Corsica on the GR20*. If so, please consider leaving a review on Amazon, Goodreads, Book Bub, or all three. Your review can be as short as a single word or sentence and will help other readers decide if *The Twenty* is for them. It's the best possible gift you can give an author.

ABOUT THE AUTHOR

photo credit: D. Tulloch

Marianne C. Bohr, published author, award-winning essayist, and former travel blogger for the Huffington Post, married her high school sweetheart and travel partner. She follows her own advice and visits new places at every opportunity. She wrote her first book, *Gap Year Girl: A Baby Boomer Adventure Across 21 Countries,* over the course of the yearlong sabbatical she and her husband took to travel across Europe. *The Twenty: One Woman's Trek Across Corsica on the GR20 Trail*, is her second book. Marianne lives in Park City, UT, with her ski instructor husband, where after decades in publishing, and then many years teaching middle school French, she skis, hikes, and writes.

SELECTED TITLES FROM SHE WRITES PRESS

She Writes Press is an independent publishing company founded to serve women writers everywhere. Visit us at www.shewritespress.com.

Brave(ish): A Memoir of a Recovering Perfectionist by Margaret Davis Ghielmetti. $16.95, 978-1-63152-747-0

An intrepid traveler sets off at forty to live the expatriate dream overseas—only to discover that she has no idea how to live even her own life. Part travelogue and part transformation tale, Ghielmetti's memoir, narrated with humor and warmth, proves that it's never too late to reconnect with our authentic selves—if we dare to put our own lives first at last.

The Fourteenth of September by Rita Dragonette. $16.95, 978-1-63152-453-0

In 1969, as mounting tensions over the Vietnam War are dividing America, a young woman in college on an Army scholarship risks future and family to go undercover in the anti-war counterculture when she begins to doubt her convictions—and is ultimately forced to make a life-altering choice as fateful as that of any Lottery draftee.

forty-eight peaks in New Hampshire's challenging White Mountains—and discovers, in the years that follow, that in order to feel truly successful, she will have to do much more than tick off peaks.

Gap Year Girl by Marianne Bohr. $16.95, 978-1-63152-820-0

Thirty-plus years after first backpacking through Europe, Marianne Bohr and her husband leave their lives behind and take off on a yearlong quest for adventure.

The Expedition: Two Parents Risk Life and Family in an Extraordinary Quest to the South Pole by Christine Fagan. $16.95, 978-1-63152-592-6

In the middle of parenthood and successful careers, a middle-aged married couple skis 570 miles while dragging 220-pound sleds—with no guide or resupply—from the edge of Antarctica to the South Pole, fulfilling their biggest dream and making history as they stretch their minds, bodies, and marriage to the limit.